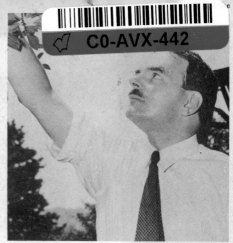

A Stone Rejected

Politics Self-Taught

Man From Main Street

The Immortal Amateur

The Treasury's Peter Pan

Far From Europe

Sorcerer's Apprentices

27 Masters of Politics

A NEWSWEEK BOOK

27

Masters of Politics

In a Personal Perspective

by

RAYMOND MOLEY

Published for *Newsweek*
by
FUNK & WAGNALLS COMPANY • NEW YORK

To the Memory of
my Father
who liked party men,
especially Democrats.

The Purpose

To SAY THAT WE LEARN politics by experience is to say that we learn it from other people. Politics is an art expressed in behavior. Its principles emerge in terms of what those who successfully practice it do, say and believe. As an art, it is transmitted through observation, written and spoken language and the measurement of the effects of specific appeals on human behavior.

This is a book on politics expressed and interpreted through sketches of twenty-seven individuals who were notable in public life in my time. It is written from my own personal point of view. While I have tried to avoid the autobiographical, I have occasionally used incidents based on personal knowledge of and association with those people. I do that to add immediate and intimate meaning to the portrait of the person involved.

I believe that politics should be thus portrayed by those who have had the advantage of such associations. The fact is that most worthwhile political writing has always been from a personal point of view.

For that reason, I have used as a basic rule of selection the inclusion only of people I have known fairly well. In every case but one, I enjoyed a personal relationship—in some instances, casual; in others, a friendship of some depth and length.

Since my contacts with most of these people go back some years, I have attempted to place my facts and interpretations in the perspective of time. My book, therefore, is a product not only of observation but of reflection.

These people, in varying degrees and against various backgrounds, knew the art of politics. Their careers have something to teach everyone, as I found they had something to teach me. I hope, therefore, that scattered through these chapters there may be a few pages of lasting and general political wisdom, open to those who care to learn more of this ancient profession, this major source of human interest and this arbiter of all our destinies.

I hope that if occasionally I have made an observation or drawn a conclusion with which some friends of these personalities may not agree, it will nevertheless be evident that what is written is in good faith, good humor and well within the bounds of fairness.

RAYMOND MOLEY

Bridgewater, Connecticut
September, 1949

Acknowledgments

In the preparation of this book I have had the continuous and discriminating assistance of my son, Raymond Moley, Jr. Valuable editorial help was provided by Marjorie Wilson, my assistant. Needless to say, my indebtedness is very great to those contemporaries, living and dead, who are the subjects of these studies.

In a few passages in the chapters on Howe, Woodin, Hugh Johnson and Byrnes, I have used language from my book, *After Seven Years,* and from selections from that book published in *The Saturday Evening Post.* In the chapter on Will Hays a short passage is borrowed from my book, *The Hays Office.* In the chapters on Flynn and Sumners I have used some material from articles written by me and published in *The Saturday Evening Post.* Acknowledgment is made to Harper & Brothers, The Bobbs-Merrill Company and *The Saturday Evening Post* for permission to use this material.

27 Masters of Politics

27 Masters of Politics

In only one respect does this book follow a sequence of time. It begins with two people whom I should call political teachers. Their creative activities, the educational value of which meant so much to contemporary politics, preceded in time those of the other personalities in the book.

This order of appearance I could hardly avoid, since without the lessons I learned from these pioneers I could not have comprehended nor could I have personally known those who appear later. Moreover, these men and others like them cultivated the ground from which many more recent leaders have gathered the harvest.

Tom L. Johnson's name is now virtually unknown except in the city in which he wrought a revolution in government forty years ago. But the ideas which he developed, in common with others in the Middle West, have since swept over the nation.

Beard was professionally a teacher, historian and publicist, not a practitioner of politics. But the impact of his ideas upon the political thinking of our time has been definitive and immensely important.

These two men were in a very real sense political teachers of the living present.

Reform without Incompetence

TOM L. JOHNSON

I STOOD in a noisy crowd before a Cleveland newspaper office on a November night in 1907 and saw in the election returns that Tom L. Johnson had soundly beaten that stalwart Republican congressman and candidate for mayor, Theodore Elijah Burton. I was so happy at the news that I almost forgot that on that same day I had been elected to my first public office—that of clerk in a village some miles to the West.

The Republicans had done their utmost that year. President Theodore Roosevelt had prevailed upon Burton to run and had made no bones about supporting him. William H. Taft, Secretary of War and President-to-be, joined in the urging. So did James R. Garfield, Secretary of the Interior and son of an Ohio President. This made the campaign a piece of national news and a test of national Republicanism.

In three successive elections Johnson had already beaten three opponents. Burton was the best the Republicans had. He was a man of eminent respectability, high attainment as a scholarly statesman and great power in the House of Representatives. But he was also stiff, ponderous and pedantic. As he accepted the nomination, he had intoned the aphorism attributed to Julius Cæsar, *Jacta alea est*. This, which could have passed in parliamentary oratory, was ill suited to the rough ways of municipal politics. Cartoonists had their fun with it, and Johnson announced a personal translation, "Let 'er go, Gallagher."

Burton was nevertheless a potent speaker, with a masterly grasp of financial and corporative realities. He had the fervid support of every element in the city which represented invested wealth and

3

finance, large business management, and the more conservative educational and ecclesiastical forces.

That campaign exceeded anything Cleveland had known in bitterness, excitement and general interest. There was wrangling in the clubs, the streets, the schools and the homes. The major issue was the nature of prospective franchises to be given to the street railway companies, the rate of fare and the extent of city control. Deeper than all that, however, the campaign epitomized a line of division between the philosophy of individualism in business, as exemplified in the Hanna-McKinley era, and the so-called "progressive" philosophy of the early years of the century.

After his election Johnson appealed to the more reconcilable people of the business community, and common ground was found with Frederick H. Goff, a distinguished lawyer of eminently conservative connections who later became president of the Cleveland Trust Company. Goff was a man of truly heroic qualities who, no doubt influenced by Johnson, was keenly perceptive of the changing times.

A product of Goff's personal philosophy was the Cleveland Foundation. Unlike the foundations of Rockefeller and others (Goff was once a member of a major Rockefeller law firm), its board of control was not self-perpetuating. A majority of its members were appointed by public officials. It was based on the principle that since wealth was created by the collective energies of all the members of a community, that wealth should in major part return to enrich the common life of that community.

Goff and Johnson established a basis of settlement. In simple terms it recognized the street railways as private property entitled to a fair return on investment. It also recognized a paramount right of the city, through its government, to control a business that used city streets as a monopoly. It recognized, in short, private ownership and paramount government control in the public interest.

The fare charged was to fluctuate automatically in line with a fiscal reserve in the company. This settlement, named after its final draftsman, a Federal Judge, is the Tayler Grant. It ended the street railway issue in Cleveland politics. It stands as probably the most constructive determination of public and private interest in municipal history.

Back and beyond and above this settlement of what was really an incidental issue, there was an idea which I learned early from Johnson and later saw illustrated in four years' association with Goff while I was director of the Cleveland Foundation. It was the belief, now widely held in all economic levels, that property—all property—is to a greater or smaller degree invested with a public interest. No man or set of men have a right to do as they choose with property which serves the public and which derives its value from public patronage.

Government is the public's agency to determine the public interest in property. It is or should be an arbiter, serving all interests with even-handed justice, never allying itself with one interest against another. For the moment that an official leader allies himself with one group against another group, he descends from the bench of justice, identifies himself as a combatant and opens the judgment seat to the tyranny of contention.

This was the philosophy of Johnson. It was the philosophy of Goff. Perhaps I invite the charge of provincialism by calling it a Cleveland idea.

Johnson won astonishing successes in business before he entered politics. He lived in an Horatio Alger era, and there was something of that "brave and bold" citizen in this young man who rose from poverty to eminence and economic power in his middle thirties. Whatever he touched seemed to prosper and to yield rich profits. He promoted and developed street railways in Louisville, Indianapolis, Detroit and Cleveland. He developed steel manufacturing in Pennsylvania and Ohio. He was a successful inventor in his own right. He had amazing judgment in picking business associates and subordinates. Had he followed business as a lifelong career, he might have left one of the country's major fortunes.

Johnson was not a man who blandly accepted success as a tribute solely to his own personal capacity. As his fortune grew from every enterprise touched by his restless energy, he began to wonder just why he should succeed while others failed. He knew that he had been guiding his attention to business situations in which a minimum of competition prevailed. Later, he pointed out that at the age of eleven he became a monopolist when a railroad conductor gave him the exclusive privilege of selling papers on his train.

He asked himself about the system which permitted monopoly. He noted that monopoly grew from the joining of politics and business. And he perceived the moral failure of a government that allied itself with a single interest. He was ripe for a great awakening.

A sudden conversion arrested his interest and almost ended his concern with money-making when, in 1883, chance in the form of a railroad news-butcher tossed in his lap a copy of Henry George's *Social Problems*. Johnson's education in economics had been in the market and workshop. He never had considered causes. He was interested in results. George appealed to him because his diagnosis was devastatingly clear and his remedy simple and all-inclusive. Johnson's next step was characteristic of a man of action. He apparently didn't bother to consult background reading. He took his Henry George books to lawyers and businessmen and talked and listened. Your true politician learns through his ears, not through his eyes.

Johnson soon sought out Henry George in Brooklyn and established a lasting friendship. No disciple ever gave himself more utterly to a master. Thereafter Johnson's life purpose was to cure inequities in society and, following the advice of George, he sought his end through politics. He would undoubtedly have written as his epitaph that he was a life-long advocate of the ideas of Henry George. He was first and last a single taxer.

He served two terms in Congress, where it would seem that he gave major attention to converting his colleagues to single tax and to the doctrines of free trade. Later, he participated in George's campaign for the mayoralty of New York and stood at the deathbed of the great reformer a week before the election in 1897.

In the perspective of time, I wonder if in his case, as in that of many others, it was not the Henry George remedy but the diagnosis that was important. I leave it to economists to debate the soundness of the single tax. But the tremendous fact which George so diligently promoted was that of social value. To point out that a piece of land in itself is valueless unless there are people who find it useful is to shake the very foundations of all ancient concepts of private property. Moreover, land exploitation is the easiest form of exploitation to understand. Johnson pursued this point in his entire attack upon monopoly and privilege in many fields other than taxation.

Johnson, intent upon giving practical meaning to the philosophy of his dead master, first sought and won the office of Mayor of Cleveland in 1901. He held this office until 1910.

The extraordinary thing about Johnson was that, while his soul burned with the zeal of reform, his practical knowledge of administration gave his city honest and efficient government. He handled the business of government with such skill that his public was induced to take good government as a matter of course. Unlike many others whose names are associated with reform government, he denied that efficient and honest government was an end in itself. It was just a detail, like shiny shoes and pressed clothes.

In his autobiography, *My Story,* written in the final year of his life, he impatiently brushes aside the truly memorable administrative achievements of his years of service as mayor. "To give 'good government,' " he wrote, "wasn't the thing I was in public life for." It was "a side issue, merely. While we tried to give the people clean and well lighted streets, pure water, free access to the parks, public baths and comfort stations, a good police department, careful market inspection, a rigid system of weights and measures, and to make charitable and correctional institutions aid the unfortunate and correct the wrong-doers, and to do the hundred and one things that a municipality ought to do for its inhabitants—while we tried to do all these things, and even to outstrip other cities in the doing of them, we never lost sight of the fact that they were not fundamental." [1]

Even his great crusade for a three-cent fare was to him an incidental matter. He believed with all his heart that the roots of evil were in land and land taxation. He said many times that if cheap transportation were gained, the public's saving would merely be paid in higher rents.

Nor did he make a fetish of non-partisanship in city government. He did not fight the Democratic machine. He took it over, controlled, directed it and measurably kept it clean. In this respect he revealed a deep wisdom, for the winning of elections was not entirely dependent upon his personal popularity. His organization won them, and even after his death the party he built won two more elections, with Newton D. Baker as a candidate.

Baker was destined to become Johnson's most celebrated lieutenant. But the annals of Cleveland's politics are full of the names of able administrators who were chosen by Johnson and taught by him to serve the public. The innovations he conceived in city government spread their influence everywhere. Home rule, municipal control of utilities, smart police administration, enlightened welfare activities conceived in Johnson's Cleveland became standard practices in many other cities.

Notable among the city departments that attained national administration and emulation under the Johnson regime were Charities and Correction, under Harris R. Cooley, and Police, under Chief Fred Kohler.

Cooley, who had been the pastor of the Disciple Church attended by Johnson, was a humanitarian and a bold administrative innovator. Under his leadership the various correctional and charitable institutions were moved out from rookeries in the city to a great farm purchased by the city. There he developed decent, humane plants—one for minor offenders, another for the indigent, another for old people, another for juvenile delinquents, and an-

---

[1] *My Story*—New York: B. W. Huebsch, 1915; p. 125.

other for tuberculous patients. Modern welfare administration everywhere owes a heavy debt to this pioneer effort.

Chief Kohler, a martinet in handling his police, was a far-sighted humanitarian in handling offenders. When Theodore Roosevelt visited Cleveland in 1910 he designated Kohler as the "best police chief in the United States." Years later, Kohler himself was elected mayor.

But it is as a teacher that Johnson deserves to be remembered. He believed that a political leader can go only by measured steps in reform and that the limit of his progress is the capacity of the public to understand, accept and learn to live with reform. Therefore, he conceived the educational function of his job to be paramount. Some years after Johnson's death, his most widely-known lieutenant and successor, Newton D. Baker, when leaving the office of mayor said, "I believed during my tenure of this office that preaching was my most important job."

Johnson's power as a public educator was so great that almost every person in Cleveland's streets was able to talk with good intelligence about franchises, property rights, taxation and a variety of other complicated issues. A visitor from abroad once asked Mayor Johnson to tell him about the street-railway problem. Johnson pointed to the street below his window and said, "Just go out and ask the first man you meet." That was hardly an exaggeration.

I hope it is not the pride of a native that induces me to believe that Cleveland is politically the most remarkable city in the nation. The ups and downs of other American cities in which massive victories for reform are followed by swift falls from grace are marks of political immaturity. In the past forty years Cleveland has had its scandals and its upsets. But a certain sophistication prevails which tempers the curves of civic morality. Behind Cleveland government is an educated public whose basic training goes back to the still revered golden age of Johnson.

When, in 1933, the nation hailed a national administration which established in rapid succession a number of long overdue reforms, an elderly man came to my office in the State Department. It was Frederick C. Howe, whom I had not seen since, as a youngster, I had attended Tom Johnson's tent meetings in Cleveland. Fred Howe was of the Johnson inner circle. He was the most academic of the lot, an orator and the author of many books on reform. In the years since Johnson he had drifted here and there, looking for the light he had seen in the Johnson years. He was infused with the idea that under Roosevelt the nation might see something of the same renaissance. Misty-eyed he talked of the old days, and I told him, as I had told many others, that whatever of permanence and worth some of us had given to the New Deal was the fulfilment of simple lessons learned long ago from Johnson in Cleveland. In so far as the New Deal conformed to that pattern, it was hardly controverted. But it never learned that reform without able and efficient public service is a song without words. The nation still waits for national leadership in the pattern of Johnson—reform without incompetence.

Challenge to Orthodoxy

CHARLES A. BEARD

Twenty-two Years passed between the death of Tom L. Johnson and the inauguration of the New Deal in Washington. They were years of extraordinary national diversions—war, normalcy, depression. But the seed planted by Johnson and other pioneer reformers in the early years of the century had been alive and growing in the minds of a new generation of Americans. There was a revolution in the texts and teaching in the schools and colleges, in literature, in the everyday discourse of the young, in newspaper and magazine comment, in the legislatures of the states, in judicial decisions, and in the policies of many business enterprises. A new order of priority in social values was appearing. In short, there was, by 1932, an educated audience for the political preaching of social progress through government.

No man was more potent in creating this receptivity than Charles Austin Beard. He appeared on the academic stage as a challenge to orthodox concepts of history, political science and economics, just as had been some of his elders, like John Dewey and Thorstein Veblen. But unlike those pioneers, Beard immensely amplified his influence by creating, often in collaboration with others, popular textbooks which reached all grades and classes of schools. Other writers of textbooks, such as James Harvey Robinson and Carlton J. H. Hayes at Columbia, were infected by his intellectual and emotional interests. Graduate students inspired by Beard moved into vastly important educational forums everywhere. When the children who had studied his texts in school reached maturity, Beard offered them the *Rise of American Civilization*, a great distillation of his historical research in popular form. Finally, his great dialogue, *The Republic,* reached millions more. I cannot believe that ever in our national life has one man wielded greater educational influence.

It was an unforgetable experience to breathe the intellectual atmosphere at Columbia as it existed when I arrived there to study under Beard's direction in 1914. His most potent piece of research, *An Economic Interpretation of the Constitution of the United States,* had appeared the year before and had rocked the academic as well as the juridical world. The sideburns of Harvard's Albert Bushnell Hart bristled as he pronounced the book "little short of indecent." Nicholas Murray Butler characterized Beard as the advocate of "a notion" linked with "the crude, unmoral and unhistorical teaching of Karl Marx." William Howard Taft shouted his denunciation from his retirement at Yale. New York's complacent intelligentsia were shocked and there was rumbling among the trustees.

All of which, of course, made Uncle Charley immensely popular with students. I have noted over many years in academic life that the easiest way to popularity among students is for a young teacher to convey, by whispered innuendo or subtle thrusts at orthodoxy, the notion—often purely imaginary—that "the powers-that-be" disapprove of him. The fact in most such simulated persecutions is that the trustees have never heard of the would-be radical. Some of Beard's less worthy disciples never tired of this trick.

Moreover, some disciples of Beard later inevitably carried his views to lengths that were never envisaged by the master himself. As in the case of Justice Oliver Wendell Holmes, discussed later in this book, Beard was badly served by sorcerer's apprentices. He underscored the great influence of economic factors in history, a theme which had been greatly exploited by Marx. But Beard never failed to make the point that this thesis was present in the Federalist papers, in Harrington, and existed as far back as Aristotle.

He never intended to postulate strictly materialistic elements as the sole explanation of historical events. He was no atheist or agnostic. I once heard him say that "this world is no pig-pen," by which he meant to affirm his belief that something more than a material destiny was shaping our ends.

But no such reservations were made by some teachers and writers who followed Beard. The breach made by Beard in the walls of orthodoxy was used by many who have sharpened class distinctions in America and loaded our political system with bureaucratic burdens.

In 1914-1917, the war in Europe intensified the atmosphere of conflict at Columbia. Radical sentiment was unshakably non-interventionist. Beard was inevitably drawn into the vortex of pacifist controversy, although he was an outspoken enemy of German militarism and contemptuously denounced Wilson's tortuous neutrality. Despite this, he ardently defended the pacifists' right to be heard.

This gave some ultraconservative members of the Board of Trustees an opening to attack Beard on the expressed ground of the war issue, although their real antagonism stemmed from their disagreement with his writings on the Constitution. At one point, when an attack on Beard was imminent in the Board, some of us in the graduate school drew up a testimonial of our faith in Beard and secured the signatures of practically every graduate student in our own and related departments. To President Butler's credit, it should be added that he used this document in a Trustees' meeting to beat down an effort to "do something about Beard."

The storm broke in 1917, when Beard, enraged by a summary dismissal of three faculty members, resigned with a blistering attack on the trustees. And here, in the early prime of life, Beard's career as a teacher and director of graduate students ended. It was a cruel loss to education. But the impact of the incident was permanent. Columbia's authorities were so careful forever after to encourage academic freedom that many an incompetent has been retained and many an issue has been avoided.

This backward-leaning is illustrated by an incident that occurred many years later. A trustee of one of the colleges at Columbia told me that Fiorello La Guardia, then about to retire as Mayor of

New York, wanted very much to occupy a teaching position in Columbia. This man had approached another very important Columbia trustee with La Guardia's ambition and was told that even a hint that a trustee wanted to promote an appointment would violently prejudice a favorable outcome! I was asked to sound out the members of my department. Their answer was a resounding "No!" and the matter died. The irony of this incident is apparent. For La Guardia was far to the left of even the Beard of 1917, but the hint of his appointment came from the timid trustees.

The mutability of time is shown, too, by a comparison of the editorial content in the *New York Times* when Beard resigned and when he died. On the former occasion, the *Times* declared that Beard was a writer of "bad books . . . grossly unscientific . . . unrelated to facts" and that his resignation was "Columbia's deliverance." When he died, handsome amends were made: ". . . liberalism was not only a tradition in his family but also a creed that was to be carried into practice. . . . Even before the storm broke he championed freedom of academic thinking. He disagreed with J. McKeen Cattell and H. W. L. Dana for opposing our entry into the First World War, but defended them against a reactionary board of trustees that had dismissed them from Columbia and resigned from the faculty himself. . . . The future will have to decide his merit as a historian; the present honors him as a defender of liberties that must be upheld if this democracy is to survive."

It should be added that before President Butler's retirement, Columbia, at the behest of our department, which was largely composed of friends and former students, invited Beard for a term of teaching. This Indian summer was happily marked by an honorary degree.

The influence of Beard upon his students is difficult to express in terms of ideas. It was made of deep personal ties and an attitude of mind.

His dramatic impact upon people was immense, for he was, like Veblen and James Harvey Robinson, a great satirist. This gave a brilliant tone to his teaching and writing. His patience and kindness were boundless. Hundreds of his friends' books bear evidence of his encouragement and influence. He was, moreover, an arresting example of industry sadly needed by a not-too-energetic academic community. Writing, especially to a professor, is hard labor. Beard never spared himself. For thirty years after his retirement from Columbia he scorned honors and acclaim and turned out an incredible number of books in the seclusion of his Connecticut home.

Beard taught an attitude of mind vastly important to the field of politics. It was hard-bitten realism. He challenged orthodoxy —even his own earlier orthodoxies. He once said in class that the best equipment of a historian was to consider at all times that the very opposite of accepted faith may be true. His last public address, to a group of research specialists in government, was a plea that they reconsider all the dogmas of political science taught thirty years ago.

His early belief, which helped to revolutionize the interpretation of history, was that great events were rooted in deep economic trends. For that very reason the personalities in his history seldom come to life as they do in Henry Adams or Gibbon. This overemphasis upon social and economic forces he himself challenged in his last years.

His recognition that great events are not always the result of economic and social forces, but are often caused by the acts of individuals is shown by his later attitude toward Roosevelt. Beard was an early admirer of the New Deal, but, largely on the issue of foreign policy, he later became a sharp critic of Roosevelt. In 1937 he supported Roosevelt's Court reorganization plan. Seven years later, he said to me, "The senators were right in fighting that plan. They knew their man. I was wrong."

Beard's challenge to orthodoxy was present in his two big books on the origins of our participation in World War II. These books were violently criticized by reviewers who represented those circles, largely eastern, who pressed in 1940 and 1941 for intervention in the war. Their point of view—that our participation was essential

—has itself become an orthodoxy. And this final orthodoxy Beard challenged. It was no break with his past. It was that great consistency that breaks even with what seems to be consistency.

Something of the same reaction was apparent in the comments of so-called liberals when Bryan died. How, they declared, could the blazing radical of 1896 become the defender of a Tennessee law to enforce fundamentalism in 1924? The answer to those critics is that Bryan could believe that laws and governments could do all things. In 1896, abolish poverty; in 1914, stop wars; in 1924, prevent the teaching of evolution.

Beard died as he would have wished—a victim of hard work induced by a passionate drive to tell the truth as he saw it. I saw a good deal of him in those last years of his life, for I lived near him in Connecticut. The last time I saw him, I talked briefly with him about a book I wanted to write some time, embodying what I had learned in and from politics in the years of my life. He was the teacher again, and I was the student. "Come back next week and show me the outline," he said. I labored over my plan and went back the next week to get the advice I badly needed.

He was not at home. He had been taken to a New Haven hospital where in a few days he died—his frail body literally charred and killed by the drive of his burning mind.

I remember well what he said as I walked with him to my car that last time I saw him: "I have written two books about this war. I will write more, if I live." There will be more books to support his thesis before the whole story is told. For his challenge, momentarily unpopular, will live.

Sidewalk Statesmanship

ALFRED E. SMITH

SOME DAYS AGO I found in my copy of Henry F. Pringle's excellent book on Alfred E. Smith the yellowing pages of an old news release. It was an account of a meeting on November 1, 1928, between the representatives of the College League for Alfred E. Smith and Smith himself, who was just completing his Presidential campaign against Herbert Hoover. The venerable educator and philosopher, John Dewey, was spokesman for the League, and he presented an impressive list of endorsements from faculty members of more than four hundred American colleges. The significance of the occasion burst in the faces of the reporters present, despite their fatigue and cynicism after weeks of following the campaign of a man who they knew had slight chance of election. Their stories next day reflected the last, best incident of a long campaign in which the issues were scarcely audible.

I remember well the great sincerity with which John Dewey reflected the admiration of people who had lived in higher education for a man who with deep truth and great feeling was able to say in reply: "I have never graduated from any school. I have not got a diploma or piece of paper to prove that I ever went to school." Dewey's tribute recounted the capacity of Smith to make the complex simple, to win public support for dull and dry necessities and to win mass support without an appeal to class.

Al Smith was the most potent political educator of a decade singularly devoid of lasting inspiration, and his ultimate rank as a statesman will rest upon that simple fact. Perhaps it was because in that decade I was engaged in education that I felt his importance so deeply.

He was, as he said, denied all but a brief introduction to formal schooling. He learned by explaining things to himself. In the vast scope of his duties as a legislator and as an executive he restated the papers and documents to himself in his own inimitable vocabulary. He then sought homely parallels and examples. Then he conveyed these meanings to millions who read and listened as if he were talking to millions of Smiths.

He was an extrovert. He had the capacity of an actor learned in parish entertainments. He added a touch of rough native humor. And he spoke in public the speech that was known in the streets and clubhouses. Except in two instances, he was irresistible in a campaign, and on those exceptional occasions he contended with cosmic national forces. There was no pretense about Al Smith, even the pretense of being without pretense.

Writing in 1928, Felix, now Justice Frankfurter, underlined a point about Smith which set him apart from his two distinguished successors as Governor, Franklin D. Roosevelt and Thomas E. Dewey. "The clue to his record in New York," said Frankfurter, "lies in his extraordinary talent for accomplishing great reforms not merely *with* popular assent, but *because* he is able to awaken popular interest in his aims and to enlist popular understanding of the technical means by which alone social policies can be realized."

This emphasis by Smith on making the public understand the means as well as the objectives of reform is a practice that needs to be noted again and again. It is indispensable not only to that vague concept called social progress, but to the improvement of government as an efficient servant of the public.

Franklin Roosevelt took a much easier course. He illuminated objectives—even fantastically unrealizable objectives. These excited and inspired. When one set of these objectives—F.D.R. loved the word—faded, he provided another. Since the interpretation of tough practical problems of administration is tortuously difficult, Roosevelt seldom sought to teach. He was content to inspire.

Thomas E. Dewey, as able as Smith as an administrator, has never been able to dramatize his achievement. He has never been able, as was Smith, to win public interest in the dull details of budget-making, road-building, institutional care or educational mechanisms.

In this capacity to make the public understand the complex but essential mass of governmental machinery, Smith stands alone in the annals of American statesmen.

While Smith had unparalleled skill in making the problems of government simple, he realized that government was no simple matter. He believed in no Jacksonian proposition that every man was fit to govern. No president or governor ever paid a higher compliment to education by the choice of expertly trained assistants.

This often caused dismay and anger among his old friends.

When he was President of the Board of Alderman, an old schoolmate asked him for a job as elevator starter in the Municipal Building.

"Don't you know about civil service? There's a stiff examination for that job."

"Examination in what?"

"Hydraulics and a lot of other things you don't know anything about."

"Listen, Al, save that stuff for the Eyetalians and Poles. I went to school with you."

Al told this often with great amusement, but with no softening in his preference for experts.

Smith never hesitated when the public service was involved to turn against powerful members of his own party. His devastating arraignment of William Randolph Hearst lives in New York's political annals. Hearst never again was a factor in the politics of the state. When it became apparent that John F. Hylan was a bungling mayor, Smith came down from Albany and supported James J. Walker as an alternative. Then, in turn, Walker's casual manner toward public duty infuriated Smith.

Always the individualist, Smith never built a strong statewide party. He won elections on his own, and since he was indispensable to party victory, the various organizations followed him. Unlike Gladstone or Asquith, he spent little time in the long negotiations and compromises necessary to great party leadership. Facing the national convention in Madison Square Garden in 1924, which had just rejected his candidacy, he pledged New York to the candidate John W. Davis. He added, "I am the leader of the Democratic party in New York State." No leader who felt sure of himself would have so asserted himself.

In the years following 1932 he grew increasingly indifferent to state and city affairs. Smith at seventy was reminiscent, detached and more and more religious. Family obligations, often embarrassingly expensive, kept his attention on his business of running the Empire State Building. He seldom frequented party gatherings, and his occasional speeches lost the spark and wit of earlier years.

It was inevitable that public knowledge and comment upon the career of Smith should, after 1928, be enmeshed with the name of Roosevelt. Actually, their careers were quite apart after Smith surrendered his Albany office to his successor. The rift widened with the years, while volumes of speculative comment appeared which dealt with the parting of their ways.

I have no desire to pursue that subject, except in so far as one aspect illuminates the deep convictions of both men. It can hardly be said that, at the time when their relations became irreconcilable, one was more "radical" than the other. Nothing in Roosevelt's policies as governor had reversed the trends established by Smith. Nor did the measures enacted by Roosevelt justify Smith's outspoken opposition. Certainly, the Roosevelt policies in agriculture and in the protection of investors, in spending on public works or in social security could not have offended the Smith who campaigned in 1928. Nor can I believe what is so often said by partisans of both men—that Roosevelt's failure to avail himself as governor of Smith's advice could have embittered so generous a soul as that of the Happy Warrior.

Smith arrived at many of his spoken convictions by a deep instinct which he rarely defined in explicit words. He was a man who was profoundly conscious of the fact that he had succeeded.

He never entered that rarefied atmosphere in which other notable men have questioned whether it is, after all, "worth while." Like Herbert Hoover, he believed that his rise from obscure poverty to high place was made possible by the atmosphere and tradition of America. He believed that he succeeded because he worked hard, lived right and that this country rewarded and approved such effort. He saw nothing inconsistent in moving from Oliver Street to Fifth Avenue, although in Tammany club houses there was muttering about Al's going high hat. He respected success. He believed, moreover, that success was individual and that an effort to by-pass individual effort by class or collective movements was dangerous and alien to American tradition.

Smith knew the reality of economic differences from bitter experience, but he passionately believed that the general welfare demanded that all avenues between groups should be kept wide open for individual effort and achievement.

Hence, his earliest attack upon Roosevelt was in response to what he conceived to be an effort to array class against class. He never spoke with more intensity than at the Jefferson Day dinner in Washington in 1932 when he said, with his mind and that of his audience on Roosevelt, "I will take off my coat and fight to the end any candidate who persists in any demagogic appeal to the masses of the working people of the country to destroy themselves by setting class against class and rich against poor."

With that declaration the die was cast. He had hesitated long and anxiously about becoming a candidate. And he had, when it was too late, made an effort to halt the Presidential aspirations of Roosevelt. He failed in this effort, but despite his perfunctory support of Roosevelt in the campaign his opposition continued to the end.

It is irrelevant to cavil at Roosevelt's motives in never summoning Smith to high place in government. Smith had made his choice and it is hardly likely that he would have accepted. Such a rapprochement would have implied an insincerity of conviction foreign to Smith's nature.

Smith died in the midst of Roosevelt's fourth campaign, with no public announcement of his choice. It had, however, been widely rumored as early as the spring of 1944 that he contemplated supporting the Democratic ticket that year. I had known Smith in those latter years well enough to doubt such speculations and wrote a piece which sharply denied this suggested change in Smith's attitude. Smith read it and wrote a note of appreciation and approval.

He died as he lived, in the belief that a so-called new deal which moved beyond the opening of the doors of opportunity to a chimerical goal of success for all was a denial of American tradition.

A Stone Rejected

HERBERT HOOVER

It FELL to my lot to play a small but intimate role in a series of events which probably weigh more heavily in the mind of Herbert Hoover than all else in his eventful career. I carried the unofficial but arduous responsibility of a policy pack-horse for Roosevelt between his first election and inauguration. I was present when the two men first met in November after the election, at the White House, and on two subsequent occasions. I helped to draft their joint and Roosevelt's several statements during that time.

The issues were critical and of lasting importance. They involved the foreign debts, the forthcoming World Economic Conference and, finally, the bank panic in February and March, 1933. It will be Hoover's conviction to the end that cooperation at that time might have spared America and the world bitter anguish and loss. It was Roosevelt's conviction that cooperation was not his duty. Interpretations of this issue will be a subject of debate for a generation.

Elsewhere, I have written the record of those negotiations factually and in detail.[2] There is little that I can add to resolve the real issues in the debate because the matter really comes down first to the unspoken calculations in Roosevelt's complex mind and, next, to the motives behind the panic that gripped people in the bank crisis. Simply stated, Hoover believes that people were afraid of Roosevelt's projected policies and of his advisers. Roosevelt believed that people were afraid of the banks. I pretend to no clairvoyance in plucking the meat from either of those mysteries.

[2] *After Seven Years.* New York: Harper and Brothers, 1939. Chaps. III, V.

Inferences are dangerous, even when based upon the observation of conduct.

Charley Michelson rushed in where others have feared to tread, however, and once said flatly that Roosevelt calculated that the bank crisis would culminate on Inauguration Day. Thus, it may be surmised, a masterly political mind would contemplate a peerless political advantage. Perhaps this is true, although Roosevelt never indicated to me that he had such a gamble in mind. For it would have been a vast gamble with the security of the nation. It deserves to be said, however, that if he had so calculated, his conduct would have been exactly what it was.

Roosevelt returned to Miami from a cruise on February 15th and arrived in New York on the 17th. He was well advised of the panic that was infecting the nation. On the 14th the Michigan banks had closed, and those in other states followed.

On February 17th Hoover wrote personally and in longhand a long letter to Roosevelt reciting the grave nature of the emergency and asking, in the interest of creating confidence, that Roosevelt make public certain assurances. Among these, Hoover suggested, should be statements that "there will be no tampering or inflation of the currency; that the budget will be unquestionably balanced, even if further taxation is necessary; that the government credit will be maintained by refusal to exhaust it in the issue of securities" and that "it would be of further help if the leaders could be advised to cease publication of R.F.C. business." He added that he would welcome the announcement of the new Secretary of the Treasury, who might be a point of working contact with Roosevelt.

This letter was delivered by a Secret Service officer personally into the hands of Roosevelt on the 18th, at a newspapermen's dinner in New York City. Several friends, including myself, were at the table at the time, and Roosevelt, after reading the letter, passed it around the table to be read. In a discussion later that night, Roosevelt seemed nettled by Hoover's request for specific statements concerning his course and held to his determination that mere statements would not improve matters.

In the rush of things in the next ten days, I learned nothing further of the fate of Hoover's letter. The fact is that it remained unanswered for at least ten and possibly eleven days. The reply reached Hoover on March 1st. It was an apology for the delay, with the enclosure of a draft letter which Roosevelt said had been written a week before. This draft had not been sent because of the misunderstanding of a secretary. It said, in substance, that Roosevelt did not believe that a mere statement would help.

This loss of time was serious, although Will Woodin had been named as the new Secretary of the Treasury and on his own account started conferences with members of the Hoover Administration and with bankers.

It is most unfortunate that contacts were not established immediately after the receipt of Hoover's letter—contacts which proved so useful two weeks later. Most, if not all the steps that were then taken might have been accomplished by close cooperation. For Roosevelt's word was law with the Democratic side of Congress. And the infection of fear might have been stemmed before it had reached the critical stage of that March 4th. All the tools which were eventually used were in the Hoover arsenal. And after Roosevelt's arrival in Washington March 2nd, he found the Hoover Administration ready and able to work with the incoming masters of the scene.

In those emergency ten days after March 2nd, Will Woodin, together with Ogden Mills, Arthur Ballantine, retiring Undersecretary, and F. G. Awalt, Acting Comptroller of the Currency, and several others spent days and nights together in the Secretary's office. I was present in an unofficial capacity. It is no understatement to say that without the expert, experienced and generous help of those Hoover holdovers, the banks could never have been saved. The pity is that this joint effort could not have had its beginning sooner.

Hoover left Washington neglected, exhausted and deeply disappointed. But he was not embittered. All the evidence points to the fact that he was carried through the shoals of political caprice by a sturdy philosophy built up in the earlier years of his incredible career.

I well remember his final Presidential appearance before the Gridiron Club, after the election. His speech on that occasion carried none of the rancor so often attributed to him at that time. It was, instead, a beautifully phrased tribute to the spirit and institutions of a country that gave him, despite his humble origin, honors, fame and high responsibility. It was a speech of high purpose and deep humility. He vanished into the ranks, marking the crowded events of the early Roosevelt years, busying himself with useful incidentals and, wherever and whenever called upon, sharing the fruits of his experience with those who asked.

But it was decreed in the stubborn mind of the man who succeeded him that Hoover should never officially be called by the nation to service befitting his talents. It was a grievous waste, compounded in later years when war magnified manyfold the reappearance of so many of the problems of the first World War. This studied neglect has often been noted and, again, I must disagree with those who attribute Roosevelt's neglect entirely to ungenerous and vindictive caprice. It was, I believe, the result of political prudence, for Roosevelt entertained a view that only Hoover among the notables of the Republican Party possessed the massive convictions and intelligence to provide an alternative to the New Deal. Roosevelt actually believed that Hoover might well emerge once more as the leader and the candidate of his party.

As proof of this, I have an interesting memorabile on the wall of the room where this is written. It is a note from Marguerite Le-Hand, the President's secretary, recalling a bet which I made with Roosevelt some months before the 1936 conventions. It says:

November 10, 1936

Dear Ray:

In the President's "Future Folder" he found a memorandum dated June 3, 1935, saying:

"How many dollars will you give me against one dollar that Hoover will not be the Republican nominee in 1936? I will give you twelve to one on all the money you can get."

He had an idea that he made this bet with you. Do you recall it? At any rate, he says he owes somebody a dollar and he wants to pay it.

Beside the note is a dollar bill, mute evidence of Roosevelt's belief that Hoover might and ultimately would regain ascendency in the Republican party. It was no part of Roosevelt's nature to build up a rival.

That fear of a Hoover renaissance surely had a part in the persistence with which the Democratic party under its skilful master perpetuated the myth that Hoover and Hoover alone was the architect of the depression and the impotent pilot of a nation in a great storm. Other lesser Republicans—like Stimson and Knox—who had been no less critical of Roosevelt than Hoover, were granted full political absolution. But Hoover was the stone rejected until advancing age had its way with his availability and a more generous soul inhabited the White House.

The concentration of Democratic policy against Hoover succeeded even beyond the expectations of its progenitors. For the Republican party itself caught the malicious infection. Candidates Wendell Willkie and Thomas E. Dewey skirted the Hoover issue with conspicuous but wasted caution. Both of these more recent candidates, by studied omission, implied that their Republican party began some time after 1933. The veil with which they covered the past was an insubstantial thing. Democrats seeing that past stark and unprotected, made it the center of their attack. Undefended by Republicans, the Hoover history as it was learned by millions of new voters was exactly what Democratic bias and vindictiveness wanted it to be. And this distortion proved in large measure to be the decisive factor in five successive Republican defeats.

Meanwhile, Hoover, in addressing four successive Republican conventions, has offered his party the moving elements of a real party philosophy. And the mounting enthusiasm with which these messages were received should have suggested their value to the candidates selected. But doing exactly what Roosevelt intended that they should do, the candidates offered a marrowless program for a party which by inference they defended by an apology. And in the hard, pragmatic test, these candidates and their strategy failed. Hoover, in the abundant resources of his own conscience, can know that he will live as the greatest Republican of his generation.

I have personal reasons to know that Hoover, in the years after his defeat, lived under no veil of bitterness. The failure of his successor to put aside political advantage for the nation's sake fundamentally disappointed Hoover. His defeat at the polls he took with the stoic soul of a real politician. For Farley and, as I learned, for me, he carried no resentment for our part in 1932.

In 1938 I met him on a train coming from the West Coast. We spent many hours together—hours that were for me sheeer and enlightening satisfaction. For Hoover, after his native shyness has been overcome, is the foremost informal talker of his time. Out of his cosmic career he has gathered vast information. He knows more than any man I ever knew and, to a greater degree than is the case of most people, a large part of what he knows is illuminating and pertinent to current affairs.

In 1939, a year after that meeting on the train, there was published in two gossip columns and later in a national periodical a strange and false story. It said that Hoover, angered by my book, *After Seven Years,* and feeling that I had therein violated the tenets of confidence, had sent to Roosevelt the suggestion that they join in denouncing me. When the story appeared, a mutual friend suggested that I see Hoover. I did so, and Hoover said the story was false, that he had never since the day of inauguration had any communication with his successor and that he did not propose to be used by my enemies to smear me. His word on this was printed in the offending magazine in the form of a letter from Larry Richie, his secretary. He did not need to do this for his own sake. He was simply moved to be just to a man who, years before, had done what he could to defeat him in an election.

Currently and at long last Hoover has attained, not only in the esteem of the more enlightened few but in the general affection of the many, the status that marks him as our foremost elder states-man. His service to the world and his country in estimating the food requirements and capacities of all nations has vividly brought him to the attention of those who were too young to know him either as a great figure in the first World War or, later, as Presi-dent. Finally, his leadership in the Commission on the Organiza-tion of the Executive Branch of the Government has brought into perspective his capacity as an administrator and statesman.

This Hoover report on governmental reorganization will linger as one of the major documents of our time. Taken as a whole, it is far more than the collected opinions of experts on the critical need of our government for greater efficiency and economy. It reflects in its every aspect Hoover's immense talent for massive organization, his enlightened conception of the needs and capaci-ties of the nation, his basic conviction that liberty and initiative are essential to our preservation and progress. Finally, it is an expres-sion of his belief, for which he was mistakenly chastised in 1932, that government must not only at times lend its powerful support to our economic system, but must be ever cautious lest it crush those individual efforts that are the only real sources of wealth and security.

History's Bone of Contention

FRANKLIN D. ROOSEVELT

THE TITLE of this chapter is intended to suggest that a definitive, not to say final, evaluation of Franklin D. Roosevelt can not appear for generations. That is not because of any difficulty in mobilizing the facts, nor is it because of the complex character of the man. It is because his personality, appeal and policies so divided people that those who loved him will hear no evil, and those who hated him will tolerate no praise. In such an atmosphere, calm and judicial evaluations are lost.

Perhaps this is because he was so good for so many and so bad for so many others. His major achievements cut deeply into the social structure of our country. Since 1933 there has been a revolutionary shift in the economic strata. Those who have benefited will revere Roosevelt's memory. Those who were dispossessed will revile it. And children and children's children will inherit those conflicting judgments.

It is not for me in this space to contribute to that debate. For the reasons stated above, it would be futile. It would take volumes to do it. And it would be foreign to the purpose of this book.

For that reason, I may disappoint two kinds of reader: Those in whom there is a lust to probe the motives and lacerate the reputation of anyone who speaks anything but praise of Roosevelt; and those who seek in every contemporary discourse on Roosevelt some new revelation of his duplicity or failure.

I am writing about people who had something to teach about politics, and Roosevelt had a great deal. I shall therefore set down some considerations and judgments of Roosevelt only as a politician. In that role he was a master—an immensely successful one. His capacity and conduct in the fields of economic and social reform, in the reaches of human affairs embraced by the Presidency will be considered only in so far as they throw light upon Roosevelt the politician.

Roosevelt's career will remind us once more that success in politics demands more than casual interest or belated addiction. It is no profession to be taken up in later life, like golf or bridge, after success in business or in a profession. It demands long experience, constant attention and, what is most important, a radical adaptation of mental processes. It demands personal and environmental advantages denied to most. It is a jealous art and can tolerate only slight time for other human concerns. Roosevelt had most of the necessary advantages and paid the price and the penalties.

We need not speculate about why or when he decided to give his life to politics, because such decisions are seldom knowingly made. The circumstances of his early environment, as well as the nature of his mind and character dominated his course.

The environment into which he was born and spent his early life is a familiar story. Economic security, association with eminent people of his time, the historical memories of the Hudson Valley and the prestige and name of his distant cousin, Theodore, were among his advantages. Roosevelt himself once wrote the following rule for a beginner contemplating the vicissitudes of a political career:

"I think we can lay down a rule covering a political career entered into with the highest purpose of serving one's community or one's country. Either the individual should have enough money of his own safely invested to take care of him when not holding office . . . or else he should have business connections, a profession or a job to which he can return from time to time."

His personality lent further advantages and incentives. He was unusually attractive in physique and in manner. He liked people, and most people liked him. His mind tended to discursiveness, except when politics was concerned. He was what highbrowism lists as activist. He did not quarrel with life as he found it. The world into which he was born was something to be worked with and to provide him with satisfactions.

His mentality was perfectly suited to the life he was to lead in pursuit of political eminence and power. His academic record at Harvard and at the Columbia Law School was mediocre. There is no evidence of even a mild interest in history, theoretical politics, psychology or economics. This is the more remarkable because in his day Harvard and Columbia offered the unparalleled incentive of courses in those fields given by brilliant and distinguished men. In this respect, his absorption of those offerings was markedly inferior to that of T.R., who avidly devoured whatever was within reach at Harvard and later at Columbia.

We are almost shocked at the contrast between F.D.R.'s casual interest in fine thinking and classical culture and the prodigious industry of Jefferson at William and Mary, of Madison at the College of New Jersey, of Woodrow Wilson in his father's study and at Davidson, Princeton and Johns Hopkins, or the mastery of the few books within Lincoln's reach.

Roosevelt simply was not reflective or philosophical. He had little patience with the abstractions of mathematics and economics and, so far as I was ever able to discern in five years of association, he was quite ignorant of such political classics as are the primary reading of the younger students at Oxford, Cambridge, or the best of American universities.

Even Bryan had manifested an interest in ameliorative and reformist literature, although he neglected basic information. But Roosevelt as a young man showed none of that broad interest in economic pain-killers which developed in his Presidential years, and even then his interest was in their adaptation to the exigencies of politics.

One can hardly recommend this sort of preparation for statesmanship, but it had immense reward for Roosevelt. It freed his mind for intense, almost passionate concern with matters which most serious people regard as the escapist pastimes of idle hours. And these, when pursued with intense concentration, are invaluable in politics.

Roosevelt's lack of capacity for fruitful and revealing reflection, his meager scholarly interests, his frail delvings into complex economic problems and his juvenile off-hour interests were positive advantages to him as a politician. They were understandable by the generality of people, whose interests were similar.

To a philosopher, a scientist or a great lawyer, the preoccupations of a politician seem to be the interests of a person too lazy to apply himself to serious things. This is a gross underestimation of the politician's job. For beneath the surface he is applying his mental faculties to exceedingly complex subject matter, and if he is to be successful he must labor with incessant energy and meticulous care. For political genius is the capacity to give continuous, undivided and sedulous attention to matters that to most serious people seem too trivial to bother with.

Whether Roosevelt chose law as the most convenient avenue to a political career or as a serious vocation is not clear. What we do know is that his residence at the Columbia Law School was not marked by unusual work and that he left before the course was finished. After admission to the bar, he worked casually and briefly in a big law office and, in 1910, turned to active politics, as a candidate for state senator in his heavily Republican home district.

This was a most orthodox beginning. T.R. had trod the same road nearly thirty years before. And F.D.R.'s campaign showed real capacity for a rookie politician. He adopted a plan which became immensely significant and unfailingly successful in 1928, 1930 and 1932. He neglected the cities in his district, because by tradition they had Democratic tendencies, and saved all his energies for winning the rural Republican votes. Thus, he wasted no time on those who needed no conversion.

He also recognized that it was essential to get attention by spectacular means. He threw his attractive personality at his prospective constituents, driving about in a shiny red automobile in a whirlwind man-to-man canvass of the backroads.

Once in the Albany Legislature, he made another shrewd move. He established a home which was pleasant diversion for colleagues wearied by hotel routine and restaurant food.

And most notable of all, Roosevelt, realizing his political inexperience, his previous lack of contact with the press and his short-comings as a writer of speeches and papers, enlisted as an assistant and tutor a veteran political reporter, Louis Howe, who was destined to remain a sort of political equerry for a quarter of a century.

Later, he seized the opportunity to ally himself with those who hated and distrusted machine politics, the emblem and embodiment of which was Tammany Hall. Thus, by the simple means of selecting a common enemy, he garnered wide-spread recognition and approval.

Those who called themselves the better people of New York have always had mixed reasons for opposing Tammany. The reasons which they do not express are that Tammany suggests alien ancestry, religious affiliations antagonistic to those of most native Americans, and generally the "lower" and poorer element. The reasons expressed are the corruption, the misgovernment and the autocracy of the machine. These latter evils are not to be minimized. The former, however, are important and pervasive. In any event, opposition to Tammany has made national reputations for Democrats and Republicans alike—from Tilden to Dewey.

Roosevelt's defeat of Charles E. Murphy's Tammany candidate for the United States Senate, Blue-Eyed Billy Sheehan, made him a national figure at small cost. For with his Republican constituency behind him and a national field of action before him, he needed Murphy only as the "heavy" in his play.

The feat, together with his active advocacy of Woodrow Wilson in the 1912 pre-convention fight, brought him favorably to the notice of the new President and, again following the T.R. pattern, Roosevelt received as his reward the Assistant Secretaryship of the Navy.

In 1914, according to Roosevelt's own account, at Wilson's specific request he ran for the Senate as an independent Democrat. Although it was a futile gesture, it was nevertheless good public relations. The war, the prominence of the Navy and Secretary Daniels' unpretentious façade provided an unusual opportunity for the Assistant Secretary. Moreover, it offered a zestful indulgence in the affairs of ships and the sea. The evidence is clear that he did

(courgeous)

his job well. His nomination and candidacy for the Vice Presidency in 1920 was, like the 1914 candidacy for the senatorship, productive of good will.

His subsequent illness was a tragic personal blow. I leave to others the resolution of the question whether adversity enriched his character. I have no clear opinion on that. But on the political side, Roosevelt performed magnificently in overcoming the handicap that his illness placed in the way of his ambition. He continued his political interests with the devoted help of Margaret LeHand, his secretary, and of Louis Howe.

At the very center of his political activity there was always a mighty flow of postal correspondence. This, as was shown by Jefferson and Lincoln, is indispensable to political success. As I note later in connection with Louis Howe, letter-writing came to be so voluminous that the dictation and signing of letters flowed beyond both Roosevelt and Howe and was carried on by several assistants. It billowed up during the governorship until tens of thousands of Americans cherished friendly missives from Roosevelt.

It hardly needs saying that every political omen pointed to a Republican victory in 1928 and that the Democratic nomination would be worthless. Echoing this general belief among experienced people, Will Rogers wrote a full-length magazine article suggesting that it was a shame to waste Al Smith in such a race and that the Happy Warrior should be saved for 1932. But Smith could not afford to wait. The maturity of his career had arrived, and he had no choice.

The effort to induce Roosevelt to run for governor raised a serious issue. I am willing to let others interpret the personal considerations involved, among which health loomed very large. In any event, Roosevelt's magnificent physical courage always dominated that consideration as it did in 1944. The political question before him was the advisability of running in a year when only a bare chance of election was offered. In a Republican sweep the New York governorship almost always went with the rest. So it had been in 1920.

But the considerations in favor of Roosevelt's running for governor were strong. It would restore his standing as a national figure. It would show that his physical handicap was no bar. If he were defeated, he would for many reasons surely run ahead of Smith. Not least among the considerations was the fact that party men respect and admire a person who for the sake of his party runs in the teeth of defeat. And, finally, there was the chance that he might weather the storm. His judgment was abundantly vindicated.

At this point there should be recorded an uncomfortable element in the mind and calculations of Roosevelt. In those years and well into the first years in the White House, Roosevelt entertained a nagging awareness that might easily but incorrectly be called an inferiority complex. He was deeply sensitive to the fact that so many among the people who knew him—particularly among those who belonged in the social stratum in which he was born and lived—believed, for one reason or another, that he lived beyond his intellectual means.

Al Smith and Newton D. Baker held this opinion. So did men like Judge Seabury and other leaders at the bar and in business in New York. This view attained classical expression in Walter Lippmann's famous column in 1932 in which he said, among other things, that Roosevelt was "a pleasant man who, without any important qualifications for the office, would very much like to be President." In cultural and pseudo-cultural circles in New York, this attitude in the years before 1933 was a fashion. It had some ground in the record. But those who shared it overlooked the intense mental effort Roosevelt had given to a career not as blessed by academic or professional prestige but quite as difficult as law, medicine or scholarship.

This opinion hurt Roosevelt, but he braced his determination to overcome it. It may be added that with this effort came a not quite Christlike tendency to beat down not only the opinion itself but those who held it.

It is not remarkable, therefore, that when he became governor he did not avail himself of Smith's generous tender of help and advice. Smith people were not retained. Roosevelt determined to take things in his own hands. From then on, the die was cast so far as Smith and all and sundry who held Smith's opinion of Roosevelt were concerned. The mighty engine of governmental power was not destined to spare those who once deluded themselves with a notion that Roosevelt was a weak man.

Once established as governor, Roosevelt began to set up the machinery by which his succeeding steps to the Presidency could be mounted. Louis Howe was established in New York City. He lived in the Roosevelt house on East 65th Street and worked in the office of a rather anomalous set-up called the National Crime Commission. This afforded maintenance for Howe and facilities for contacts with visitors in New York and for correspondence—always correspondence.

In Albany Roosevelt had as his counsel Samuel I. Rosenman, who had grown up in a Tammany environment. Rosenman maintained contacts with New York City politics and with Democratic members of the Legislature. He performed valuable service in handling state legislative problems and in helping Roosevelt with speeches in state matters. There was always bitter feeling between Howe and Rosenman, but such was the care with which Roosevelt delegated authority that their clashes were not often serious.

Roosevelt's major staff acquisition was Edward J. Flynn, boss of the Bronx: In his book, *You're the Boss,* Flynn has described the persistent, almost frantic effort of Roosevelt to get him to accept the position of Secretary of State, a near-sinecure of some prestige and a convenient means of establishing at close quarters a man to whom Roosevelt delegated great power as a political deputy. Later, James A. Farley was selected by Roosevelt to be the political drummer of his cause.

In 1931 I came to be actively associated in the scheme of things and in early 1932 was designated to handle for him all matters relating to the issues, speeches and statements of the national campaign—first for the nomination and then for the election.

It is astonishing that Roosevelt so ordered the various divisions of his political activity, so sharply delegated authority and so clearly maintained personal contact with each of us that there was never the semblance of conflict and never an overlapping of function. This was a mark of superb administrative ability in the political field.

I have known something of the administration of Republican campaigns in the four election years that have followed 1932. In every instance, even under the meticulous Dewey, there has been friction, jealousy and lost motion.

I can best illustrate Roosevelt's capacity for political administration through my own case. He made it clear that I was to gather together the people necessary to the background and substance of his national policies and to be responsible for those people. I insisted on a promise that he would work through me exclusively in these matters. He so notified party leaders in the nation in writing.[3] He never deviated from this in the four years that followed. I exercised arbitrary authority in my limited role, but only in that way could chaos be averted.

I am glad to set this down, because one of the most frequent charges against Roosevelt in his administration of government and one of the traits most irritating to the members of his Cabinet was his habit of telling two or three people to do the same thing, tactfully refraining in each case from telling either what the other was up to. There was no such muddling in the mind of Roosevelt the politician.

Mrs. Roosevelt scarcely ever participated in the meetings, conferences and general activities of the campaign period or, in postelection days, in such affairs around the White House. Roosevelt never seemed to consult her beyond minor questions of housekeeping or family affairs. Except for her great dependence on Louis Howe and her minor contacts with Farley, she kept out of our way. Roosevelt seemed to place no reliance on her political judgment and, so far as I know, never permitted her to interfere in major decisions of government. She was generally regarded as a

[3] For text of letter, see my *After Seven Years*. New York: Harper and Brothers, 1939, p. 45.

kindly woman who had torrential energy. Certainly, her curious economic and social ideas never crept into our concerns.

I have elsewhere described in some detail the methods followed in preparing speeches, statements and public papers.[4] It is only necessary to repeat here that in the ordinary sense of the word, "ghost writing" was out of the question. Such cheap deceit would have been repugnant to my own sense of workmanship and a disservice to Roosevelt. An important speech needs to be tailored, with many fittings and revisions. The ideas of many people need to be incorporated. The finished product must be a part of the personality and ideas of the speaker. He must feel it as his own.

But F.D.R. wanted help and made no bones about the fact that he received it. Only once in that entire campaign did he depart from the text, and that was when, in Baltimore, he took a swipe at the Supreme Court. The hornet's nest thus opened insured subsequent caution.

After Roosevelt's accession to the Presidency, my relations with him in assisting with speeches, public papers and statements continued for more than three years. The scope of subject matter was enlarged, however, and the methods employed were revised. In the first six months of that period I served as Assistant Secretary of State. a position with no statutory duties, which permitted me to serve Roosevelt directly on a wide variety of subjects. I left that office to assume the editorship of a magazine, but still served Roosevelt unofficially.

In those years it was possible to use officials, Cabinet members and others as sources of material and memoranda, but always Roosevelt used me in the final formulation of speeches and public papers. It would probably be news to the top brass in the State Department of those days, who jealously resented my access to the White House, that during that period Roosevelt always secured from them and submitted to me their memoranda for use as raw material in preparing speeches and annual messages.

The country as a whole was unaware of the fact that in about

[4] *After Seven Years.* Chapters I and II, and this book, pp. 149-150.

the middle of the year 1935 Roosevelt radically shifted the whole strategy of his political career. In that year he apparently decided that the earlier New Deal was no longer adequate to sustain his power. Consequently, he shifted his appeal to labor, to minority racial groups and to the masses of the cities. This was not only a repudiation of Jefferson's famous dependence upon agriculture and small towns, but it reversed the policy built and carried through from 1910 on by Roosevelt and Louis Howe. In 1932 Roosevelt felt keenly that he was unable or unsuited to evoke the enthusiasm of large city audiences. He once said to me, "Al Smith is good at that. I am not." By 1935 his mood changed, and the whole course of political history was altered.

The proof of this will be apparent to anyone who will note the course of his legislative program. Social Security, the Wagner Act and a revamped WPA came in that year, and the radical Roosevelt tax program was launched. Perhaps he took a lesson from his dreaded enemy, Huey Long; but also he calculated the ease with which this new course could be taken. He was, in short, bartering acreage for population.

He realized that he could—by cementing the labor vote by the privileges and powers of the Wagner Act, by unemployment and old-age benefits, by the liberal use of relief money and by class appeals in his speeches—win the solid support of great masses in the larger cities. He was thoroughly aware of the continuous drift of the population toward cities, partly because of the growth of urban industry and partly because of the mechanization of farms.

Comfortable alliances with such bosses as Kelly of Chicago and Hague of Jersey City through patronage and the use of relief funds were part of the strategy. Advocacy of civil rights helped with the gathering hosts of Negro voters in northern cities.

To be sure, such a shift would start the return of rural counties and districts to the Republican party. The statistics of subsequent elections show that return. He could also be sure that he would set southern Democratic leaders on their guard, if he did not stir their opposition. But he could calculate that, while they might cause trouble in Congress, they would be impotent in elections—locked in the one-party system.

Meanwhile, vast majorities were assured in the cities, which would overwhelm Republican majorities elsewhere. This strategy proved itself in his three successive elections. It sufficed for the duration of his life. What will come of it remains to be seen.

His third-term candidacy, I have reason to believe, was fore-ordained. I felt that he intended to try it because of a remark he made in 1933. One morning after Lewis Douglas, then Budget Director, had completed his early morning conference in the Roosevelt bedroom and had left, I said something in his praise. Roosevelt agreed and then added thoughtfully, "In twelve years he would be a good Democratic candidate for President." There are ironic touches to this, considering his subsequent break with Douglas and his own drift far to the left of the Douglas fundamentalist economics. Roosevelt's statement, I always felt, indicated a purpose in his mind, even at that early date, to break tradition and to try for a third term.

In the two years before he "consented" to run in 1940, Roosevelt's zest for subtle mystery was fully satisfied. Indirect but not conclusive suggestions that he wanted to return to Hyde Park were merely to divert speculation and to enable him to choose time and place. He never seriously considered any other candidate. As Farley and others say, he systematically eliminated all other prospects. His casual notations of Harry Hopkins' assets and liabilities, solemnly presented by Robert E. Sherwood in his *Roosevelt and Hopkins* as serious evidence that he favored his good friend, can be discounted. This encouragement was merely a way he had in friendly dawdling with intimates. He knew, as many master politicians have known, that to tell a harsh truth to a friend is dangerous, especially when the truth is certain to hurt. And by nature he hated to inflict hurt—directly and face to face. He knew, and Hopkins should have known, that the idea was preposterous.

Roosevelt's lack of directness and sincerity, so abundantly shown in the record now being made public by those who worked with him, can best be understood by a consideration of the mentality and code of conduct exacted by a lifetime of concentration in the art of politics. If the politician were to live wholly by the code of those whom he dominates, he could not expect to win the mastery to which he aspires. His code of right and wrong, his reactions to stimuli and his conduct cannot conform in their entirety to those patterns which are set up in the copybooks to guide the youth of the land. In this divergence arises much of the conflict of opinion about Roosevelt the man, the politician and the statesman.

This is because to an ultimate degree Roosevelt attained what may be described as the political mind.

I have been asked many times by those who know of my long association with Roosevelt: "Is he"—or was he—"sincere?"

When time permitted, I always answered that sincerity, as a quality known to the generality of people, is not fairly applicable to a politician. Or to put it another way, in a category of virtues appropriate to a politician, sincerity occupies a less exalted place than it does among the qualities of a novelist, a teacher or a scientist. And that is in no way damning the politician, for he may exalt virtues such as kindness, understanding and public service far beyond those who sniff at his lack of sincerity.

Perhaps a fairly simple explanation of my meaning can be conveyed by a classical parable written in Plato's *Republic*.

A character in that dialogue describes an underground cave with its mouth open toward the light and, within, a wall facing the light. Inside the cave, and looking toward the wall, are human beings chained so that they cannot turn. From childhood they have seen only the wall and the reflections cast thereupon.

Behind them and toward the mouth of the cave is a fire. Between the imprisoned human beings and the fire men pass with "statues and figures of animals made of wood and stone and various materials."

The objects thus carried are reflected upon the wall—the fire supplies the light. The human beings see the shadows, never the substance. And by manipulation of the objects, those who carry them determine what the enchained human beings conceive to be the reality—the truth.

Roughly translated into the terms of political behavior, the human beings are the public. The carriers of the objects are the politicians, considering not the substance of what they carry but the effect produced upon those who see the shadows.

The politician creates illusions. His words must be selected not because they are the most forceful or descriptive in conveying exact facts and situations, but because they will produce in the minds of hearers or readers the reaction desired by the speaker or writer. What therefore, does sincerity, as we talk this virtue to our children, have to do with the calculations of a politician?

Ultimately, the considerations of a politician are not based upon truth or fact; they are based upon what the public will conceive to be truth or fact.

This produces what is called a "political mind." It is an adaptation enforced by the necessities of environment and survival, just as is the fur of a polar bear or the coloration of a ground-hog. A sort of natural selection operates in the political environment which promotes the survival and success of minds capable of what some may call dissimulation and others call insincerity.

The classical definition of a political mind has been provided by Bernard Hart in his great work on psychology. He said:

"When a party politician is called upon to consider a new measure, his verdict is largely determined by certain constant systems of ideas and trends of thought, constituting what is generally known as 'party bias.' We should describe these systems in our newly acquired terminology as his 'political complex.' The complex causes him to take up an attitude toward the proposed measure which is quite independent of any absolute merits which the latter may possess. If we argue with our politician, we shall find that the complex will reinforce in his mind those arguments which support the view of his party, while it will infallibly prevent him from realizing the force of the arguments propounded by the opposite side. Now, it should be observed that the individual himself is probably quite unaware of this mechanism in his mind. He fondly imagines that his opinion is formed solely by the logical pros and cons of the measure before him. We see, in fact, that not only is his thinking determined by a complex of whose action he is unconscious, but that he believes his thoughts to be the result of other causes which are in reality insufficient and illusory. This latter process of self-deception, in which the individual conceals the real foundation of his thought by a series of adventitious props, is termed 'rationalization.' "

If this be shocking to those unacquainted with the life of politics I hasten to assure them that the public has developed immunities which measurably serve as a sort of protection.

I realize that Roosevelt himself would and Mrs. Roosevelt probably will deny the foregoing evaluation. That, however, would be a logical extension of my argument. For no real politician would wish his words and judgments to be known as political. To eschew political motives is a first rule of politics.

Frederick the Great wrote a discourse refuting Machiavelli's *The Prince*. Someone said that Machiavelli, had he been alive, would have heartily approved Frederick's action in writing the book, because a first consideration in a Prince must be to repudiate the methods by which he actually rules.

To quarrel with this interpretation of a politician, his habits of mind and his motives is to quarrel with human life, and, I may add, with politics as we know it. This suffices to explain the contrast between Roosevelt's words and actions and the verities and results written in the record.

There are, however, in any master of an art shortcomings due to character or failures in judgment.

For reasons that we need not explore, Roosevelt lacked the generosity that would have added to his stature as a politician and a statesman. The truthful but wistful account of Farley reveals how little it might have taken to cement the loyalty of a genuinely susceptible soul. Failure to praise or to acknowledge a real obligation helped in a major way to alienate a powerful lieutenant. This was no isolated case. Marguerite LeHand commented many times to me that it was difficult to get Roosevelt to express gratitude to those who helped him. This is always a major failure in politics. Burke once remarked that "Magnanimity in politics is not seldom the truest wisdom."

Roosevelt unnecessarily and capriciously provoked antagonism. His suspicion denied him the help of many who could have enriched the achievement and distinction of his administration.

He was, in an unusual degree, susceptible to the heady wine of power. In 1932 he was patient, amenable to advice, moderate and smilingly indifferent to criticism. As time went on and victories mounted, he grew impatient of advice, however well intended. He succumbed to the unlovely habit of telling, not asking. He developed self-certitude to the extent that he tended to ascribe self-interest, cowardice or subtle corruption to those who crossed him. He closed, one by one, the windows of his mind. Perhaps this is a disease that haunts the White House. In any event, Roosevelt developed pernicious attacks of it, and this lessened his capacity as a political leader and statesman.

Finally, as Roosevelt's political power came to be more and more personal, there developed under his Presidency litttle improvement in the unity or coherence in the Democratic party which he dominated. His genius in promoting his own success and in winning elections had no counterpart in a capacity to build organization from the bottom up. Perhaps this is not possible in the Democratic party because of the Solid South. The two wings of the party may always be destined to have antagonistic aims. Meanwhile, it remains to be seen whether organized labor, under American conditions, can ever be assimilated in a party.

It may be a strange anomaly that the achievements of Roosevelt in winning masses of voters by positive benefits, in conducting a war and in the field of diplomacy may live longer than his constructive party activities.

That may well be because his political capacity, which was of a supremely high order, was so largely devoted to his own career. The issues he created, however, and the potent influence of his name will be assets of his party for a long time.

The Immortal Amateur

WENDELL WILLKIE

THE DRAMAS of American politics have never even re-
motely produced a parallel to the shoot-the-rapids feat of Wendell
Willkie in and before the Republican convention of 1940. That
feat had daring, suspense, size, sound and color. But as drama it
had the weakness of shooting the works in the first act. Nothing
that Willkie could do thereafter would fail to be anticlimax. And
the final scene, four years later, was, as theater, un-coordinated, unrehearsed and unconvincing.

That the nomination of a great party could be kidnaped was
owing to the disunity of that party. It was also possible because of the inexperience and newness of the two major aspirants—
Dewey and Taft.

But it could not have happened, except for Willkie's singular
charm, his breathless energy and his abounding faith in himself.
He embodied the effervescent zeal of a great salesman who believed in himself, without much critical analysis of his product.
His enthusiasm threw deep shadows over the grave deficiencies in
his experience, equipment and potentialities. In the four years that
followed his nomination, those shadows vanished, and basic weaknesses stood stark and irrefutable. Willkie died the amateur in
politics, rejected by the party that had married him in a mid-
summer night's burst of emotion and adventure. But he died also
in the cherished memory of a group that will always defy party
assimilation and that will never achieve political maturity.

I use the word "un-coordinated" in speaking of the Willkie
denouement because his ultimate failure was due to no lack of
the elements that make for durable political leadership. The sum

46

of those elements should have added up to matchless availability as a public figure.

The circumstances of Willkie's birth were, politically, happy ones. He was the son of successful, intelligent, middle-class people in the heart of the nation and descended from as staunch German liberal stock as that of Carl Schurz. His boyhood was typically Midwestern. He knew his country in detail but not in synthesis. He harvested wheat in Minnesota, dressed tools in the Texas oil fields, operated a cement-block machine in Wyoming, picked vegetables in California and taught high school in Kansas. He attended two colleges redolent with the best American traditions; practiced law in Ohio and New York, trying cases in variegated ranges of jurisprudence.

Nothing that was American escaped his eager interest. One day in the early spring of 1940 I invited him to meet a group of people in Santa Barbara, California. He plied them with vigorous concern about their city, its problems, population and interests. He gathered information as a cocker gathers burrs—rapidly and indiscriminately.

His contacts with people were fresh, easy, casual. His personality, voice and manner carried the irresistibly captivating force of a great jury lawyer. He was free of all pretense, studied dignity, formality. He "dropped in" on people, never bothering about precedent or protocol.

He loved crowds, perhaps to a degree that induced dangerous forgetfulness, for in campaigning he frequently permitted his immediate hearers to lead him into ad-libbing which was incomprehensible to the vast radio audience beyond.

In the habit of many men of massive physique and vitality, he never reckoned with the rules of physical conservation. In that respect he drained life's cup to the dregs of untimely exhaustion and death, recklessly squandering many years of measurable influence and leadership for a short, brilliant impact upon this country and the world.

His abiding faith was in the ideals and memory of Woodrow Wilson, for he had grown and lived, until the advent of the New

Deal, a Democrat and a believer in the League of Nations. His belief that the Republican party had betrayed the Wilsonian faith was ineradicable. It was almost an obsession. And it stood, at first a hidden, but ultimately an obvious bar to any permanent leadership in the Republican party.

His nomination in 1940 was the child of unusual but hardly miraculous circumstances. The possibility was logical enough in the weeks before the convention, although few people versed in politics would concede him any chance. In that period I felt that he did have a chance, perhaps because I felt that he had the qualities indispensable to success against Roosevelt. I wrote at that time: "For some curious reason, after the professional politicians heave the last shovelful of conversational sod on Willkie's chances, they still cannot leave him for dead."

It was clear that Dewey and Taft, unwilling to face the realities of their individual weaknesses, were not going to permit a compromise among their delegates. Willkie's growing popularity began to make an impression among a few realists who felt that he had a better chance against Roosevelt. And powerful interests in the East were capable of throwing to his support a manufactured but immense impact of propaganda.

In the weeks before his nomination Willkie had the benefit of plenty of press support, not only because the unusual attracts journalists, but because the Willkie personality made wonderful copy.

I cannot concede that the Willkie nomination was captured by a hurricane of telegrams or by galleries systematically stuffed with Willkie shouters, although both those circumstances helped. There was logic in his nomination—hastily improvised logic, perhaps, but momentarily irresistible.

Only after the noises of the convention had died away, only after delegates and party chieftains in the quiet of their homes began to unpack suitcases stuffed with rumpled telegrams and soiled shirts did the reality dawn. They had yielded their party to a Democrat whose political antecedents were shrouded in obscurity and doubt! They had, professionals as they were, in hot, humid haste nominated an amateur to lead them in a desperate effort to regain their lost glory. They had gambled their all on what they regarded as a copybook statesman, inexperienced—perhaps uncontrollable.

For Willkie was destined to remain an amateur, innocent or contemptuous of the timeless code that rules the club house, the court house, the convention and the canvass.

Presuming upon a friendship of some years, I sought and obtained an interview with him at the very summit of his career, two days after his nomination. My assignment was the preparation of a magazine article about him. We talked through a large part of a long, rainy night in New York. It was not easy to pin him down to the personal details that I needed for my article. He persisted in talking about plans for his campaign, reversing the order of questioning by seeking information from me concerning the Roosevelt campaign of 1932.

I soon saw that here was no Roosevelt who, while exploiting the impression of the unusual and unorthodox, fundamentally followed the rules he had learned in a long, intensely political career.

Willkie unfolded a plan to dispense with the traditional national chairman and to place his party machinery in the hands of a committee of five, with Charles Evans Hughes, Jr., as moderator. Hughes, Jr., while enjoying the prestige of his father's great name and no inconsiderable ability of his own, was actually as much a political amateur as Willkie. Another member of this proposed steering committee was to be Russell Davenport, as inexperienced as Willkie himself—and visionary as well. Political interests were to receive a salutation by the appointment of John Hamilton, retiring national chairman.

Sensing the disaster inherent in such a scheme, I proposed that Willkie listen to a seasoned veteran who had, 20 years before, restored the Republican party to power—Will Hays. After some persuasive argument against Willkie's objection to any association with such an orthodox Republican, I won his consent to call Hays on the telephone. I implored Hays, "For heaven's sake, come quick!" Hays at once, through the midnight rain, rushed to the aid of his party.

He listened to Willkie's plan with gathering and hardly hidden dismay and then, in the inimitable Hays habit of indirect but wise comment, said:

"There are a million little people running the Republican party. Upon them depends your success. They work on the doubtful, keep the party fires going, get out the vote. They must, when they look up through the ranges of party machinery, see way up at the top a chairman they can understand. One who speaks their language, knows their needs—one who will not forget them."

The committee plan was abandoned, and Joe Martin became chairman. But Willkie pursued his own course in the campaign that followed. He plunged along with improvised speeches, improvised trips and appearances, frequent omissions of political amenities and creating, at the end, a great doubt among his listeners about how his proposals differed from those of his opponent.

Weeks were wasted before his acceptance speech—weeks spent at Colorado Springs with daily off-the-curb remarks about this or that. There were unending interviews with all sorts of visitors, and there was little preparation for the great September and October assizes.

Edward J. Flynn, who directed the Democrats that year, says that Willkie would have been elected without a speech, had the election been held in July: "But when Willkie made his long acceptance speech at Elwood, Indiana, we knew we could beat him. He made matters worse with every speech. The organization Republicans failed to show enthusiasm. There was passive resistance."

"The Willkie defeat," continues Flynn in his book, *You're the Boss,* "cannot be attributed to lack of finances. . . . the amount spent by the Republicans was fantastic . . . during that campaign, in Phoenix, Arizona, I saw at least five headquarters for Willkie on the main street . . . money was being grossly wasted." [5]

[5] *You're the Boss.* New York: The Viking Press, 1947. p. 169.

Grossly wasted, too, was an asset more precious than money. The sudden nomination of a candidate who owed nothing to bosses, machines or to any of the conventions of politics inspired thousands who had never before felt an interest in politics. These people proudly but ineffectively cherishing a belief in "independence," were now able enthusiastically to participate in the sport of a political campaign without imperiling their detachment. Many of these professed independents belonged to the moderately and over-moderately moneyed status—the "station-wagon set," as Tom Dewey was fond of calling them. There were also innumerable young people, conservative by background, who had attained political puberty since Hoover had left the White House and who never really knew what Republican power was like. These young people had learned too well in college that politics is a grimy game and they yearned for the game without the grime. They mobilized for Willkie in great numbers.

In all these newcomers the Willkie movement had a potential asset of great importance. Rightly managed, and with tact and patience fused with what remained of the Republican party, an effective majority party might have been created. This fusion failed in part because impetuous amateurs imagined that they could just once participate in a campaign without mingling with regular Republicans; in part, because of the deep conviction of regulars that these novices were determined to supplant them.

All this inspired power crumbled away after the election, because neither Willkie nor those with whom he was most closely associated had either the desire for or the instinct of party building.

A national campaign is an intricate and supremely arduous enterprise. Millions of words must be spoken, and under modern conditions these words must be planned and written. Willkie's speech and policy architects collectively were a department of utter confusion. There had been little preparation before September, and improvisation prevailed after that. There were too many, too inexperienced cooks.

Hence, the issues were not clearly drawn. People could nod in approval when Willkie talked about more jobs and more production. But the specifications of how these were to be achieved were never sharply stated. Willkie himself was a man of broad, generalized gray language. His policies blended so comfortably with Roosevelt's that the public was unable to discern what all the shouting was about. Nor was there an issue drawn in foreign affairs. Finally, Willkie made little of the third-term issue. He was content with calling his adversary the "Third Term Candidate" and with a few quotations from the fathers. In politics, a quotation is never an adequate substitute for a fact.

These were not matters of detail. They were matters of substance and of critical importance.

Commentators who earnestly wanted to write favorably of Willkie were driven to distraction in their effort to clarify in the press the vaguenesses of Willkie's appeal. I, for one, had to resort to innumerable paraphrases of Emerson's great verdict on Lord Chatham that "there was something finer in the man than anything which he said." But I realized to my despair that a man has to explain himself.

Nevertheless, Willkie emerged from the campaign with what he would have called a great "reservoir" of respect and affection. He had demonstrated incredible energy, personal magnetism and profound honesty of purpose. He gathered more votes than had any Republican candidate before him.

No leader in a generation had a better opportunity to recreate a party than had Willkie when he addressed the country by radio a week after the election. He sensed the opportunity, although he did not grasp its implications. He spoke of his party as a loyal opposition and promised vigilant watchfulness.

But later he sought the sweet satisfaction of merging irreconcilable roles. He essayed to lead a party and also to be independent. He tried to be a free commentator on public affairs, while serving as an actor in those affairs. He tried at once to be Grantland Rice in the press box and Joe McCarthy on the field. A great party leader lectures his followers behind closed doors. Somehow, Willkie conveyed a growing impression that he was, however loyal, the active opposition to his own party. That is not party leadership.

Let us take an example of a great political leader from the dust of the last century—William Ewart Gladstone. Whenever, in his long careeer as opposition leader or prime minister, Gladstone decided to bring his party to a new course of action, he labored incessantly, patiently and earnestly with his fellow leaders. In the standard life of Gladstone by his faithful supporter, John Morley, chapter after chapter is devoted to describing these exercises in persuasion. Gladstone made more speeches in a year than Willkie made in all his life. But they were mostly in the homes of his colleagues or in the cabinet room. The net of it all was that Gladstone ultimately brought his party around to almost every position that he thought wise. That is party leadership.

Mr. Willkie took positions on public questions and then scolded his party for not anticipating them. He had influence, but it was the influence which comes of criticism outside the party. In the role of critic and publicist, he did much to bring his party to the Mackinac Declaration. But in so doing, he lost his position as leader. He promised the "loyal opposition" on November 11, 1940, that he would be its leader. But his course in the years which followed made that leadership dwindle away. The loss was serious to him, to the party and to the country.

A victorious candidate is in a position to make the rules. The professionals will generally follow them in order to remain in favor. But the defeated candidate has little latitude, if he hopes to retain his leadership for battles yet to come. He must devote himself to the trying tasks of consultation, strategy and planning. The sunshine politicians will make themselves known for what they are in the hours after the rout. The ranks of the dissatisfied will swell. To the party leader falls the labor of keeping as many of these individuals in line as possible.

Infinite patience, buoyancy, confidence and the ability to instil confidence; knowledge of how to deal with other party chieftains, which can come only from experience and association with them— all must be part of the make-up of the party leader, if he is to command the respect of those powerful, unhappy few. With them, the future of the party is his. Without them, the prospect of personal victory is dark indeed.

Wendell Willkie, the great, lovable American, proved to possess few of the characteristics which one must have to dominate a political party over the years. His great charm and idealism, his contagious faith in America were not enough.

Despite his detachment from party affairs for the three years after his defeat, the event proved that he desperately wanted renomination. I had seen little of him in those years, but late in 1943 he invited me to breakfast. He claimed that he could and would get the nomination "on the first ballot." He also spoke of his desire to establish a friendly and politically advantageous relationship with Herbert Hoover. That never developed.

Willkie moved ahead with his campaign and for some incomprehensible reason selected Wisconsin as a testing ground. He met utter disaster.

I saw him last at a small luncheon immediately after that defeat. He was no happy warrior. He showed traces of bitterness toward what he called "machine" and "Old-Guard" Republicans, and especially toward the then ascendent Dewey, whom he branded as opportunistic and incapable of high statesmanship. I asked him what had happened in Wisconsin. He replied that the county leaders had done it.

Those who, in the long years between, run politics, select delegates and control primaries had turned to other alliances. Willkie had toured the world, consorted with kings, prime ministers and generalissimos; had lectured his country from Moscow and England and Nanking. Returning, he found his admirers still flatteringly enthusiastic, but he found those upon whom party continuity depends bound to new candidates—mainly to the indefatigable Dewey. Willkie was Enoch Arden peering over the threshold over which he had once carried a slightly giddy old party.

Now, in these years after his death, we can imagine the shade of Willkie grimly casting up the accounts. He might hear his irreconcilable rival, Dewey, declare that the Republican party after two more defeats is hopelessly divided. He could know that no one since 1940 has so inspired that marginal vote which follows no party. He could know that his party, despite its rejection of his leadership, has embraced most of the objectives for which he fought so gallantly and, it seemed, so hopelessly. He could know, too, that he gave to the annals of politics one of its brightest, almost unbelievable pages.

Politics Self-taught

THOMAS E. DEWEY

IN ANY ANALYSIS of the art of politics the significance of Thomas E. Dewey must be in the amazing fact that he went so far with so little natural political endowment. His success is a tribute to hard work, courage, perseverance, analytical intelligence and a superior sense of order. If ever a man circumvented the designs of Providence, it is Dewey. Having made the choice of a political career, he doggedly studied his lessons and almost reached the summit.

It would be interesting to speculate on what he might have done, had he emulated Will Hays or Ed Flynn and devoted his talents solely to political organization, leaving the "front" job to others. Even there, his lack of intuitive discernment, affability and effective dissimulation would have been a handicap.

There was no handicap in Dewey's background or antecedents. Those have been well exploited and need no recital here.

He made the best of his educational opportunities, which were excellent—at the University of Michigan and the Columbia Law School. He worked at odd jobs for part of his schooling, which is good for favorable copy about a candidate. He plunged into the practice of law and attracted the attention of important people. He moved ahead in the law and in law enforcement.

The quality and bent of mind, temperament, demeanor and off-hour diversions of Dewey, carefully analyzed, would suggest great success in law, medicine, business or in the Episcopal clergy. For politics they simply do not apply.

To witness Dewey as a politician is to recall Samuel Johnson's oft-quoted remark about the dog that walked on two legs: "He doesn't do it very well but the amazing thing is that he can do it at all."

Dewey's mind is active, inquisitive, analytical. One can imagine him as a boy repeating hundreds of times, as is the wont of some bright lads, the single word, "Why?" I can imagine the disturbing effect of this incessant inquiry upon elders whose desire to be let alone surely must have been moderated by admiration for a boy who really wanted to know. Curiosity is boundless in Dewey, the man.

Unlike Roosevelt, who always greeted verbal information with smiles of appreciation and unnecessary "yessing," Dewey comes back with questions. He "frisks" the mind of a visitor with penetrating inquiry. He makes him prove things, which is generally embarrassing to people who never bother to verify what they say. This habit of Dewey's disturbs people who do not know him well. It makes them feel foolish or unwanted or intrusive. But it is meant as a compliment, and it is also an expression of a valuable attribute in a public official, who needs all the accurate information he can get.

Dewey has another mental trait, an extension of his inquisitorial powers, which is certainly not an attribute of a salesman although it is respected among his associates. Very often, when a suggestion is made that he do this or that, he replies with a positive "No." Then the suggester presents an argument for the idea, which is brusquely rejected. Then another reason is given, and Dewey knocks that down. If the person making the suggestion is durable, this goes on for a long time. It is not meant to be unpleasant. It is not meant to be total disagreement. What Dewey is trying to do is to gather the best of all reasons for his own decision, and he knows that only by pulling several layers of irrelevant stuff off his conferee's mind can he get at real substance. I well remember an instance of this, in 1943, when Dewey, as well as Governor John Bricker were subjects of Presidential discussion. I knew Bricker well and had seen him a great deal that year. Dewey said, "Tell me about your friend, Bricker." I did so, with a number of praiseful generalities. Dewey interrupted with the crack, "You haven't said a word that makes him any better than Harding."

This nettled me, but restraining myself I set to work and for twenty minutes I expounded with ample detail about Bricker the administrator, the politician and the man. Dewey seemed better satisfied, and when I saw him next, he said, "I have grown to think Bricker is pretty good." Then, possibly without knowing that he was giving my speech back to me, he elaborated on Bricker the administrator, the politician and the man.

In March, 1948, when Dewey was trying to decide whether he would go to Wisconsin and make a speaking campaign, I saw him in his hotel apartment in New York. He said that this was the most difficult decision he ever had to make. He knew he was going to lose the primary, although he thought General McArthur and not Harold Stassen would beat him. I felt that he should go. So did his able secretary, Paul Lockwood, who participated in the conversation. Lockwood and I were subjected to a beating that lasted three hours. We turned our brains inside out, but Dewey brushed off every argument.

I went home weary, disgruntled and firmly of the opinion that Dewey did not intend to go.

That night, he spent hours with two of his political managers, Herbert Brownell and Russell Sprague. After giving them the same beating that we had received earlier, Dewey, at one in the morning, said he would go. This is the way of perfectionism. Roosevelt would have responded to a hunch.

This precision of mind reflects itself in dress, manner and demeanor. Only once have I seen Dewey thoroughly disheveled and completely informal. That was in his bitter slugging match with Stassen in the Oregon primary in May, 1948. Somehow, in the fight his instincts got the better of his mind, and this revelation of Dewey the "regular fellow" won the state.

Perhaps this indicates, more than anything else, the ultimate shortcoming of Dewey the politician. Despite his dogged courage, there is fear—fear of his instincts, which are good, fear of making spectacular blunders. There is reliance on the rational and orderly in a field where reason and order have little authority. His speeches are a bit too precise and distilled, his demeanor too studied, his photographs too posed.

He turned an honest penny in his early days with his voice. That, too, has not been a political asset. There have been voices that helped in politics—witness "Honey Fritz," mayor of Boston who gathered ballots with his ballads. But when Dewey sings he means it. When he speaks, you know that he knows he has a message.

There are classical distinctions among orators. In some cases it is said that the audience reaction is "How well he speaks." In others, it is "Let us take up arms against his enemies!"

Dewey's speeches suggest Billy Phelp's story of the effort once made by Mark Twain's wife to cure her husband of swearing. She came to his room and with some difficulty uttered a string of Mark's favorite oaths. Mark replied, "Dear, you have the words but you haven't got the tune."

Some may attribute the lack of effectiveness of Dewey's speeches to the absence of a sense of humor. Neither ridicule nor irony nor figurative language comes naturally to him. But it is well established that a keen sense of humor is bad for a national political figure. Al Smith's humor was spontaneous, infectious, and exceedingly funny. But in that Al Smith was *sui generis*. Even Roosevelt, whose love of a joke was boisterous, was corny and repetitious when he tried to be funny. Dewey's lack of humor was no handicap in a nation that has taken to its heart so many dry and impassive Presidents.

The ineffectiveness of Dewey's speeches which reached an attenuated summit in the 1948 campaign, resulted from overstriving for perfection, overcaution and too many cooks. Throughout his career Dewey has practiced teamwork in speech preparation. No doubt taking a leaf from the Roosevelt book, he assembled assistance—often able assistance. The work was done with great care and at great length. He himself participated vigorously. His rule was that a minute on the air was worth an hour in the drafting room.

Ultimately, in 1948, a host of speech-writing assistants was enlisted. There were experts on agriculture, labor, finance, foreign affairs and what-have-you. There was also a special writer whose purpose was to put in "spiritual stuff."

Here was the apogee of organization. Everything and anything was considered. As I saw this machine in operation in the west I felt that the effect was overrefinement, overtraining. By the time a least common denominator of everyone's ideas was reached, there was precious little left. The result was generality without even originality in expression.

The breeding of perfection in speeches produces something like the overbreeding of animals. They are too frail for the inclement atmosphere of a campaign.

A speech in politics must be something to talk about. The Dewey utterances reflect a lack of feel for language—pungent, homey or at times strong and beautiful. Few or no unforgettable phrases or images leap out. Dewey's speeches bear no more relation to native eloquence than do Cardinal Spellman's poems to literature.

An honest soul like Dewey's finds it hard to adapt itself to the habits of mystery, of subtle deception and ambiguity which are indigenous to politics. Any such effort has usually been self-defeating or clumsily rationalized.

When Dewey accepted the nomination for governor in 1942, he said, "For my part, let me say right now, that I shall devote the next four years exclusively to the service of the people of New York State."

Now, when the issue came, as it was bound to come, native politicians would have merely shrugged it off, as they have done in numerous similar situations. Instead, Dewey begat rationalizations. When his bandwagon started to move, his contention was that neither he nor any agent had supplied any motive power. He held that when a man enters public service as a career, he is subject to the rules therein. The Presidential nomination being a responsibility of the delegates therein, they have plenary power over a party member. And since a nation is supreme over the state, a debt to the state of New York could be canceled by the national voice of the convention and the electorate. Following that reasoning, he pointed to the words carefully, not to say artfully, inserted in the statement above, "For my part." They meant that so far as he was concerned, he would continue as governor.

Such statements as well as the rationalizations thereof are not regarded as serious matters in practical politics—the more's the pity. So those who sought Dewey's nomination without authority labored to nominate him, and he accepted.

In 1947, while sedulously holding that he was not a candidate, Dewey made a western trip. He disclaimed any political objectives, although in his journey from state to state he talked often with politicians. It was generally believed that he did take the trip for political reasons, and his disclaimers were not only disbelieved but resented as an affront to the normal political intelligence of politicians and news men.

His silence at that time on the major achievements of the Republican Congress was resented. Some of that reticence about Congress crept into his 1948 campaign utterances. The obvious pretense, lack of frankness and failure to stand by his party unquestionably injured him seriously. In this respect he had somewhat artificially and unconvincingly adopted what he deemed to be a political course which a greater master of politics could have avoided.

The 1948 campaign will, of course, be written as the greatest failure of the Dewey career. There were many contributing factors in that great Republican disaster that cannot be attributed to Dewey. There was overconfidence among Republicans generally and many weak state candidates, from Ohio to Colorado— inclusive.

But Dewey must bear a major responsibility. He did little or nothing to alert Republicans everywhere to the danger of overconfidence and the possibility of defeat. But beyond that was his own apparent reliance upon mechanical indices of voting preferences.

For Dewey was always a firm believer in opinion polls. In his pre-convention campaign in 1940, one of his supporters had a polling device which, by tests taken before and after a speech, was designed to register the exact effect of a speech in winning converts. In 1944, public faith in the polls practically nominated Dewey, despite little or no effort on his part. They heavily favored him in 1948. But the fatal weakness of the polls was in failing to register the slide that must have taken place in the last two or three weeks of the campaign.

To that slide Dewey contributed the major impulse. In previous campaigns, caution had prevailed, but other factors saved him. In his gubernatorial campaign of 1942 he made a strong anti-New Deal speech at the outset but objections by some of his former associates in the district attorney's office ended that tactic. He refrained from criticizing the sitting governor, Herbert Lehman, largely, it must be frankly said, because of religious considerations in New York. Hence, his campaign speeches said nothing but generalities interspersed with attacks on machine politics. The weakness of his opponent made election certain. He swayed, in 1944, between slashing attacks on the Roosevelt regime and fine tributes to international cooperation. In 1944, it is true, the difficulties of his position were great. The war was growing in intensity. To exploit the Pearl Harbor disaster, in fact any criticism of the conduct of the war, would have been met by screams about national security. General Marshall visited Dewey and earnestly asked him to omit the Pearl Harbor story, and Dewey patriotically refrained. The real issue of the campaign—Roosevelt's health and the qualities of his running mate—from a political point of view had to be unspoken. Dewey labored under difficult circumstances.

In 1946, as a candidate for reelection as governor, he had a record and a good record to exploit. He was elected by a huge majority as a recognized success as an administrator of state affairs.

This should have given him the clue to the theme for 1948. The facts were, as has been shown by the Hoover Commission, that the Federal establishment was unwieldy, inefficient, wasteful and abominably administered. Above all, the country needed a new deal in administering its affairs. Dewey might well have endorsed the foreign policy of Secretary Marshall in one speech and then devoted his campaign to a detailed exposé of incompetence at home. The facts were there for his staff to assemble. Moreover, he might have convincingly defended the Taft-Hartley Act and the economy measures of the Eightieth Congress. He might have vividly dramatized the meaning of good administration of public business, something of which he was an acknowledged master.

As early as July he seemed to agree that the crying need of the country was good administration. It was a natural thing for him to exploit this need, for his supreme qualification for the Presidency was effective management. But practically nothing was said about the subject. Moreover the impression was created that he did not favor the acts of his own party in Congress. The tragedy of Willkie was repeated. There were somewhat tiresome reminders that the United States had a world mission, that Communism was bad and that we must march boldly toward the future. The result is history and tragic history.

Perhaps I have created the impression that Dewey can be rated as a failure in politics. That is not my intention, and certainly any such conclusion would be false and unjust. Dewey has been a brilliant success in politics. Consider the facts on that point. In his early thirties he won the nation's admiration as a prosecutor. At thirty-six he almost won the governorship, and at thirty-eight, just missed a Presidential nomination. Now, at 47, he has twice been his party's choice and has ably conducted the affairs of New York State for nearly seven years. No man of such dynamic qualities is through in politics. He has plenty of time to confound his critics, and this one hopes that he will.

It is a melancholy and disturbing observation on the facts of political life that Dewey's main defect as a political figure is the fact that the admirable man that is Dewey has so often been obscured by the mask of Dewey the rational politician. It is a big man, too, who so betrays himself.

No American has ever devoted himself with more intensity to the service of a not-always-grateful public. In his prosecutions of rogues and shabby politicians he moved relentlessly to the realities of each case. To try to convict a man like Jimmy Hines, whose doings were hidden in the half-light between crime and politics is not easy. In that case Dewey had almost completed his case and had revealed his evidence when the judge declared a mistrial. So, weeks later, when the glue had thoroughly congealed, Dewey retried the case and won a conviction.

The layman little realizes how tough a mind is required in such mass prosecutions as Dewey won. He must through his assistants, who may be of uneven ability, direct many cases at once. He must protect his witnesses, deal with police over whom he has no administrative authority, sift his clues, watch the selection of juries and match wits with skilful and well paid defense lawyers. He must also deal with a capricious press and bring favorable public opinion to his side. All this the youthful Dewey did superbly.

In the realm of political organization he reorganized a state Republican party which had lost twenty years of state elections and built it into a strong, organized force. In this respect he did better than Al Smith, Roosevelt or any Republican in fifty years. He has avoided factionalism and has got along better with his legislature than any governor in recent history. Moreover, he has developed a smart, efficient, and effective state administration. He has blasted the pious fraud, always a slogan of New York Democrats, that only under them can there be what many of them call 'umane government.

He has probably taken the bitterest and most subtly cruel cracks that cynical and oversensitive reporters have ever invented. Most of them do not deserve repetition. One, however, attributed to a woman, was that "you have to know Dewey to dislike him." The actual refutation of this is the fact that those who were most intimate with him years ago are still with him. No man ever held his subordinates in more willing service and loyalty. The secretaries, lawyers and other administrators who are around him were there when he first entered politics. Some date back fifteen years. Compare this with the processional of the disillusioned who have left other notable men. A man must have generosity and other personal qualities of a high order to elicit such devotion.

Dewey has taken defeat over and over, sometimes when victory seemed assured. He has never suffered embitterment or discouragement. This is moral courage which most successful men never have been compelled to show. Al Smith was beaten only once, before 1928, and then defeat was foreordained. Coolidge never lost. Nor had Warren, until 1948. Dewey's capacity to come up from the floor cannot be underestimated.

The real tragedy of 1948 was that the nation needed just what Tom Dewey had in a superlative degree. It needed harsh, direct inquisition on why this or that was needed. It needed someone to bring strong and devoted people into public service. It needed efficiency and economy. It needed a man in the Presidency who for two or three years could forget reelection and literally clean house. It needed sharp questions such as have been the wont of Dewey: Why? For what? What will it cost? Does this really do what it seems to do?

All this was denied by the voters in 1948. The blow that struck Dewey may have struck us all. That is the pity of nature's neglect of Dewey's political equipment.

He'd Rather Be Right

JOHN NANCE GARNER

ON MY MOST recent pilgrimage to Uvalde, I suggested that, instead of living a comfortable life in that city, John Nance Garner might have been President of the United States.

"No, I'd be dead by this time," he answered.

I would find it hard to quarrel with that judgment, because Garner is not only a shrewd judge of his own physical powers, but he is unparalleled in his appraisal of the burden that rests upon a President.

For this massive personality has served on official, friendly and often most intimate terms with eight Presidents. And in each case it was no master-and-servant relationship but, under the Constitution, strictly coequal. Garner represented the 15th Texas district in the House for fifteen continuous terms and was elected for a sixteenth. But in that year he was also chosen as Vice President. He had attained the Speakership in 1931 and for years before that had been, by reason of his position on the Ways and Means Committee, a powerful influence in the House.

Thus, for thirty-eight years Garner watched the processional of the great, near-great and pseudo-great in the nation's capital. In that time Garner saw 3,000 members come and go. He won profound respect and influence in the national legislature—perhaps beyond any other figure of his time. He was a professional's model for professionals in politics and statesmanship. His flexible mind comprehended the immense range of national problems in those years. He knew nearly every significant American of his generation.

But Garner so maintained the constancy of his personal way of life and his habits of mind and articulation that when he left

Washington he resumed almost the precise place in his home community that he had left long before. Except for the physical changes of age and the breadth of his intellectual interests, he was and is the same John N. Garner who was first elected in a district as large as Pennsylvania.

The simple integrity of his habits bespeaks the simple integrity of his inward convictions. His rugged speech, personal appearance and actions after his nomination for the Vice Presidency became a treasure trove for cartoonists and writers of anecdotes. Some people in the remoteness and isolation of the metropolitan East mistook him for a "character," a glorified clown who spent his time thinking up his next wisecrack or selecting the next funny hat he would wear. A large part of the eastern conservative press portrayed him, when he was nominated with Roosevelt, as a dangerous but picturesque demagogue. They thought him a radical, a wild man. And they prayed, *mirabile dictu*, that Roosevelt might live.

Perhaps this impression was sharpened by news-hungry Washington writers who were, in those days, busy introducing the candidate in their home papers. One of the characteristics of such writers is that they lose the capacity to take a man as he is. They have seen so many phonies in their day and they are so afraid of being taken in by phonies that they conclude that nothing is what it seems to be.

It is quite clear that Garner is picturesque. What made him so distinctive in Washington was the fact that his method of living contrasted so sharply with the show that goes on in the national capital. But he was living his life as he wanted to live it, and the least of his wants was public attention. He refused to go to dinners because he wanted to go to bed early and get up early. He smoked cigars, played poker and struck a liquid blow "for liberty" because he liked those things. At home he went hunting because he likes to hunt and live out of doors. He wore Amon Carter's gift Texas hats because he liked Amon, because that kind of hat was worn in Uvalde, because they were comfortable and because they didn't cost him anything.

There never has been anything of an act in Garner's way of life.

No man who is putting on an act could remain in Congress through all those years and keep the affection and respect of the discerning minority of hard-headed, sharp-eyed men who are there.

Garner's ease of manner deludes no one who knows him well. He is "Mr. Garner" to his close friends, associates and even to his relatives. That is how Mrs. Garner always spoke to and of him. His only son, Tully, addresses his father as "Mr. Garner." Those who knew him well winced a bit when Roosevelt and Farley used the name "Jack." Like Andrew Jackson long before him, this citizen of the frontier has magnificent manners with women. His economical use of words in public life in no way marks his participation in personal conversations. On such occasions he addresses his listener by a variety of names. With Roosevelt it was occasionally "Captain," but always for emphasis, "Mr. President." With others it may be a foreshortened first name, but when he wants Mr. X to remember something, he is "Mr. X."

As a man who profoundly respects the institutions of his country he manifests deep respect for the offices held by others, just as he expected respect for his.

Since he has always avoided time-consuming social functions and political picnicking, Garner reads more than most politicians: newspapers, the Congressional Record and a great many books— good and trivial. But like all politicians, he learns most from talking with people.

Garner is a realist, impatient with pedantry and pretense. The garden of his mind is carefully pruned. He doesn't try to raise too much per acre. What grows in his mind has room to get to the air and sunlight, to fill out, nourish itself. His mental life is no aggregation of half-suffocated plants, and there are very few weeds.

Garner is no sectionalist. He loves his state, his district and his country. But years of service at the center of government have developed his sense of the nation. He was generally rated as a southerner because he came from Texas. But a glance at the map explains a great deal about Garner. Uvalde is near the 100th meridian, which is west of Minneapolis, Des Moines and Kansas

City. He lives where the foothills of the Rockies begin to rise from the great level spaces. But his district originally followed the Mexican border five hundred miles and the Gulf a few hundred more. This was and to a degree is still cattle country. It is not cotton country, which explains a lot. Some of the deep incompatibility which always characterized Garner's relations with Cordell Hull arose from Garner's protectionism. Even Sam Rayburn, who was for years a protégé of Garner, is anti-tariff, for his district is in far-away Northeast Texas.

Garner was never an enemy of business, since his own career was a study in economic shrewdness and business success. For public utilities, however, he developed a hard attitude, feeling that their excesses in the 20's invited strong governmental intervention. During the battle in Congress over the Holding Company bill I heard a senator plead earnestly that Garner intervene and bring about a softening of the legislation. Garner was obdurate: "They have brought it upon themselves. They cannot be permitted to go on as they were."

Garner's greatest legislative battle and achievement was his fight against the tax program of Treasury Secretary Andrew W. Mellon in 1924. The Mellon plan proposed to reduce taxes all along the line at a fairly uniform rate. It received the enthusiastic acclaim of the conservative well-to-do community but stirred up a hornet's nest elsewhere. The issue was made to order for Garner, considering the fact that a Presidential election was in the offing and that this bill had every appearance of an effort to help the rich. Garner, as ranking minority member of the Ways and Means Committee, offered a graduated schedule of reductions favoring smaller incomes. After a two weeks' debate, Garner won a complete victory.

Two of Garner's closest friends in the House were the Republicans Ogden Mills and Nicholas Longworth. Their relations were close, convivial and pregnant with mutual respect. Mills, the ablest Republican congressman in matters of taxation and finance, became Hoover's Secretary of the Treasury. Longworth was Speaker of the House.

Garner spared neither in debate, however, and his uncanny skill in outguessing Treasury experts in the anticipation of tax receipts became legendary. With little research assistance and aided only by pencil, paper and a keen sense of values Garner offered an active and annoying opposition in the years of Republican control from Wilson to Roosevelt. Everyone then connected with the Treasury testifies to Garner's consummate ability in finance.

Meanwhile, Garner refused to bother himself with those concerns that capture the energies of most congressmen. He introduced very few of those minor bills which fill the House hopper in thousand lots. Nor did he cumber the Congressional Record with remarks, although his eminence might have won the floor almost at will.

James F. Byrnes, on the occasion of Garner's retirement, said on the Senate floor:

"I came to the House of Representatives in 1911. I am certain that for at least six years thereafter Representative Garner withheld from the Congressional Record all remarks made by him on the floor of the House . . . While the Record will disclose few speeches made by him or bills introduced by him, those of us who served with him know that there is hardly a measure of importance which was enacted in the last quarter of a century to which John Garner did not effectively contribute."

Perhaps the reason why Garner's nomination in 1932 was received with such unjustified fear by eastern conservatives was his controversy with President Hoover in that year on the question of unemployment relief. Garner introduced and secured the passage of a measure providing for a public works program of $1,200 million and an additional $1,000 million of credit from the R.F.C.

Hoover angrily vetoed the measure, characterizing it as the "greatest pork barrel measure ever devised." Neither Hoover, it may be added, nor Garner had hardly scratched the surface of the spending yet to come.

Despite differences in outlook in that time of depression, Hoover held a high opinion of Garner, as, in fact, had two earlier Presidents. T.R. was amused and intrigued by the young congressman from the cow country. Later, Woodrow Wilson in war years selected Garner as his primary means of liaison with the House. This relationship was not publicized, because the official House leader was Claude Kitchin, with whom Wilson had irreconcilable differences. To implement this liaison, Wilson fixed two long periods a week for conferences with Garner. Sometimes these policy sessions would last for hours. For the greater part of two momentous years, this intimacy continued, and the impression left by Wilson on Garner was permanent.

Bascom N. Timmons, in his biography of Garner, quotes Garner on Wilson: "Wilson was the greatest intellectual aristocrat I have ever known. No President ever had a deeper philosophy of government. His messages to Congress were the most statesmanlike of any I have ever heard or read—they lay over all others like a dollar lays over a dime." [6]

It would be absurd to believe that Garner in the latter half of Roosevelt's second term did not harbor the ambition to gain the Presidency. There was almost irresistible logic in the idea, for Garner through long and brilliant service deserved first honors from his party. He was no longer young, of course. In November, 1938, he reached the age of 70. But his health and mental powers were as good as ever. Moreover, he was deeply disturbed about the course of government policies and felt that he had the formula for their correction.

It is unthinkable that if Garner had agreed, the Democratic conventions of 1940 and 1944 would not have renominated him for Vice President, despite any objections of Roosevelt. As we now know the history of his continued good health, he would have outlived Roosevelt. But he did not so choose for reasons that are a credit to his deep integrity and devotion to classic principles of government.

The story of the last two years of Garner's service as Vice President is told in infinite detail in Timmons' book. Much of that story is verified in James A. Farley's account of the Roosevelt years. I may add that, since I saw Garner often then, I can con-

---

[6] *Garner of Texas.* New York: Harper and Brothers, 1948. p. 86.

firm what both Timmons and Farley say of the deep unhappiness of Garner at that time, of his distrust of Roosevelt and his policies and of his fears for the welfare of his country.

He could not accept a Vice Presidential nomination because, as he said to many people, he opposed a third term for any President. Moreover, he had exchanged pledges not to run again with Roosevelt, and he was a scrupulous respecter of his word.

This is how Timmons puts it, and since Garner authorized the Timmons book, it may be regarded as authentic:

"That day (January 20, 1936) Garner got an important piece of information. Roosevelt told him that he never would run again for public office. Garner also gave Roosevelt some information.

" 'Neither will I,' he said."

Garner so scrupulously observed this pledge that he authorized Timmons, who was a delegate in 1940, to take the floor if necessary and tell the convention "that Mr. Garner would not again take the Vice Presidency under any circumstances."

Garner's opposition to the renomination of Roosevelt was fairly well known at the time. He hoped and believed for a long time that Roosevelt himself would not seek it, for the simple reason that as conditions stood after the defeat of the "purge" in 1938 it was by no means sure that Roosevelt could be elected if nominated. The onset of war in 1939 changed the whole situation. From then on Garner believed Roosevelt wanted the nomination and would use the foreign crisis to justify and compel it.

Meanwhile, Garner's stature became more and more apparent to the country and his popularity burgeoned. He was the man in Washington that visitors wanted to see. He was accorded ample space in the newspapers. Businessmen liked him because he offered a possible alternative to Roosevelt. Party men loved him because of his political regularity. All of Congress respected him and sought his advice. The traditional impotence of the Vice Presidential office could not submerge his vital activity. As a legislative leader he had risen to the power once swayed by Speakers Thomas B. Reed or Joseph G. Cannon. He had made a throne of a political sarcophagus.

Relations between the President and the Vice President cooled and hardened. Garner had been non-committal toward the Court bill in 1937 and outspoken against the purge in 1938. In both instances his judgment was vindicated by the outcome.

He didn't like the people around the President. Morgenthau he weighed and found wanting. Wallace he regarded as a radical, impractical and dangerous. He bitterly opposed the advocates of spending for spending's sake.

In 1939, with the beginning of war in Europe, Garner shrewdly decided that Roosevelt wanted to run again, and he was determined to do everything in his power to forestall him. Polls and other means of sounding Democratic opinion indicated that Garner was overwhelmingly favored as an alternative. In December he announced that he would accept the nomination. Apparently Garner had decided that Roosevelt's intention of being a candidate overrode their mutual pledge of 1936 not to run again for public office, and thus released him from that pledge. To all his intimates Garner said that he had no hope of getting the nomination, but was permitting his name to be entered as a protest against a third term.

But it was clear to all of us who saw Garner often in those years that his opposition to Roosevelt ran much deeper than an issue of constitutional custom and propriety. He had formed a shrewd, sophisticated judgment of the President which gave him ample ground for fear.

He had found Roosevelt unreliable. Timmons quotes him as saying, "He was a hard man to have an understanding with. He would deviate from the understanding."

He felt, moreover, that power and popularity had gone to the President's head. Garner had observed enough Presidents in office to recognize the effects of the heady wine of authority. In Roosevelt he detected a special case of this intoxication.

The two men violently disagreed on methods of handling Congress. Over the years Garner had gained a profound respect for legislative independence as well as appreciation of congressional psychology. He opposed the high-handed pressure that had been imposed by Roosevelt and the men about him.

He disagreed on two of Roosevelt's major policies—the enlargement of the power of labor leaders and the theory of channeling the people's savings into great government projects. He once said to me, "The troubles with this country are too much John L. Lewis and too much spending."

The rest is history. Garner, like Farley, projected himself as an avowed candidate. Roosevelt waited until the last moment to declare himself. And an angry and confused convention acquiesced not only in a third-term nomination but in the thoroughly unpopular acceptance of Wallace.

Garner, as had been his habit in other campaigns, spent the summer and autumn at home. This time, he omitted his customary single speech.

He returned to Washington in January, 1940, to preside over the Senate and to attend the ceremonies that mark the inauguration.

Eloquent tributes were offered on the Senate floor. It was noted that never during his eight years had a ruling of his been reversed. This was a remarkable, perhaps an unparalleled parliamentary achievement. He said to a group of friends in farewell, "I am going home to live to be ninety-three years old."

On the occasion of my most recent visit to his home in Uvalde in April, 1949, there was ample evidence that this ambition, like most of the others that have marked his career, will be amply realized. The young man who at the age of 24 arrived in West Texas with tuberculosis in his lungs and $151.25 in his pocket is rich in the lusty health of age and in worldly goods. He is as keen in his judgment of the national scene as ever. When President Truman visited him in 1948, Garner offered unvarnished advice about the state of the nation.

He reads fourteen newspapers, the *Congressional Record* in full, a weekly budget of clippings sent by Jim Farley, and such books as please his mood. He directs his multitudinous business projects —land, house-building and banking—with skill. Out on the screened-in back porch he will still "strike a blow for liberty," as he did in the convivial days with Mills and Longworth and others in the Capitol "Board of Education."

He hunts and fishes with the old zest, faring forth in the appropriate seasons for days at a time, in his old car whose front fenders are worn destitute of paint by the bodies of slain deer.

Unlike most retired statesmen, Garner is not interested in preserving his recollections in personal memoirs. He doesn't need the money, he doesn't like to write, and he is content to leave the record as it stands in the affectionate memory of his friends.

Bascom Timmons, sage and honest newspaperman and friend of long years has written the authoritative biography—short, spicy and frank—in the Garner manner and character. In the Timmons book in direct quotes are Garner's views on every conceivable subject and on every phase of the long Garner life.

Garner burned the voluminous papers which accumulated during his public service. This was a loss to history, but it was nevertheless the act of a man who will never need to prove the integrity that is so well known to all with whom he came in contact.

Never since he left in 1941 has he visited Washington.

It was a major affliction when Etty, his wife, died in 1948, after a long illness. For Mrs. Garner, a woman of education and fine intelligence, had disclaimed the social life of her time and in all the years following Garner's election as county judge in 1895 had served as her husband's secretary, counselor and homemaker. Her official post is unfilled. Garner writes his own occasional letters, usually with lead pencil, to the great and lowly alike.

He is not happy about trends in government and economic life. He believes that the public through reckless political promises has been led to think that government largess is unlimited. He fears the effect of further deficits upon the savings of the people. He believes that government is too big, too unwieldy and too incompetent.

When I arrived for my most recent visit, he was studying a huge chart of the government published by the Hoover Commission on the Organization of the Executive Branch of Government.

"Look at that," he said, "No President and no Congress can control that under present conditions."

But he is no pessimist creeping toward the end with mumbling expressions of hopeless fear. He believes in doing things. He accepted membership on a committee to follow up the Hoover commission and to get action. He accepted this at the invitation of his old friend and political opponent, Herbert Hoover himself.

Garner will leave little in the written record to mark the wisdom he won from the years. On two subjects, which he regarded as paramount in free government—representative government and party alignments—two classic comments deserve preservation.

He once said to his constituents: "If you reelect me I'll go up there and do the best I can for you as long as it is the best for the country as I see it. As to details you'll have to trust my judgment. Don't write or wire me to support some bill just because the word has been passed around to devil your congressman. Even if you have read the bill, which will be unlikely, you won't know what it will be like in the final form. I will know this and I will vote to do what I think is right—for the Fifteenth District and for the Country."

And to Bascom Timmons he expressed his view of the New Dealer's idea of a new Democratic party:

"This talk about dividing the country into two political camps—one progressive and the other conservative—is all so much stuff. There will always be agitation of this realignment, but in my considered judgment, it will never come. If it did you'd find you'd have a radical and a reactionary party and neither of these could serve the nation. Each of the two parties is in a sense a coalition. Any party to serve the country must be a party of all sorts of views, and through a reconciliation and adjustment of these views you get harmony and a program for good legislation and good administration. The country is neither radical nor reactionary. A party has got to strike a balance.

"There are around forty-five million voters in the country. You've got a bedrock of around fifteen million in each party who will never scratch the party ticket and they serve a great purpose of stability. You have another fifteen million who swing often or occasionally, or go fishing or stay at home on election day, and these fifteen million serve a great purpose, too. That is where you get your changes. No one can figure a better system than that—a third Democratic, a third Republican and a third independent. Most American people have the same general ideas and concepts. Both the Republican and the Democratic parties are more than eighty years old and are here to stay. No third party has strength for more than one election and this when special conditions have given it a temporary following. The pendulum swings from party to party on personality of candidates or on issues."

Corn-fed Proletarian

HENRY A. WALLACE

FOR YEARS it has been the preoccupation and joy of political writers to ponder and comment upon the ways, habits and motives of Henry A. Wallace. They have been like bird-watchers intent on a rare fowl winging its way within their ken. For such writers Wallace has been a profitable object of concern, for he makes salable and notable copy.

Wallace, however rare a species, defies the adaptability for catalogue analysis offered by birds. The man's inner life can hardly be inferred from any pattern of behavior. He has fluctuated too violently for that. In the years ahead scarcely anything he does will be a shock either to his followers or to his enemies. Inconsistency is his normal state.

Henry followed his father in a bolt from traditional Wallace Republicanism. Rewarded for this by appointment to the post in a Democratic Cabinet once held by the elder Wallace in a Republican Cabinet, he followed the New Deal line. His oratorical support of his boss in three Presidential campaigns was as intolerantly partisan as that of a paid party spieler. This philosopher and bookish man on the stump could find no wrong in his party, while associating the opposition with Nazis and blackguards. Rejected by his party for renomination in 1944, he swallowed personal rancor and supported the ticket with all his power. For this he was rewarded by another Cabinet post. But a year later he so shocked the regularity of President Truman that he was summarily fired. Then an exile from two parties, he blazed a courageous but fanatical and visionary trail of opposition in foreign policy.

But there has been consistency in Wallace's devotion to one creature—his "common man."

The common man has been the hypothetical hero of the political drama of Henry Wallace. This character is, like Frank Fay's invisible rabbit Harvey, a creature who is heard about but not seen. He was certainly not in evidence when Mr. Wallace called him to the polls in November, 1948, to support his newly formed Progressive party. For the common man is an abstraction for which there is no concrete embodiment. He is the premise of an argument, not the supporting proof. The vast differences among the actual people to whom this name might be applied defy actual length, breadth and thickness. Mr. Wallace's hero is, in effect, a figure of speech.

At the Jackson Day dinner in 1946, it was a bit awkward for Wallace to use Andrew Jackson as an example of the man of the people. The best that can be said is that Jackson was a man for the people, rather than of the people. For Jackson was neither plain nor common. He was a natural aristocrat, a disciplinarian, a leader, a fountain of authority.

And it could be said of Wallace, as Woodrow Wilson said of Jefferson, that he "was a patron of the people . . . he shared neither their tastes nor their passions." Mr. Wallace, the politician, would do much for plain people.

His life has been far from ordinary. Upon his graduation from college he stepped into the routine of editorial work on the family farm magazine, *Wallace's Farmer,* succeeding his father as editor in 1921 and continuing in that job until 1933. During that time he developed remarkably successful statistical methods for estimating farm yields, prices and price trends. His experiments with the breeding of corn are credited among several genuinely important contributions to genetics in the past half century. He has also been eminently successful in the improvement of breeds of hogs and chickens. We hear a good deal about the great financial success Wallace made in these lines. But no serious student of farm economics would underestimate the practical benefits to American farmers made possible by the Wallace studies.

I first met Wallace when he came to Hyde Park to meet Candidate Roosevelt. Rex Tugwell, with whom I was associated in the campaign, was captivated by the quiet modesty, the charm and the bold intellectual radicalism of the man from Des Moines. At that time Roosevelt seemed to be only casually interested in this new disciple.

Wallace had little part in the development of Roosevelt's farm policy launched in September in a speech at Topeka. That program was not easy to formulate, since Roosevelt himself had casually endorsed another scheme earlier in the year. Henry Morgenthau, Jr., told me that when he reminded Roosevelt that the plan he was adopting differed from his earlier favorite, the answer was, "Oh, that was last February."

The major contributions were from M. L. Wilson of Montana, Rex Tugwell, George Peek and Hugh Johnson. After the outlines were drawn up, Wilson was sent to Wallace, who brought back Wallace's suggestions. Finally, after the suggestions and recommendations of at least twenty-five people had been gathered, it was my task, as in the case of all the candidate's speeches in that campaign, to put the pieces together in a consistent whole.

When Cabinet-making was in progress, it was largely Rex Tugwell who persuaded Roosevelt to appoint Wallace to the Agriculture post. There was opposition, for Henry Morgenthau, Jr. wanted it and was strongly backed by that venerable collector of party funds, Morgenthau, Sr. About a month before the inauguration Roosevelt wrote to Wallace offering the job and, as he left on a fishing trip, told me to get Wallace's acceptance.

I called Wallace, who was in Des Moines, on the telephone. Did he get the letter? Yes. "Well," I said hurriedly, for I had to deal with several other shrinking appointees that day, "What about it?" There was a long pause, which I vividly remember to this day. Finally, after another verbal prod from me, I got a hesitating and rather tremulous acceptance.

Perhaps that pause was the breathless suspense of a man who knows that his whole life will be shaped by a word. Maybe it was a moment taken out by a methodical breakfaster for another gulp of milk. My conviction then was that it was the sincere hesitation

of a genuinely modest man who was not quite sure of his capacity
to assume such power.

I still believe my interpretation was right. For later, when
Wallace asked Tugwell to take the job of Assistant Secretary
under him, he said that he hesitated to make the suggestion: "For,
Rex, I really ought to be working under you."

The impression that Wallace created in the inner life of Washington in those early days was that of a plain man with no pretense
—charming, kindly, interesting.

Henry Wallace, as Sherwood Anderson wrote in 1933, "might
as well have been . . . farmer, college professor in some small
middle-western college, country town store keeper, country town
postmaster. I think Will Rogers is the type, he just accidentally
being a big movie star. There is something in common between
Will Rogers and Henry Wallace. There is the same little smile
. . . an inner rather than an outward smile . . . perhaps just at bottom sense of the place in life of the civilized man . . . no swank . . .
something that gives us confidence.

" 'I may not solve anything for you, probably won't, but I
won't let you down, sell you out. I won't lie to you. I won't tell
you one thing when I mean another.' " [7]

In the years since I have seen little of Henry Wallace. But with
other millions I have observed his strange quixotic journey through
the countryside of politics.

As Secretary of Agriculture, Wallace took over a place easily
adaptable as a temple of strange intellectual sports, mystical in-
cantations, occultism and statistical vagaries. His habits were
wholly inconsistent with orderly administration. Some time after
Wallace had got under way in the vast department, Tugwell said
to me that Wallace was delightfully oblivious to administration.
"He is a mystic," Rex added.

It was Franklin Roosevelt who remarked that a Cabinet officer
may get along without administrative ability but that a President
cannot. Yet in 1940, to the dismay of party leaders, Mr. Roosevelt, perhaps capriciously, saddled the Administration with Henry

[7] *Today,* November 11, 1933. p. 4.

Wallace as Vice President. Of course, Americans have cherished the Vice Presidency chiefly as a source of innocent merriment. But the joke—if they persist in the whimsy—is on them. Of twenty-six individuals elected to the Presidency, seven have been succeeded by the Vice President elected with them—a fairly large proportion, all things considered.

From 1940 to 1944 Henry Wallace stood in line to succeed Mr. Rooosevelt as President. Fortunately, Mr. Roosevelt's health withstood the trials of those years. For Mr. Wallace would have been as suited to direct the Federal government as a man with St. Vitus's Dance to conduct the Philadelphia Orchestra. The Presidency involves the most grinding administrative work in the world. Every major decision, every major squabble comes inexorably to the big Presidential desk. Whenever that desk gets cluttered up, trouble ensues. The man who sits at that desk cannot pass the time of day swapping stories, snatching catnaps, whittling sticks or dreaming mystical dreams. It is a place for decisiveness, clear thinking, efficiency and dispatch.

Since Henry Wallace has been proclaimed a mystic and metaphysician of sorts, he no doubt is fully aware of the idea of dualism, well known throughout ancient religions. Stripped of lingo, it is the belief that within the thin shell of man there live two spirits or personalities—sometimes in balance and harmony, often in conflict.

This hypothesis had great vogue in the more practical sphere of New Deal politics. Thus, when some fervent Administration official made a speech which collided violently with some well-considered Administration dogma, Mr. Roosevelt explained that it had no official significance. The man was speaking as a citizen, not as an official. The speech was, in short, not *ex cathedra* but, perhaps, *ex proprio motu,*—on his own, or something like that.

The strange constitutional position of Mr. Wallace during several months of his Vice Presidency not only violated principle but created bad practical results. Mr. Wallace was at the same time Vice President of the United States and head of an Executive agency, the Board of Economic Warfare. In the latter job he was a subordinate of the President. As Vice President he was not.

It is clear that the Vice President is exclusively a Legislative officer. Under the Constitution, he becomes an Executive officer only if the Presidential office is vacated. But under Executive order, Mr. Wallace became an Executive officer as head of the Board of Economic Warfare. In short, duality doctrine was invoked.

Now at about this time one of the most publicized talents of the versatile Mr. Wallace was his ability to throw the boomerang. There are two kinds of this aboriginal weapon—the war boomerang and the return boomerang. The first, when thrown, hits the enemy. The second returns to the sender. It all depends upon what is called the "skew." During those hectic days of his dual role in the government Henry Wallace attacked Mr. Jesse Jones, thus violating the President's order prohibiting public quarrels. The feud concerned the functions of Mr. Jones' agency and Mr. Wallace's agency. As Vice President he was not subject to the President's order, but as head of the Board of Economic Warfare, he was. In his attack Mr. Wallace must have had the wrong kind of skew, for the missile thrown by the Vice President came back at the head of the Board of Economic Warfare.

On the political front, the demise of the BEW meant two things: that Mr. Wallace was not to be renominated, and that the ideology of the New Deal had suffered a serious setback. The ideological boys had lost their Gandhi, now that Gandhi had lost his second garment. He was the ideal and inspiration of every little world-planner in Washington. They launched their tiny skiffs in the torrent of his wordy discourse. They burbled their admiration of his cloudy philosophical exercises. They spoke in hushed tones of the master's mysticism, his delving into Asiatic religious lore. And they snatched at his curious economic ideas like seals seizing their daily portion of fish. After Roosevelt had abolished the BEW and turned its functions over to Jesse Jones, it was clear to them that they must forsake their high priest and follow the President.

As the 1944 convention approached, the President began to hear from devoted followers some plain talk about renominating Wallace. Boss Kelly of Chicago flatly said that, while he could carry Illinois for Roosevelt, he could not carry it with Wallace on the ticket. The President, tired and already gravely ill, asked his trusted friend, Edward J. Flynn, to make inquiries among Democratic leaders about the advisability of keeping Wallace. Flynn, after a trip, reported that a Roosevelt-Wallace ticket could not carry New York, Pennsylvania, Illinois, New Jersey and California. And so Jonah was cast overboard.

The Wallace uprising at the convention was skillfully suppressed by the big state bosses.

Wallace, once more the calculating politician, decided that the time had not come to desert the party, and he stumped lustily for Roosevelt-Truman. He was rewarded not only with the cake of the Commerce Secretaryship, but the frosting of supplanting his old rival, Jesse Jones.

After Wallace's installation in his new Cabinet post, it became apparent that he had only begun to speak his mind. He began to lead what might be called a left-wing New Deal. He started by going after the railroads through an attack on the Interstate Commerce Commission. And since the President had appointed or re-appointed every member of the ICC, it was an attack on the Administration as well.

From then on, Mr. Wallace appeared as the savior of the left, reviving all the old war cries of the Populists to stir the farmers, wooing the CIO and by indirection pointing the finger of blame at those in the Administration who were lukewarm toward the Great Crusade.

Mr. Wallace remained on. Probably the idea of a third party was already in his head. But for a time he chose to remain within the Administration, speaking his piece. Certainly party regulars would have been happy to dispose of Mr. Wallace. But his following appeared too formidable. After Roosevelt's death, Harry Truman kept Henry Wallace on, and Henry's needling continued.

The clean break came in the fall of 1946. Henry Wallace

chose as his subject the Administration's foreign policy. At Madison Square Garden on a September night he denounced the Truman-Byrnes policy toward the Soviet Union.

Within the week he was forced to resign from his Cabinet post. The road was clear to form a third party.

I doubt if Wallace was sorry. His martyrdom somehow suited him at the time. A cause, which he felt was all-important, called him. With his faith in the Democratic party gone, he would lead his cause alone.

At times, particularly in the year or so preceding the 1948 election, Wallace's behavior seemed almost like that of a religious fanatic. His intolerance toward those who expressed views differing from his own ran high. To him they were dark and sinister figures who would go to any length to uproot and destroy all civilization, all humanity. To him his fight was not only the good fight, but the only fight. Those who were not behind him were against him.

The amateur crusader had full sway, and what little political prudence he had acquired was forgotten.

Had Henry Wallace at this time exercised the slightest shred of political judgment he could have polled a much greater vote in the 1948 election. Many who served him should never have been given control. But as in his New Deal days, Mr. Wallace showed his disregard for organization. Others, however, were eager to take over this task. In the diverse elements which shared the Wallace convictions and prejudices there was highly trained organizing ability, but it was among the Communists who promptly seized control. There can be no question that Communists and near-Communists dominated the New, or as they chose to call it, Progressive party convention.

The platform that emerged largely paralleled the Communist party line. It denounced the European Recovery Plan and the Truman Doctrine. It called for peace with the Soviet Union on Stalin's terms. It demanded an end of aid to anti-Communist countries, including China, Greece and Turkey.

When the Vermont delegates in Convention Hall proposed an

amendment that the covention "does not give blanket indorsement to the foreign policy of any nation," they were hooted down.

When Wallace arrived on the scene, he was prepared for the question he knew the newsmen would ask. Before the question was posed, he told them not to ask him to repudiate Communist support because he wouldn't. "So you can save your breath."

The rabble that made up the convention was a strange sight. There were the dreamers and the disillusioned, the frustrated, the naive—and the ruthless Communists.

The convention proved to be the crest of the Wallace movement. The show itself ended in anticlimax.

The expectation that Wallace could poll some millions withered day by day. Labor had the fish of the 80th Congress to fry. The Negro vote that Wallace had so assiduously cultivated preferred the realization of Truman to the anticipation of Wallace. The farm vote had long since forgotten the Iowa boy. The Wallace vote, 1,137,957, was relatively less than any of the notable third-party efforts of history. It was even less than that cast for Governor Thurmond, the States' Rights candidate.

Wallace, seeking eminence as a leader of the masses, cannot convey in his oratory the notion that he knows what the masses want. He cannot enlist the zeal of the necessitous, because he cannot reduce his offering to concrete terms, as could Huey Long.

As a leader he calls for the generation of power before there is any consideration of control. He calls for action against something or other, without clearly thinking of what action should produce. He asks us to be earnest, without defining what it is we are to be earnest about. He calls us to a "cooperative way of life," without describing how we should reach it or what it should be like when we do reach it.

Behind such earnest but muddled leaders, since the beginning of time there have gathered camp followers who are not so inspired and who are not so earnest, but who know very clearly just what they do want. These had their way with Wallace.

Knight of Non-partisanship

EARL WARREN

IF THE READER who has the common habit of perusing a book from front to back will hold his finger at this page and turn to my article about Hiram Johnson, he will find there a good deal that will make Earl Warren easier to understand. For Warren is very largely a product of political conditions which were created, almost alone, by Johnson. If Warren is good for California, and he is, he is a product for which the good people of the state ought to thank Johnson. If, on the other hand, it is a misfortune that only men of very loose party affiliations, like Warren, can be elected to high office, the blame must be attributed to the Johnson crusade which pounded the ruling party into so many fragments that no one has ever put it together again.

Moreover, the Johnson regime revised the election laws to a point where it is doubtful that real two-party government in the state can ever revive. This lack of party responsibility, which in California bears the pleasant name of non-partisanship, I hope in the course of succeeding pages to show is net loss, despite the fact that it sometimes produces and elevates a public servant like Earl Warren, the "parfit gentle knight" of non-partisanship.

There have been labored attempts by many writers who have found Warren good copy to press a relationship between Warren and Johnson beyond this point. But there is little similarity between the two men, either in personality or policies. Johnson was emotion incarnate. He hated and he loved intensely. Warren, the Scandinavian, is quiet, almost stolid in temperament. Johnson as a prosecutor was flamboyant, flashy. Warren was matter of fact, efficient. Johnson gambled recklessly in politics. Warren is cautious, slow and secretive. Johnson soared into national politics even before he was governor. Warren's rise has been slow, methodical. Thirty years passed between his first public office and a national nomination.

Those who stood in Johnson's way were "the enemies of God, corrupt, vicious." Warren's critics are "mistaken." Warren is more likely to find common ground with a variety of governors and party leaders over the nation—even Republicans. Johnson always walked alone.

Warren was never an associate of Johnson. Johnson had gone to Washington well before Warren entered public office. There is no evidence of anything more than casual contacts between the men. Warren admired the older man, however, and reveres his memory. Only one of the many governors' portraits in the Sacremento capitol hangs in Warren's office. It is that of Hiram Johnson.

The atmosphere and action of the Johnson story is an heroic epic, full of dragons, stratagems, spoils and the clash of arms. Warren's is a California Idyll. Johnson suggests Beowulf or Siegfried. Warren recalls gentler, quieter heroes.

Fate must have worked overtime to provide Warren with a suitable background and equipment for the politics of the second quarter of the Twentieth Century. Fine, sturdy ancestry, neither poor nor rich; labor affiliations; work for a good education; a handsome and healthy physique; a gentle and winning disposition—all in a growing country already past the rough days and in a political system fairly well cleared of wildlife. Fate, aided by Warren, provided a home background of singular attractiveness—a happy marriage blessed with handsome and worthy children.

Partly because of good fortune, partly because of an agreeable and disarming disposition, largely because of caution, patience, industry and excellent intelligence, Warren's political progress has been an almost unbroken story of success. It cannot too often be stressed that until the Truman miracle of 1948, Warren had never lost an election. In thirty years of public office, he has moved with caution from one step to another, keeping his own counsel about decisions, shrewdly timing his moves from office to office, doing the day's work and making no serious political enemies. He has iron in his soul and can fight, if need be, but he would never fight for a fight's sake. That would be misspent energy. With his genius for making friends and his capacity for generating commonsense solutions of difficult situations, he has had little occasion for violent controversy.

It was in 1927 that I first came to know Warren well. In that year, I was engaged in gathering the material for a book on district attorneys.[8] I traveled extensively and visited practically all of the major county law enforcement offices of the country. My observation led me to believe that the best service in a district attorney's office may well make the fewest headlines. It is more important in a big office to conduct the run-of-the-mill cases efficiently than to go all out in the few sensational murder or graft prosecutions. It is more important, moreover, that the district attorney himself stay at his desk and direct his subordinates than seize personal glory and political advancement by trying the sensational cases himself. On the basis of this standard I have always felt that many of those who have risen to high place from that office fell below the ideal.

In my visit in Oakland in 1927 I found that Warren met the test. After my survey I declared without hesitation that Warren was the best district attorney in the United States. I was pleased to note that this judgment was recorded in Warren's campaign literature when he sought the Presidential nomination in 1948. It was, so far as observation, measurement of results and subsequent events were concerned, a sound judgment.

In the Warren years experienced crooks made it a cardinal point never to linger in Oakland. They preferred to take their chances across the Bay in San Francisco, where more colorful but less efficient prosecution prevailed.

It is noteworthy that, unlike other district attorneys who used the great public curiosity about criminal law administration as a means of reaching high office, Warren made no early effort to seek

[8] *Politics and Criminal Prosecution.* New York, Minton, Balch & Company, 1929.

a better job. His decision to remain in Oakland was not the mark of low aim or of indifferent service. It was a mark of genuine respect for his job and the business of law enforcement.

But when 1938 rolled around and the Republican party began its rise from the ashes of six years of humiliation, Warren quietly decided to move. As district attorney he was well known to his fellow D.A.'s everywhere in the state. Their respect and good will offered him an easy assurance of promotion. He was nominated for attorney general by the Republican, Democratic and Progressive parties and was elected practically by acclamation. It is significant that in Warren's official biography not a line is devoted to his achievements as attorney general. It is an office of dignified and often important routine, and he did his work thoroughly and without fanfare.

Nomination for governor in 1942 came to a somewhat hesitant and irresolute Warren. He first tried to induce the notable president of the University of California, Robert Gordon Sproul, to run. But Sproul had a better job, he thought, and Warren yielded. He won the Republican nomination easily and almost crowded the incumbent Democrat, Culbert Olson, off his own ticket. Olson vanished under the Warren tide in November. Four years later, Warren swept both primaries.

In running for governor Warren used the term "non-partisan" in official literature. His candidacy was promoted individually. His name was not linked with other Republican candidates. After attaining office, his major appointments, almost evenly split between the parties, have been devoid of partisanship and have done little to build a party organization in the state.

There has been no lack of muttered complaint among professed Republicans during Warren's years as governor. They have said that Warren is hard to see, that he is unfeeling about the need for a party organization. But Republicans have had no acceptable alternative. Under the laws of the state, Warren can always gain the Republican nomination and harvest a host of Democratic votes. The alternative to Warren is always someone from the piebald Democratic party or a nondescript vendor of nostrums. When

Warren goes, the Republican party will be, as it was before 1942, factional, disjointed, weak. Warren's government is popular, efficient, humane—but personal.

Warren respects competence and expertness. He can and does attract good assistants and knows how to delegate work. His extreme care in making appointments slows things up considerably. There are always scores of vacancies waiting while Warren explores every corner in the record of prospective appointees.

Warren is a thrifty administrator, despite the crying needs of a growing state and the organized pressure for public benefactions. During the war the state treasury gathered a veritable windfall of a surplus. This Warren succeeded in locking up for future needs. In his first term he eased the purse strings on old-age pensions just enough to prevent a revival of California's wild ideas on that subject. His health insurance plan, which has raised the blood pressure of the medical profession, is a Warren proposal, but still unfinished business.

Real modesty, together with a frank appraisal of his own past concentration on state issues, has restricted his utterances on national and international subjects. Once, when he was urged to sound off on international problems, I heard him answer, "What on earth could I say that hasn't already been said by Vandenberg, Dewey, Stassen and the others?"

His love of California is deep and genuine. He has consistently opposed Federal intrusions. This trait, which is indigenous to California, is often learned by outsiders sharply and after considerable damage. Warren has always resented the coming of national candidates to his state. Stassen once ventured in that direction and found a very determined and not-too-pleasant rival in his way.

When Thomas E. Dewey felt assured of the nomination in 1944, he set his heart on getting Warren on the ticket. Not only have the personal and official relations of the two been uniformly pleasant, but their combination on a ticket seemed most appropriate. Warren was determined not to run. Since Dewey was aware of my long friendship with Warren, he asked me to convey some inducements to the California governor. I was to say that Dewey, if elected, would see to it that the Vice President would have a house suitable to the needs of the large Warren family, that the salary of the office would be raised, and that there would be provided for the Vice President some administrative work other than wielding a gavel in the Senate.

I carried the message and Warren's answer was "No." His specifications were no doubt utterly sincere. He had been elected to clear up a mess and he wasn't through. He had a duty to California to fulfil. Moreover, on the political side he said that Californians would probably vote against the ticket to keep Warren at home. Nothing could move him from his position.

In 1948 things were different. He had given six years to the governorship and he was ready to move. Fate, the ineptness of the Dewey campaign and other circumstances that need not be recalled here brought about Warren's first defeat.

Warren's campaign in 1948 was the first chance that the nation as a whole has had to see a real non-partisan in action. It was difficult to determine from what he said whether Warren was running as a Democrat or as a Republican. He was out to make friends for himself and for Dewey. His charm was unquestionable; his acceptance by those who heard him, clear. No one can know what votes were thus gathered. Certainly, Warren lost no prestige or favor by his unsuccessful candidacy. There lingers the impression of a man of good will who, without bitter partisanship, sought the votes of unprejudiced people.

It cannot be denied that more partisan-minded Republicans were irked by Warren's lack of fervor in preaching party loyalty. Senator Taft was reported to have found his appeal quite unusual for a Republican candidate. But it was Warren as he had always campaigned, summoning all good men to come to the aid of a good man, regardless of party.

Warren can hardly be blamed for his non-partisan attitude, because he came into politics in a state which had all but proscribed parties in its laws. There, candidates may by petition get on the primary ballots of any or all legal parties. This, of course, makes it virtually impossible to hold parties responsible for their own candidates. Party registration means very little in California. For one reason or another, a million more Democrats are registered than Republicans, but this never represents the relative party strength in an election.

Under this law, the most fantastic things may happen. Sometimes they do. For example, Warren, an exceedingly popular man, could win a delegation to a Democratic national convention.

The system, which was designed to produce a truly democratic result, often defeats the very principle which it was ordained to sustain. A few years ago, an able and distinguished Democratic congressman named Costello ran for renomination in both primaries. He won in the Republican primary, but a well-organized minority defeated him for the Democratic nomination. Because he was a Democrat, he could not appear on the ballot in the election, although he had won a nomination. Only if a candidate wins his own party nomination can he appear as the candidate of another. He was the clear choice of an overwhelming majority who voted in both primaries, but that majority could not vote for him in an election except by "writing in" his name.

Those earnest men who, like Hiram Johnson in the first decade of this century, saw political machines, in corrupt alliance with privileged business, exercise ruthless and undemocratic power, sought legal means of curbing them. When those reformers looked for a place to transfer the power which they tore away from the machine, they turned back to the theoretical repository of all power, the voter. They were, as they put it, "giving government back to the people." Their idealism contemplated the free citizen, free of party allegiance, voting for the very best officers for the very best government. They anticipated the rise of all good men with good government as their only objective. They conceived that voters, freed from bossism, would be wise as well as good.

In reaching these conclusions, their zeal exceeded their good sense and their grasp of history. They failed to realize the considerations that caused equally earnest but greater men, more than a hundred years before, to fear unrestrained popular rule. The makers of the Constitution were concerned with turning government over to the voters, too, but they were also careful to provide the voters with machinery that would enable them to delegate details to representative institutions. The two representative institutions which developed as agents of popular power were the political party and the legislative assembly.

The main devices of progressives of forty years ago—the direct primary, non-partisan ballots, the initiative, referendum and recall—struck at the heart of the party and the legislative assembly. The voter was theoretically free to take matters into his own hands.

But the independent voter, like Henry Wallace's common man, is a myth, born of the zealous hate of the progressives for machines and for "special interests." These monstrous excrescences could be indeed struck down by law, but the multitudinous ties of the voter to other loyalties remained. With the parties shackled by law, other forms of collective action were free to invade the political field and claim the loyalty of voters. They arose from all sorts of social and economic situations. Religious prejudices and loyalties, labor and business groups, associations for isms and nostrums—all took the place of parties, especially in states like California where "progressivism" was pushed to its logical end.

The result was a vermiculate entanglement of compulsions in which the voter was held in servitude far more confining than the party control from which he was rescued. In such a chaos small, compact minorities exercised far more real power than their membership justified. And the evil of this irresponsibility lay in the fact that most of the real nature and aims of these groups were quite extraneous to government. Except for their purposes of using government for the promotion of their irrelevant ends and for getting monetary gratuities from the government, they were not concerned with government as such.

Under such conditions public officials are subjected to the pressures of interests quite as unwholesome as those of the pre-Johnson age. And these pressures are exerted not through the orderly process of a legislative assembly or through a responsible party, but insidiously, in propaganda and at the polls.

Those who used to accuse parties of hypocrisy because they

publicly eschewed allegiance to this or that religious or racial group, to this or that economic group, or to other specific forms of association, should now realize that in that seeming hypocrisy there was a certain value. The party, in seeking votes everywhere had evolved a crude form of general public interest which should be the major concern of all government. The ideal that there is a big public interest superior to the aggregation of all little interests is lost in non-partisanship.

A most serious aspect of such "direct" government is the usurpation of the field of representative government by direct votes on proposed laws and constitutional amendments, thus compelling the expenditure of public money with little or no provision for meeting such charges by equitable taxation.

Warren has had this trend literally explode in his face. His 1949 budget message called for expenditures of more than a $1,000 million dollars. He points out that one-third of this great sum, or $350,589,000, was voted by the people within three years. This is a portent of tragic consequences. By the simple device of asking a great, variegated population to say "yes" or "no" to the question whether it wants this or that benefit, a legal obligation to pay is laid upon the government. The orderly process of weighing and considering ways and means by a responsible legislature and governor is roughly pushed aside and the rapacious and capacious hand of an uninformed public is thrust into the public treasury. There can be no end to this but bankruptcy and fiscal chaos. For there are clear limits to taxation. This is another of the bitter fruits of well-meant but shallow-minded reform.

The weakening of parties and representative institutions, moreover, gives great advantage to strong personalities to whom voters are drawn on the leadership principle. Sometimes this has happy results, as in the case of Warren. It may well be that under a strong two-party system Warren would now be a useful, prosperous but little-known lawyer in San Francisco or Oakland. His firm independence, vital conscience and tendency toward independent judgments would have been difficult, perhaps indigestible materials in a disciplined party. If he had been willing to accept party limitations, he would certainly have found it harder to make the decisions and create the policies that have marked his admirable administration as governor.

But while non-partisanship occasionally opens opportunities for good men, it also opens the way for the demagogue and the power-hungry adventurer. California has had experiences with those, too.

The unfortunate aspect of good personal government is inherent in the short and fleeting years of a human life. When Warren leaves office, he will leave solid material achievements and a potent lesson in personal integrity and intelligent leadership. But there will be no organized force to carry on his ideals. When his shadow passes on, the party in which he has had somewhat nominal membership will be as it was before—factional, confused, leaderless. Almost anything can happen, and if an economic decline sets in, almost anything will certainly happen.

Jefferson was as profound a believer in the people as any man in history. But he appreciated the need of providing institutions through which the people might rule. He labored incessantly to create a party and succeeded.

Statesmanship requires not only faith in the people but a clear comprehension of means and ends.

Man from Main Street

WILL H. HAYS

IF SOME GROUP interested in preserving in a crypt beneath a national monument the most characteristic mementos of this age should ask me to nominate the most authentic politician, I should without the slightest hesitation, select Will Hays. There, embalmed for a thousand years, the remains of this man should keep their vigil. When I say that he is the purest of the species, I use that characterization not to signify mere garden-variety virtue, which he possesses in common with others, but virtue in the Aristotelean sense, which means most perfectly suited to its purpose.

And while I am defining words, permit me to ask the reader of this book to put aside the unfavorable connotation which the word "politics" has for most Americans. I speak of politics as a process devoid of good or evil, in the same sense as atmosphere, water and the earth—a prevailing something, indispensable to life and universal as the ether.

That Will Hays is not enshrined as the public's most perfect exemplar of the political art is a deficiency inherent in the art itself. Perfect virtuosity in the political art demands that most of its processes elude the eye and ear. The cognoscenti of politics know Hays as a master, and the immense durability of the man proves the talent that has guided his life. Such artistry demands that he know Americans. It also demands that Americans know only a part of him.

It is not easy to write a clinical analysis of this phenomenon, for our language is short on words properly to convey the nuances of true art. Only a few broad lines can be drawn. The shades, the detail, the surrounding atmosphere are perceptible only to emotions and the misty imagination.

Hays was born right. In the roughhouse of Indiana politics rivals reach far back into the family tree in search of evidence that hurts and kills. But no evidence of decay or infection has ever rewarded such efforts. There was only a long line of Hayses—prudent, shrewd, God-fearing and enemies of sin. The legal lineage of the Sullivan Hayses is attested by the sign over the door of the law office in Sullivan, Indiana. "Hays and Hays" it has been over three generations.

Born right, too, geographically as well as geneologically in the "great throbbing heart" of the nation—West Central Indiana. Close to the center of population. Here permit me to yield to Edward G. Lowry's inimitable portrait, written in 1921 when Hays, at 40, was Postmaster General. "He is not rustic. But neither is he urban. Certainly he is not suburban. Groping for the right phrase, I should say he is like a visiting Elk who knows his way about." [9]

Hays was bred in politics as was Mozart in music. At 40 he could say truthfully that he had been in politics all his life. He was precinct committeeman when he cast his first vote. Then there were 19 years of successive chairmanships—of the county, of the state advisory committee, of the state speakers' bureau, of the state central committee and of the national committee. There he had to end his career in organization politics. His party had no further chairs to bestow.

Coming to the party chairmanship in the spring of 1918, when in the crisis of war it was well to speak little of politics, he found his party defeated, divided, discouraged. Wilson was winning a great war which should have cemented the Democrats in power for a generation. With infinite skill, Hays turned to a patriotic theme. Up and down the country he spoke only of Americanism and win-the-war until, in October when Wilson seemed to question Republican loyalty, the country in an instinct of fair play extinguished Wilson's majority in Congress.

[9] *Washington Close Ups.* Boston: Houghton Mifflin Company, 1921; p. 88.

Hays then built the party fences for 1920, eschewing allegiance to any candidate, but incessantly preaching Republicanism. His role, to use a phrase which he coined in those days, was to "elect, not select."

And elect he certainly did! The weakest candidate in the nation's history won by the largest percentage of votes in American history, with the doubtful exception of Monroe.

Hays brought his party to the 1920 convention united and sniffing the anticipation of victory. At the conclusion of a convention a national chairman steps out and the Presidential candidate supplants him with his own choice. Harry Daugherty had that tradition on his side. But Harding, though a slave to tradition, hesitated. And well he did, for the committee itself would have broken loose. Hays remained as national chairman, the only person thus honored by his party in a generation.

When he became Postmaster General, he had exhausted the range of purely organizational honors. True, there were further elective honors to which he might have aspired. But with true instinct he knew that an organization manager is miscast as a candidate for elective office. In a sense, a political manager, with real professional self-esteem secretly regards his candidate as a "front man," as a mere snare to catch votes—sometimes as a stuffed shirt. In the judgment of a politician like Hays—a judgment, I may add, which Hays would never utter—Jim Farley invited only frustration and disappointment when, in the second Roosevelt term, he fell a victim of ambition to run for office himself. Once a manager, always a manager.

To a politician the job of Postmaster General is interesting only in the first year, when the faithful are rewarded and political obligations are paid off. After that, it is dull routine, interesting only to a bureaucrat or a stamp collector. Hays decided to move.

The opportunity very profitably to practice his political art, to remain in public life and, incidentally, to keep his status as a member of the Sullivan bar came from an extraordinary source, the motion-picture industry.

By early 1922 the grim threat of public wrath had gathered

over this giant business with an adolescent mind and, it must be recorded, at that time vague morals. The industry had grown like a street crowd after an accident. It had prospered. It had captured the enchanted devotion of the public, and its leaders, a group of hucksters and showmen, didn't know what to do next. As the producer Max Gordon once remarked in another connection, "They didn't know what to do with a hit."

They dimly realized that above and beyond their growing audiences there was something—vast, menacing, irresistable—that people called the "public interest." They sensed that when aroused it could hurt people, business, businessmen. "It could," I have written elsewhere, "strike like a rattlesnake, envelop like poisonous gas, shatter like a shell. It channeled to a myriad-armed thing called government, ensconced in Washington, in forty-eight lawmaking bodies, in innumerable city councils. It was something that might strike justly or unjustly, but none the less mortally. It could act through newspapers, as well as through governments, through magazines, pulpits, schools, clubs and welfare associations. It could sweep away dollars, credit, business standing, personal reputation, personal happiness. It was the unseen partner in every business, the indeterminate factor in every business calculation, the unwritten figure in every balance sheet. It could not be ignored, damned, even effectively fought.

"Only slowly did the bewildered movie men begin to realize that the mysterious abstraction called 'the public' was nothing more or less formidable than the elder Marshall Field's 'the Customer.' 'The Customer' was always right. Or at least he must always be dealt with as if he were right. Regardless of how irritating his foibles might be, they had to be respected, satisfied.

"And when this realization came, it came not from quiet, philosophical meditations. It literally exploded in the movie makers' faces." [10]

These showmen were as individualistic as the medicine peddlers who roamed the frontier a generation before them. The history

[10] From *The Hays Office,* by Raymond Moley, copyright 1945. Used by special permission of the publishers, The Bobbs-Merrill Company; p. 24.

of their business was a dizzy tale of ruthless competition, chican-ery, daring speculation, wanton waste and sheer genius. But the threat of retribution for the lewd pictures of those postwar years literally drove them into unity born of common danger. It was sheer inspiration that turned them to Hays, for the event proved that only such insight as he possessed could save them from cosmic disaster.

The Will Hays of the succeeding twenty-two years demon-strated refinements in the art of managing men and opinion far beyond his brilliant success in formal politics.

It was a fascinating but arduous task in writing "The Hays Office" to unravel the threads of that story. I had to contend not only with the tangled skein of industrial history but to extract from the subtle mind of Hays and the fulsome volume of his own verbal circumlocutions the essential principles and methods that he employed in his task.

I learned before I finished that to interpret Hays' success in life merely as I have in the foregoing pages—as a product of birth, environment, experience and formal political achievement—would be a naive understatement of his capacity.

He is, as Lowry said, "the one hundred per cent American. . . . Submit him to any test and you get a perfect reaction. He doesn't even stain the litmus paper. Apply any native or domestic stand-ard and he complies with it to a hair-line. He is as indigenous as sassafras root. He is one of us. He is folks. . . .

"He is a human flivver, the most characteristic native product; a two-cylinder single-seater, good for more miles per gallon than any other make of man. He takes you there and brings you back, in the blessed phrase, thus satisfying a great national ideal. He is as much a national institution and as purely native as the prac-tice of buying enlarged crayon portraits or talking machines on the installment plan."

But he is something more. Lowry concludes: "If some alchem-ist in biology (if you know what I mean) could extract the essen-tial juices from Mr. Addison Sims and all the typical Rotarians, he might produce a sort of pale, synthetic Will Hays, but there still would be qualities missing."

Hays has something approaching genius in conveying an impression of the commonplace while he calculates with no uncommon skill. His generalities, profuseness, overdone emotionalism and underdone philosophy are matters that may win the interest, amazement or ennui of the listener. But Hays is never deluded by these verbal excrescences. In the depths of his mind he is never hypnotized by his own conversational over-simplifications and wishful thinking. He may talk in terms of the general, but he thinks in the terms of the particular. Sometimes in the years when I was working on his story I felt that he didn't even hear what he was saying. It seemed that the mechanism of his mind was so constructed that a flood of predigested and thoroughly innocuous words could be turned loose to hold attention and win time while his solid faculties underneath were assessing all the circumstances involved in a course of action.

I often consult him on matters of current politics, but I have learned in doing so never to bother about his explanations for his initial opinion. I ask a sharp question and listen carefully to the first sentence. That is generally very important. What follows is pleasant but irrelevant. This faculty is one of his greatest weapons and his greatest defense. With him artlessness, forgetfulness and sometimes even helplessness are conveniently assumed means of creating an illusion. With him they are weapons and defense.

In his years with the Motion Picture Producers and Distributors of America, it was clear that no intelligent Hays could be blind to the limitations of some of the Hays aids and associates. But he was always able to see those people on the background of their special usefulness. He might neither admire their outlook and standards nor cherish them as friends. But no one, least of all the man concerned, was ever apprised of his judgment. Impersonal enthusiasm prevailed with his subordinates and his board of directors.

When Hays took the job with the motion-picture industry it

is a good guess that his employers thought that ninety percent of his value and his task would be to free them from the threat of political censorship. This, I suppose, some of them believed could be done by a garden variety of fixing legislatures, city councils and officialdom generally. It may be assumed that those leaders were not much concerned with the methods that might be used, so long as they worked.

But Hays certainly realized that crude fixing was not only unworthy of a real maestro in politics, but that it could not permanently solve the industry's problem. To do so would have meant endless blackmail and ultimate exposure and disaster. The remedy would have to come in a public opinion that recognized the futility of censorship and from a reformed and self-governing industry that didn't need political coercion.

Any great politician knows that a sense of timing is indispensable to success. Boldness is sometimes of the essence, and when Hays took his new job there was a threat so imminent that not a moment could be lost. A state referendum on censorship was pending in Massachusetts. Instantly Hays saw that this fight must be won, or the industry would be overwhelmed by state regulatory laws. He moved into the battle with every weapon— and I mean every weapon—that he could summon. Censorship lost that test by a vote of more than two to one. That was the Waterloo of censorship. After that only two state laws on the subject were enacted—one, in Connecticut, was shortly repealed; another, in Huey Long's Louisiana, was never enforced. This achievement in itself saved the industry, for it is easy to see that with the vagaries of state boards and laws to contend with, motion pictures with sound could never have become a commercial success.

But Hays not only knew how to act quickly in an emergency. He knew how to wait—for months and years if necessary—with a patience indigenous only to the land of Uz. It took ten years to bring his chaotic and competitive industry around to self-censorship. There were good resolutions, and then the breaking of those resolutions. There were solemn declarations, without means of enforcement. But Hays, despite delays, disappointments and trials that would have turned Job into a raving maniac, refused to use even the limited powers that he possessed to whip his companies into line.

Some observers believed that, like Judge Landis in baseball, he should have wielded a big stick. He knew that in a moment of crisis he might have knocked heads together, but that when all was quiet those heads would have got together amicably to get rid of Hays.

Instead, he warned, cajoled, entreated, flattered and occasionally pounded the table. But coercion, he knew, must come from without. And he waited for the moment when help would come from a new quarter.

It may be overstating the influence of Hays to imply that he had in the late 20's and early 30's anything to do with the drive of the Catholic Church against the motion-picture industry. It is not, however, too much to say that he welcomed the aggressive action of the primates of that Church, as a marooned sailor greets the sight of a sail. With the militant Church's Legion of Decency thundering at the door, Hays presented the dotted line to the movie overlords, and self-censorship became an enforced reality.

His tactics differed when threats came from social workers, educators, and the Protestant clergy. Then, he created all sorts of committees, review boards and sundry avenues for the access of outside criticism to the industry. This structure of busy-work was once designated by a Hays employee as the "Wailing Wall." Hays, steeped in Republican history, called it the "Open Door" policy. He found work for the hands of reformers—work which had some usefulness, it is true, but which served chiefly as a means of setting up a rubber wall between the industry and a not-too-happy public.

Two bits of evidence reveal Hays' love of the indirect as a means of achieving an end that a less subtle man might seek in futile action. He once told George Eastman that he served motion pictures not as a czar but as a means of sensing the signs of approaching danger. Hays was intrigued by Eastman's answer, "You are, in short, the cat's whiskers."

On one occasion in connection with Hays I used the word "catalyst" to describe an agent through which a change can be effected without itself becoming changed. Hays seized the word as his own.

After twenty-two years, Hays retired from his active participation in the industry, with a good contract for more years of advice, with the genuine friendship and gratitude of most of its leaders, and with a sense that in the formative years of a great industry he had brought more order, more cooperation and vastly more decency. There are those who complain that self-censorship itself is a denial of freedom. But Hays can answer out of the wisdom of years that the choice is not between perfect freedom and control. It is between self-control and government control. No one ever had a better chance to know that than Hays, the super-sophisticated politician.

Prometheus Unbound

JAMES A. FARLEY

JAMES ALOYSIUS FARLEY, despite his happy demeanor and his celebrated capacity for awakening cheer and optimism in others, has probably suffered more internal turmoil than any other figure portrayed in this book. Prometheus was bound to only one rock, and surely before many years the vulture which fed on his vitals must have become full-cropped and lethargic. Moreover, Prometheus might have released himself by a simple act of submission to one master. But Farley had many masters. Farley has been bound and bound again to a succession of loyalties, and ever-changing flocks of torturing decisions have come for an answer to his mind and soul. His life is a study in competitive loyalties. Farley would have given Josiah Royce a long footnote to his *Philosophy of Loyalty*.

Farley was born a sensitive, active extrovert. He grew up in relatively simple surroundings, if any human environment can truly be called simple. He was schooled in elementary matters of acquired knowledge. He was spared the mental tasks of answering for himself many questions about why he was alive, what was right and wrong, and what the world meant. For the Church into which he was born had the answers, and Farley was a born believer.

His duty was clear, for those whom he loved needed him and he met their demands willingly. He had to go to work at an early age, and since he did well and had decent employers, he had no worries about his successive jobs. He married Bess Finnegan, whom he had known a great many years and with whom he found complete understanding and domestic tranquility.

Politics entered Farley's life inevitably, easily and pleasantly.

Its practice demanded energetic activity, but no serious alternative decisions. He was born to his party affiliation; he recognized its importance; he could easily identify his party friends; and the road to political success was well marked. One rose as on a ladder, rung by rung, giving service and receiving rewards. Far beyond the foothills of Stony Point were Nyack, Albany—and Washington, like Everest shrouded in mist and known to Farley only from his schoolbooks and the newspapers.

In the middle 20's, in his own late thirties, Farley was comfortably on his way with a profitable business, a zestful career in politics developing, a growing family and a host of friends. By 1928, when Franklin D. Roosevelt was first elected governor, Farley was Secretary of the New York State Democratic Committee, and upon him devolved the responsibility of building up the party in the state. This was a job that needed doing, for, despite Al Smith's four successful campaigns for governor and vast Democratic state patronage, the party was not the well-knit machine that Farley thought it should be.

Smith was a potent figure commanding hearty enthusiasms. But he was not, as I have noted earlier, a strict party man. He did little to build a party in the state. Much of this deficiency had to be made up by Farley between 1928 and 1930, and he labored at it indefatigably.

Incessantly he traveled the pathways of the state, winning friends and remembering people. Farley possessed and cultivated, more than any man of his generation, the primary talent of a politician mentally to catalogue names and faces, to learn and retain the facts of association among people, to know who is related to whom by blood, business or politics, to labor with meticulous diligence by mail or otherwise to make and retain contacts. It is an understatement to say that beyond doubt he was a superlative salesman. He astonished and needled the egos of countless humble people by remembering their names, their habitats, their days of happiness or sorrow, their needs and the needs of their friends.

Largely as a result of this effort and not without the active collaboration of Roosevelt himself, a triumphant majority was achieved when the new governor ran for reelection.

In the memoirs of Edward J. Flynn, written long after the friendship of the two political mentors of Roosevelt had flickered and faded, it is written that Flynn had a decisive part in the selection of Farley as the "political drummer" for the New York governor's quest for 1932 delegates. Farley had revealed in New York State precisely the essential qualification for that job. In the universality of his love for people, sectionalism had no place. To him, men and women, especially politicians, were simple mechanisms responsive to simple formulas of enticement. The success that crowned his travels proved his faith and his worth.

Wherever Farley went Roosevelt was "sold."

Flynn, among the city machines, had a more difficult job. Roosevelt never won confidence there until he had been President for some time. In the final vote of the 1932 convention, most city delegates sat sullen and unhappy. It was the states that Farley had so assiduously cultivated that voiced the accents of happy satisfaction.

In the campaign that followed the 1932 nomination, Farley not only underlined the citation he had won as a salesman but established with sharp authenticity his qualifications as a party administrator. He knew and did the work of an organization leader with a professional touch.

Here I can offer first-hand evidence and sincere tribute. Roosevelt probably more than any other leader of his time, had a keen appreciation of the distinction between the task of political organization and the formulation of the public policies that are the means of attracting the generality of voters, especially of those who have no party contacts and affiliations. Roosevelt designated me as his agent to assemble material on public policies, to correlate them in a consistent whole and to direct their formulation in speeches and statements.

Farley and I agreed strictly to distinguish our functions. There was little contact between us, although what there was had no element of friction.

Farley never questioned the content of a speech or stated that this or that needed to be said. In any case, he never went over my head to Roosevelt on such matters; in fact, he never discussed them with the candidate. What was said in speeches Farley printed and distributed. I believe that if Roosevelt had decided upon the Koran as the subject of a discourse, Farley would have enthusiastically sold the product.

Farley's attitude toward the ideological side of the Roosevelt regime may provide some part of the evidence that his subsequent ordeal was not over matters of legislation or policy. There is still sharper illustration in the fact that Farley vigorously sought the passage of the Court bill in 1937 but demurred even to the brink of a break when Roosevelt sought to purge the senators in 1938. The one was a matter of public principle and policy; the other, a matter of party unity and personal loyalty.

Farley as national chairman was an engaging public figure, a master of party detail; and as a Cabinet member he was crisp and business-like. By tradition, the Post Office Department runs itself. Its politically appointed head seldom delves below the surface of its closely-knit maze of bureaucratic detail, and Farley made little change in this rule. The Postmaster General is a maker of morale, and Farley did a great deal in that respect. The political perquisites of the office are bountiful, despite the measurable influence of civil service in curbing spoils.

There were jobs, and they were given to loyal party men, with something more than a mere gesture to competence in office. A long-neglected need for buildings was a favorable outlet for the New Deal millions, and numberless post offices were built—and almost always dedicated by the Postmaster General in person. Commemorative stamps first became a matter of news and lively comment.

The first four years in Washington were for Farley full of innovation and political achievement. They were surely the happiest of all his years. Occasional glimpses of a lack of consistency in his "boss" opened few doubts in Farley's mind. Nor was Farley aware, as others were, that by 1935 Roosevelt was shifting his ideological ground and his long-term political calculations from the generality of the country toward concentration on the urban and labor vote.

The thumping victory of 1936, which was a first reflection of Roosevelt's shift in emphasis, was accepted by Farley as a smashing party victory. It added cubits to his stature before the country, not only because he was the commanding general of the victorious host but also because he accurately predicted the victory.

The year had not passed, however, before the seeds of distrust were planted, and Farley has written that the tale of division without reunion began then. The real ordeal began in 1938, and nothing so clearly shows this than a comparison of Farley's book of that year, *Behind the Ballots,* with his *Jim Farley's Story* of ten years later.

Both these autobiographical books must be considered in any analysis of Farley's attitude and course of action. Individually, they illustrate two ways in which a public servant may meet the alternatives which confront him when he decides to make a public record of his experience. One way is to write under the normal rules of political behavior, to reveal little, to protect or praise political friends, to increase party solidarity and, above all, to convey a favorable impression of the central figure and of his achievements. The penalty risked is to meet the skepticism of the reader and to invite him to withhold serious judgment pending the examination of other evidence or the "verdict of history."

The other way is to gamble with the whole truth, or almost the whole truth, and risk the uproar and vituperation that will most certainly follow.

Farley tried the first method in a book that he frankly confesses was written because he "needed the money." He followed the second in his *Jim Farley's Story.* In the latter, Farley has made two contributions to history. He has, better than anyone else, portrayed the tortuous ways of Roosevelt with his friends and associates. Also, he has torn the mask from the smutty face of high politics—perhaps more than he himself realizes.

How well he has served himself will be a debatable point. No doubt, he has relieved himself of a painful mental congestion by talking frankly. And he has resolved a long struggle among conflicting loyalties by giving his final loyalty to his conscience and his truth. This, I wish to remind the reader, might be easy for one who had no political ties, for one who had not lived his life bound by the reticences of politics. But it ran violently against the instincts of Farley the politician.

Clearly, Farley's purpose in writing for the record was to reveal his struggle to protect his party; the obstacles that Roosevelt threw in the path of his effort; the almost unbelievable indirection and capriciousness of Roosevelt in dealing with the people who helped him attain the Presidency; and most of all, the efforts of Farley himself to carry the responsibilities that went with his job of leadership. Frankly, too, Farley reveals his own thwarted ambitions which he felt justified in nourishing.

In speaking of Farley's personal ambition, I do not use the word to describe a selfish or ignoble passion. The simple code which had governed his life from childhood was that a man could expect advancement if he worked hard, lived a moral life, helped his friends and told the truth. He learned in bitterness that this code could be violated in high places and not fatally injure those who violated it. Farley thus confronted a conflict between loyalty to the methods which he always felt were the ways to achieve legitimate ambitions, and a realization of the denial of his lifetime beliefs. He decided that he would stick to his early principles and contend with all he had against what opposed them. And slowly he came to believe that Roosevelt embodied the sole opposition to his legitimate hopes. He came to believe that Roosevelt was an unreliable friend.

His first intimation came very early in 1935. Huey Long, no doubt aiming at Roosevelt and seeking to further his own ambition to defeat him in 1936, made a series of vicious attacks on Farley. Farley was well defended in the Senate, but he felt that conspicuously among those who offered no public defense was Roosevelt himself. Farley never forgot that. He would have had some difficulty in doing so, in fact, because Mrs. Farley accepted the episode as a test of the Roosevelt character and made no bones about saying so.

Bess Farley is, like Jim himself, a person of great charm. Farley's strongest mundane ties have always been attached to her. She never cared for Washington and only occasionally went there. And after the Long incident, she never cared for F. D. R. or for any of the Roosevelts. Her outspoken comments were, of course, brought back to the White House, where they were the source of some irritation among the immediate and official family and weakened the White House confidence in Farley himself.

I well remember being told in that period by a member of the White House staff: "Jim Farley is keeping a diary." This simple fact was hissed out with indignation appropriate only to the revelation that Farley was secretly a head-hunter and that the President was next on his list.

During the campaign of 1936 Farley was deeply offended at receiving a hint from White House Secretary McIntyre that Farley should not appear with the President on the train platform "because of the Tammany situation." Of course, there was no Tammany situation that year, and Farley drew the inference that a man who was about to receive a majority of 11 million votes was jealous of the partial acclaim that would greet the man who had helped him. Over and over in the years that followed, Farley noted the failure of Roosevelt to express specific and written gratitude for the Farley loyalty and services.

A man in Farley's position was never free of reminders by his friends that he was not getting adequate recognition and that Roosevelt was jealous of him. But Roosevelt no doubt was not comfortable with Farley, was doubtful of Farley's sympathy and was really jealous—there is no other adequate word—of Farley's great personal popularity among the countless party workers who had had individual contact with him.

Some of Roosevelt's coolness Farley interpreted as social snobbishness, an attribution which in truth was an injustice to Roosevelt, for Roosevelt's catholicity in his taste for companions was sometimes distressing. Roosevelt was eager to be amused, his interests were manifold, and he hated to concentrate long on one subject. Farley's life and interests were concentrated on politics. As in the case of many self-made men, business and recreation were at one. He was concerned with public policies largely as they became political assets and liabilities. He was no bon vivant, being a lifelong teetotaler.

This Roosevelt knew, and he probably tried to restrict his contacts with Farley to set political strategy meetings in his office. Flynn, Roosevelt's other major political adviser, always seemed bored with politics, had read widely and could amuse Roosevelt with items far from statecraft and politics. He was always a close social companion, from Albany to Yalta.

It might be asked at this point why Harry Hopkins became such an intimate. For Hopkins was no compendium of universal knowledge, no wit and no anecdotal treasury. The answer is that Hopkins had a faculty, not altogether happy, of giving Roosevelt lusty exhilaration by needling his prejudices, especially those regarding conservatives and businessmen.

Farley liked business and businessmen. He respected business success. In Cabinet meetings he spoke of the importance of providing "confidence" for business. "Confidence" was a horrid word to Roosevelt. He neither tried to understand it nor to provide it. Farley's convictions, while neither complex nor broadly ideological, were firm and of long standing. He could not sway with the doctrinal eddies that prevailed in those days.

In the great Court fight, Farley, indifferent to the basic constitutional principle that moved the Democrats who went into opposition, labored with the tools of his trade to carry the measure through Congress. But neither appeals for party unity nor threats of patronage reprisals were effective. It was Farley's conviction that Senator Joe Robinson never believed in the measure, but because he actively supported it deserved as a reward appointment to the Supreme Court. He was authorized by the President to tell Robinson that the appointment would be made.

After the death of Robinson, issues arose on which Farley resolutely refused to take orders from the President. These, it is significant to note, again were matters of party ethics, not of public policy. In order to achieve the election of Alben Barkley over Pat Harrison as minority leader, Roosevelt asked Farley to move Mayor Kelly to nudge Senator Dieterich to switch his vote to Barkley. Farley refused. Hopkins was then delegated to do it, and the vote was delivered.

Next year came the attempted purge of recalcitrant Democrats. Again, Farley refused to take any part, and Roosevelt used Hopkins, Thomas G. Corcoran and others. This clash of loyalty Farley resolved on the side of the party. Roosevelt, in turn, retaliated by ignoring Farley more and more in making political appointments.

At this point Farley began to look toward 1940. Mention of his name in connection with the Presidential succession had become commonplace. The polls were consistently bringing out the Farley name, together with those of Garner, Hull and others.

Farley, partly to clarify his course as national chairman and unquestionably to test his own chance of getting Presidential backing for the nomination either for President or Vice President, began what was to be a succession of conferences with Roosevelt on the subject. Farley's accounts of their meetings constitute a vivid commentary on political minds at work. Name after name came up and was dismissed—sometimes on grounds that to the average American would seem frivolous or irrelevant reasons to disqualify a man for high office.

It was apparent to Roosevelt that Farley felt himself entitled to his support. Roosevelt pointed out that Farley could prepare himself for 1940 by running for governor of New York in 1938; that his services as national chairman and Postmaster General were insufficient preparation for the Presidency. Farley would have none of the governorship.

From then on until the 1940 convention, it was a question of eliciting some clear decision, first, as to Roosevelt's intentions about his own ambition, and, next, as to Farley's own course of action.

It suffices to say that Farley and Garner, despite Roosevelt's somewhat nebulous disavowals, decided that he did intend to run and that they would try to prevent it. Both indicated a willingness to accept the nomination and permitted their friends to seek delegates.

One of Roosevelt's most remarkable superstitions was a belief that better luck attended him if things remained, so far as possible, the same from campaign to campaign. He persisted in wearing the same hat, and he wanted the same people around him. For this reason and also because Farley's capacity was unique, Roosevelt exercised every art to retain the national chairman who had done so much to win two elections. To that end, Roosevelt in July 1939 played what he considered to be a trump card. He inspired Cardinal Mundelein to appeal to Farley to remain faithful and support the third-term effort.

The Cardinal was no novice in politics, nor was this the first time he had lent a hand to Roosevelt. Early in the pre-convention race, in 1932, when Al Smith was the chief opponent, it was arranged to have Cardinal Mundelein call at the Governor's Mansion in Albany and be photographed with Roosevelt.

On the Farley occasion, the venerable Cardinal began his plea in a "James, what is this I've been hearing?" tone. Farley realized that here was no matter of infallible faith and morals. It was in the free field of politics—in his own domain. And, as a Catholic himself he knew, perhaps better than had Roosevelt, that he was not in the puissant presence of the Church, but in that of just another politically-minded American.

With respect and restraint Farley rebuffed the Cardinal's plea with a pointed reminder that this was the first occasion in his career when a responsible officer of the Church had attempted to influence his political decisions or conduct.

There was something anomolous in this enlistment of a Roman Catholic Cardinal to deal with Farley. Ernest K. Lindley had published a story, which to this day has every earmark of veracity, that Roosevelt had indicated that Farley could not be a candidate for President or Vice President because of his religion. This, says

Farley, wounded him beyond anything that had ever happened to him politically.

There was strong logic in the Lindley story, because on another occasion Roosevelt had crossed James F. Byrnes off the eligible list because he had left the Church. Apparently Farley was ineligible because he remained a Catholic and Byrnes was so because he had not.

Farley carried on in this atmosphere of conflict until the convention of 1940 when, just as he had predicted, Roosevelt found reasons to justify another term. Farley then cut the frayed ties. Loyalty to his party, his family and his own right to make his way had become wholly incompatible with loyalty to Roosevelt. He resolved the issue against Roosevelt.

That this has lost him the friendship of people in politics and elsewhere who have placed their admiration for Roosevelt above all other considerations is unquestionable. But for many others, it has confirmed a hope that a man can come through the vicissitudes and temptations of politics and retain his self-esteem and his basic loyalties.

The Autocracy of Good Judgment

EDWARD J. FLYNN

THE BOROUGH AND COUNTY of the Bronx stretches from Long Island Sound westward to the Hudson River. There more than a million and a half of New York City's population live, vote and die. They trace their origins to almost every one of the world's racial, national and religious strains. It is a bewildering miscellany. Collectively, it raises every problem known to city life in America.

According to a commonly-held maxim of political history, such a place presents the best of all breeding grounds for bad government. But despite the occasional prevalence of scandal in other boroughs, despite the propinquity of Tammany-ruled Manhattan, the Bronx for more than a quarter of a century has enjoyed good and clean government. This is not due, as reformers would like to prove, to the active civic interest of so-called independent voters. It is not due to non-partisanship in the Californian sense. In hardly any other urban area in America do the people collectively have so little to do with the direction of government. Good government in the Bronx is not due to the absence of a machine, for the Bronx machine is a model of efficiency. Nor is it due to the absence of a boss, for the Bronx has a boss whose power has never been seriously challenged.

It is—and this presents an incontrovertible challenge to all the aphorisms of reform—due to the quality of the decisions and the capacious power of one man, Edward J. Flynn, who was first selected twenty-seven years ago, not by the people of the Bronx but by the Tammany boss of New York City, Charles F. Murphy.

In theory, government in the Bronx is as democratic as the voters choose to make it. But they do not so choose. They are measurably satisfied. They might, with much difficulty, it is true, overturn the machine and the boss. They have the legal power to cut the political bonds in which they are held.

But they have not done so, and at this writing there is no more evidence that they intend to do so than at any time in the past. Occasionally, there is a murmur that this is "autocracy." Assuredly it is. But the autocracy under which the people of the Bronx live gives them what they think they want and certainly all that they deserve.

I have known Ed Flynn a long time and have perhaps enjoyed a relationship with him as close as that of anyone outside his closest circle of friends and associates. I have studied him in action, have witnessed the quality of Bronx government at first hand and have seen his handmark on the wider stages of state and national politics. I can say with full assurance that the prime factors in Flynn's long tenure of power have been his shrewd judgment, his uncanny sense of timing and, most of all, his utter realism. For Flynn in the accepted practice of politics may, within the bounds of truth-telling, deceive others; but he never deceives himself. His judgment lies in his ability to determine the time and place for decisions, in his sense of public opinion and in his acute perception of the character of those with whom he works.

I have included in his attributes a keen sense of public opinion, because I have seen it proved again and again. Prior to the congressional election of 1946, I talked with Flynn several times in the course of appraising the probable results. Early in October, the country was beset and deeply exasperated by a meat shortage. This was especially felt in metropolitan New York. Flynn said that he could not predetermine the election until he could tell whether people were just mad about meat or whether their dissatisfaction was due to deeper causes. "I can tell in three weeks," he said, "after Truman lifts the ceiling on meat."

Three weeks later, the ceiling had been lifted and Flynn said that the trouble was still present. Then with complete accuracy he named the districts in New York State that would go to each party.

Judgment of public opinion is not due, as wiseacres would have us believe, to multitudinous and intimate contacts with men-in-the-street. Such contacts more often than not confuse and confound judgment. Detachment and shrewd appraisal of the conclusions of those who seek opinions are best.

Flynn has amply proved this, for he lives in what has been called regal isolation. The use of the word "regal" is hardly appropriate, however, since in kingdoms the comings and goings of royalty are well known. But no court calendar discloses Flynn's whereabouts and doings to the public. He leaves all personal contacts with voters to his leaders, and his leaders are seen only by appointment and at ample intervals. In his illuminating book, *You're the Boss,* Flynn says with crystal candor:

"I intended to keep my personal life entirely separate from my political life. As a result, while I have enjoyed a personal friendship with each of the members of the Executive Committee over a long period of years, it has never been an extremely intimate association. I have not visited the homes of any of these men and women, nor have they been inside mine. I meet them only when occasion requires. Personal relationships in any business (and a political machine is my business) are apt to cause jealousy and dissatisfaction. No one in the Bronx can say that he was ever 'closer to the Boss' than anyone else." [11]

Flynn's city residence is far from the madding crowds of the Bronx—a penthouse atop a high apartment in the westernmost corner of the borough, over the Hudson River. Access is attained only by a private elevator.

There is an office in the County Building, where Flynn meets selected leaders and public officials for an hour or two when he is in the city. He and Monroe Goldwater, partners for many years, have extensive offices in Manhattan where Flynn occasionally drops in. Nor is this the usual type of political law firm. Under the very able direction of Goldwater, it handles a large range of what, for lack of a better word, deserves to be called legitimate practice. It is not a place for pandering of influence,

[11] *You're the Boss.* New York: The Viking Press, 1947; p. 61.

but, rather, a place where people of ample affairs go for genuinely expert service.

Except for a few weeks before elections, Flynn is rarely in the city. He has a farm in Maryland and another place in Westchester. Unlike most politicians, he reads a great deal and, it should be added, his literary taste is of the best. Except when he was Chairman of the Democratic National Committee, he has never talked for publication, and he never meets the press. His life, like that of his early sponsor, Charles F. Murphy, has been a masterpiece of reticence.

In recent years, however, Flynn has manifested a desire to put into the record his ripened experience in politics and his ideas about why politics is as it is, and how it could be improved. For several years he has given occasional lectures before my class in politics in Columbia University. Frankness, and literary and personal charm mark his classroom performance and, it may be added, the students deeply enjoy and profit by such occasions.

A perusal of his book will show why, in going over the manuscript for him, I suggested that it be called *A Reluctant Politician*. He eagerly appropriated that title for his chapter describing his introduction to public life. For Flynn's rise to leadership of the Bronx was an unusual procession of chance and circumstance. Certainly, there was not the slightest notion in the mind of the rollicking 26-year-old Flynn in the autumn of 1917 that in five brief years he would be the victorious contender for the Bronx bossdom. He had not the slightest interest in politics.

The youngest of the five children of a dignified, cultured father who made the pursuit of leisure an accomplished art after his studies at Trinity College in Dublin, and of a brave, sweet-faced mother whose labors for many years explained the miracle of the family's subsistence, Ed was born and brought up amid the homey intimacy of the little Bronx community that centered in 143rd Street between Third and Willis Avenues. When Ed graduated from Fordham University Law School in 1912, he opened law offices with Bill McKeown, whose prowess as pitcher on the Fordham baseball team had made him a local hero. Flynn, too, had a host of adoring friends. He was a gay young blood in those years—witty, quick-tongued and completely engaging. Such moments as he didn't spend on the law were given over to convivial excursions with his high-spirited coterie.

Edward J. Flynn, the young counselor-at-law, had neither the time nor the inclination to break into local politics. And so it was with genuine astonishment that he heard the offer to run him for the Assembly, the lower house of the New York State legislature.

Flynn, not knowing whether to laugh it off or leap at it, took counsel with family and friends and finally decided to run.

His first campaign has now become part of the comic legend of the Bronx. The entire district took sides in the internecine war. Husbands and wives, fathers and sons ceased to be on speaking terms for the duration. The only people who came through it with unaffected good humor were Flynn and McGuire, the principals.

He was elected in 1917. He was reelected to the Assembly three times thereafter. He had been sheriff just one month when the Bronx boss died. This was February, 1922. By now politics was in Flynn's blood. But he had begun to acquire that taciturnity which, a few weeks later, would make it possible for him to sit across a desk and exchange calculated silences with the great Murphy of Tammany Hall.

That occasion was brought about by Flynn's announcement for James W. Brown, his own district leader, as new boss. This had not set well with the mighty Mr. Murphy, who had other ideas about who was to be top dog in the Bronx. At the time, Tammany considered the Bronx a fief—its boss ruling by Murphy's sufference. Murphy sent for Flynn, and they met at Tammany Hall. After a long spell of silence, during which Murphy's cool gray eyes were fixed on the young upstart, Murphy asked disapprovingly what was this he heard about Flynn's coming out for Brown.

It was true, Flynn said; he had.

Then came another silence, which Murphy apparently intended him to break. Flynn held out. The second play again had to be Murphy's.

Murphy threw in three verbal chips—blue ones. "Brown won't do," he said.

Flynn replied that he was pledged to Brown. Again there was a silence.

Murphy was an amazingly shrewd judge of men. He had discovered and nurtured Alfred E. Smith, Robert F. Wagner and many others of this generation's political notables. His canny philosophy of leadership always permitted him to sustain a few independent spirits who took positions flatly contrary to his.

Perhaps he found in Flynn's show of spirit a very sure mark of the courage he covertly admired. Perhaps he was still testing Flynn. At any rate, he presently suggested that a triumvirate run the Bronx for a time and implied that Flynn could be one of the members.

Flynn turned the tempting offer over in his mind. Then he answered that, in honor, he could say nothing about the proposal. He was still pledged to Brown. He would not ask Brown to release him.

There the exchange ended. But the next day, presumably nudged by Murphy's long arm, Brown came to Flynn and released him.

So began the short-lived triumvirate which preceded Flynn's final selection as boss. Once a week, Flynn and the two other members would hire a limousine from a funeral parlor and ride down in state to Manhattan to report to the "commissioner," as Murphy preferred to be called. Each week, after shaking hands solemnly with the three, Murphy would ask, "How are conditions in the Bronx?" Each would reply that conditions were fine, and, after another round of handshaking, the three men would file out.

This went on until late April or early May, 1922, when Flynn again disrupted the works by answering "Rotten" to the commissioner's "Well, young man, how are conditions?"

What did he mean by that, Murphy asked.

Simply that the triumvirate wasn't working, Flynn said hotly. Whenever there was anything to be done, the triumvirate could never be got together to do it.

Well, then, Murphy said with a ghost of a smile, the time had come to end the triumvirate and choose a single leader.

A mad scramble for votes followed, and Flynn with quiet help from Murphy emerged triumphant.

Flynn ignored precedent when he assumed the leadership of the Bronx. He immediately changed the methods of administering control which forerunners in the job had regarded as indispensable. No longer was the chief available to all members of the party at all times. A sort of political chain-of-command was set up.

It was a revolutionary switch, but highly effective. Flynn recognized that the personal element had received altogether too much emphasis. It lead to jealousy and dissonance within the party. By establishing himself as an important leader, having office hours at specified times, and by foregoing political or personal association with his lieutenants during off hours, he observed an old political maxim, too often disregarded by politicians.

In the course of most prominent politicians' lives there are times when they are faced with decisions which may radically affect their political futures. Unlike mistakes in other careers, political error at these times of decision may put an end to a leader's career.

In 1925 Flynn came to such a situation. When he chose to support Jimmy Walker for mayor against the incumbent, John F. Hylan, he was gambling his political life. Mr. Murphy was gone, and this was the acid test of Flynn's political sagacity. Ranged against him were other county leaders—McCooey of Kings, Connolly of Queens, and Rendt of Richmond. Mayor Hylan hailed from Brooklyn.

It was a bitter primary between powerful groups which required the highest degree of organizing skill. Political survival of several of the participants hung on the outcome.

Flynn and Walker's supporters did the tedious work of establishing strong counter-organizations in Queens, Richmond and Kings. The result was Walker's nomination.

Flynn, victorious, found himself more firmly in control than ever before.

It was shortly before Murphy's death that Flynn met the man who was to affect his political course more critically than anyone except Murphy. In the winter of 1923-24, Flynn learned that the Democratic party's defeated Vice-Presidential candidate, after a long illness, was back at work in New York. It seemed kind and courteous to call on Franklin Roosevelt. And so Flynn stopped by for the first of those casual, friendly visits that characterized the two men's relationship until 1928, when Al Smith was nominated for the Presidency, and he and the other New York State leaders agreed that Franklin Roosevelt must run for governor.

After a vigorous campaign Roosevelt was installed as governor. The next thought of his political advisers was to prepare for his reelection in 1930.

The burden of the incidental missionary work might have been expected to fall upon Flynn. But Flynn, in conference with Roosevelt, not only agreed that Jim Farley was the man for the job; he strongly advocated that Farley be chosen.

A romanticist might weave a beautiful story of how Farley's wings sprouted under the benign influence of Flynn. The hard facts are that there was nothing either benign or noble or ignoble about Flynn's position. Farley rose because his personal characteristics precisely fitted the need of the moment.

There was never any question of precedence in the relations of the two. Moreover, Flynn considered the gaddings about that Farley had to do in Roosevelt's interest much as, in an earlier day, William H. Taft might have regarded his own participation in T. R.'s tennis cabinet. He wouldn't if he could, and couldn't if he would. Jim's job just wasn't Flynn's cup of tea. Flynn didn't covet it in 1929, and he didn't covet it in 1940, when he became Jim's pinch-hitter.

A final consideration determined Flynn's attitude. He realized then what he has never forgotten, even during the grinding, unremitting, nerve-racking job of directing that delirium which is a Presidential campaign. He realized that if he wanted to stay boss of the Bronx—and he did—he could never for one instant take his hands off the reins.

Cinch though it may seem, the job of a boss like Flynn can neither be neglected nor delegated. The organization over which he rules is a species of feudalism, in which the idea of the personal bond, hierarchic and continuing, dominates. It is based upon a series of personal and deeply felt obligations. They bind the vassal to obedience and loyalty. They bind the liege lord to protection and a living, usually in the form of a job.

To keep his district leaders efficient, satisfied and loyal, the boss must maintain his direct line of contact with those state and Federal agencies that provide jobs. He must always be the channel, the exclusive channel, through which patronage flows to his leaders. The boss can't permit his leaders to find any back doors to the pie counter. That would be fatal to his control.

Only wide-eyed innocents suppose that the business transacted in the boss' weekly conferences represents mere greed and self-seeking. A political organization rests upon many men's necessities. These are more than jobs and favors. They include friendships, encouragements. The district leader is often not only the sub-broker of jobs but the minister of charity and mercy. And the terms "charity" and "mercy" have been known to include everything from the distribution of turkeys and matzoths in season, to intercession with judges in behalf of the district leader's "wayward children." These things are the stuff of the district leader's daily life. Of necessity, they loom large in his dealings with the boss.

Flynn has grown used to hearing that he is one with other machine bosses. But unlike most, Flynn won't lift a finger for any of his henchmen or appointees who get caught off base.

Here again Flynn's profound judgment has verified itself. When the days of reckoning came, others fell by the wayside for indiscretions. But not Ed Flynn. He simply does not indulge in indiscretions. His realism has always told him that to deviate from scrupulous honesty, to stand in the path of justice to defend wayward party men, or to associate with racketeers are sure ways to bring ultimate disaster to the leaders and their machine.

His people are supposed to behave themselves. When they don't, on their own heads the sin and the sentence lie. When Tammany chieftains were moving heaven and earth to snatch loyal Democrats from the inexorable grasp of Samuel Seabury, Flynn permitted those of his men who got into trouble—and there were relatively few—to go it alone. That was revolutionary in a system where the yeomen look to the lord for unfailing succor in distress.

Judge Seabury poked into every nook and corner of city business. Yet he found no "tin boxes," either on Flynn or his district leaders.

Flynn's attitude toward those who fall by the wayside doesn't mean that he deviates one iota from the political principle that the jobs belong to the victors. He insists that good men can be found within the party to fill every appointive job. But once they are appointed, he also insists that they be let alone to do their jobs. This is shrewd political judgment. Among other things, it explains the excellent reputation of the district attorney's office in the Bronx.

Ed Flynn firmly believes that politics is the art of uncompleted contracts; that the potential power of a boss is measured by the number of favors he has done for which he has not collected a direct *quid pro quo*.

District Leader James W. Brown expressed this philosophy in simpler terms during the course of the Seabury investigation. Asked why he had interceded with a magistrate for one of the people of his district, Brown said, "That is the way we make Democrats." And questioned as to what he had told the man who had sought his help, Brown replied that he had said, "The only thing you can do for me is to vote the Democratic ticket."

Ed Flynn's personal habits offer a complete contrast to usual boss pattern. Flynn doesn't sit around until dawn in night clubs.

He doesn't lean against boardwalk railings and dole out largess to hangers-on. He doesn't preside at picnics or boat rides for the peasantry.

In the company of close friends, Flynn is apt to display amazingly swift changes of mood. Every so often, a kind of black, almost savage pessimism about things in the large, and his job in particular, breaks through his ebullient gaiety. Even in his lighter moments, his humor reflects a deep-lying skepticism. He will begin a sentence about one of the persons he most admires with the caveat, "If So-and-So has told me the truth, which I doubt," and laughingly conclude his sentence with a compliment to So-and-So.

Political differences of opinion have never stood between Flynn and his friends. He likes a man to have convictions. He's not concerned about what those convictions are. As far back as his first political fight with the McGuire forces, he acted on his belief that life goes on despite political change. To him, politics is something more than a game. But it's not a bloody war, an irreconcilable conflict. He's too highly civilized to permit political differences to affect his friendships. Once, one of Flynn's friends, in his presence, excoriated Roosevelt. Flynn didn't shout, "You're wrong," He didn't even say, "You're too bitter." He said, "You're bitter." And in that simple reaction he revealed his whole philosophy of politics.

So it is impossible to imagine Flynn, as a political leader, commanding such a purge as was attempted by the President in 1938. Yet, paradoxical as it may seem, Flynn conducted for Roosevelt the only successful purge of the 1938 campaign—the defeat of Rep. John J. O'Connor, chairman of the House Rules Committee. Flynn took the assignment partly because the President himself turned to him after Farley had flatly refused it, partly because he bore an old grudge against O'Connor, and partly because the job was a challenge to his professional skill. Like a master surgeon dressed for a night out, who is suddenly called to perform an operation commensurate with his talents, Flynn did the job.

He did it competently. He learned from it. But when he speaks of it, it is possible to detect in his voice a note of regret for the hours he could have spent more amusingly.

While Flynn was managing the campaign against O'Connor, there occurred the episode that caused the ultra-New Dealers to view Flynn's appointment as national chairman with so much alarm. Late one night, Tom Corcoran telephoned Flynn to talk about something or other relating to the campaign. Corcoran has probably never received a more paralyzing rebuff than Flynn gave him on that occasion.

Flynn subsequently made it clear to Roosevelt himself that if he was to be expected to eliminate O'Connor, he would do it according to the Flynn prescription. He explained that he wanted nothing in the way of help or support from the amateur politicians who were perpetually getting under Jim Farley's feet. And he saw to it that none came to him again. Farley bore the amateurs in resentful silence. Flynn blasted them in a twinkling.

There can be little question about the predominant influence of Flynn in bringing Roosevelt around to the selection of Truman in 1944. His account in *You're the Boss* checks with all the available evidence.

Flynn approached the selection of a candidate for Vice President with the same calm and detached realism that had characterized his support of Jimmy Walker years before. He was seeking not the best of all possible men, but the most available of all possible candidates or, as he puts it, the candidate for Vice President who would "hurt him (Roosevelt) least."

In 1943 and early 1944 Flynn had noted Roosevelt's failing health with increasing concern. After a four weeks' vacation in April, 1944, Roosevelt, according to Flynn, had made little progress toward recovery. His condition "grew steadily worse as spring passed on into summer." Flynn urged him not to run, because he "felt strongly that he would not survive his term."

Others, however, persuaded Roosevelt to run, and Flynn, accepting that decision, turned to the immensely important question of the Vice Presidency. On Roosevelt's invitation Flynn went to Washington to discuss it. The President, according to Flynn, had "a lack of interest in the problems facing him . . . he seemed to procrastinate and to lack the power to make decisions." Clearly, there was need for the help and support of those in whom Roosevelt had a firm and lasting confidence. And prominent among those upon whom Roosevelt leaned in this hour was unquestionably Flynn.

Byrnes, for reasons which I give in some detail later in this book, was discussed and, for the moment, disposed of. Then, as Flynn recounts his conversation with Roosevelt, a conclusion was reached: "Rayburn was a good man (I personally am very fond of him), but he was from Texas and couldn't be considered available. We went over every man in the Senate to see who would be available, and Truman was the only one who fitted. His record as head of the Senate Committee to Investigate the National Defense Program was excellent, his labor votes in the Senate were good; on the other hand, he seemed to represent to some degree the conservatives in the party, he came from a border state, and he had never made any 'racial' remarks. He just dropped into the slot. It was agreed that Truman was the man who would hurt him least."

Roosevelt asked that Flynn get a group together and inject the name of Truman. This group, consisting of Robert Hannegan, national chairman, Mayor Kelly of Chicago, Frank Walker, and George Allen, assembled at the White House. Flynn did active missionary work, making clear to each that the President wanted Truman. This was not easy, nor was it conclusive, as later events proved. But they met with the President, and, says Flynn, "the President told us that we should get behind Truman."

Flynn realized that the President in his indecisive mood had already told several aspirants that the race was wide open and, because of his physical condition, had permitted "all aspirants to believe that he had no commitments."

Flynn remained behind the others, in Washington, and apparently took occasion to try to cement Roosevelt's attachment to Truman. This precautionary measure was dictated by Flynn's long knowledge of Roosevelt's occasional fitful changes in decisions. It was especially necessary at that time, because of Roosevelt's difficulty in making and remembering decisions. A letter to Hannegan naming Justice Douglas and Truman was written by the President before he left Washington. But apparently it was not sent then.

Meanwhile, Byrnes had been in touch with various leaders, and they had apparently been convinced that Roosevelt had not only given Byrnes the green light but had expressed a positive preference for him.

And so when Flynn arrived in Chicago, it was evident that Byrnes would be nominated, unless forceful intervention of the President could be introduced. Flynn plunged into that task with great vigor. He assembled a small group and hammered it with arguments. "I browbeat the committee, I talked, I argued, I swore, and finally they said if the President told them again he was for Truman they would agree."

Flynn called the President and insisted that he tell each man that he wanted Truman. Roosevelt complied. Thus history and a President were made, with Flynn probably the predominant factor. Certainly, the leaders in Chicago would not have taken Truman without decisive Presidential direction, and there would have been no decisive Presidential direction without the decisive intervention of Flynn.

When the 1948 convention rolled around, Philadelphia was crawling with advocates of alternatives to Truman. Flynn was sitting quietly in his hotel room. At that time I think he was partly amused and partly annoyed by the capers of political hacks and amateurs who were blithely committing political hara-kiri. He could have told them so many things about politics—things that he learned from a Mr. Murphy of New York City many years ago.

There was no question that the incumbent Truman would be

nominated in 1948. Those who gathered in the hot hotel lobbies and bars of Philadelphia to talk of ditching Truman were unaware of the cold logic of the situation. They were too blind politically to observe the dictum Ed Flynn has always lived by—never confuse wishes and facts.

What's in a Gnome?

LOUIS McHENRY HOWE

THE STORMS of controversy and criticism that have attended the preliminary construction of the history of Franklin D. Roosevelt and his works have dealt gently with the memory of Louis McHenry Howe. When that small man emerged from the obscurity of his role as a faithful Man Friday and appeared on the national scene as a strange little king-maker, the ravages of chronic affliction were taking full toll. Howe was given barely three years of painful glory. And as the unremitting suffering grew more intense, his hands slipped from the instruments of power, and his friend and political pupil moved up and away into the realm of high destiny.

It was known—it could not help but be known—that Howe had given up the pursuit of personal fortune, fame, family, even health, in the concentrated pursuit of one aim—Roosevelt's election to the Presidency. It was written in every account of this new and interesting figure in Washington that his life had been a study in loyalty and that he had realized the height of success only at the cost of mental torment and physical deterioration. Sympathy for his suffering and admiration for a virtue not too common in politics arrested even the most virile critics of the New Deal.

There was no exaggeration in those public accounts of Howe's illness. Campaign associations and, later, life around the White House gave me a most intimate picture of Howe's infirmity. He was able to sleep only by fits and starts. Chronic asthma made it impossible for him to lie in bed, and he accommodated his frail breathing apparatus by an interminable series of postures. To while away the hours, he read detective and adventure stories of all types, with trash in the ascendency. Bed, floor, chairs were piled with newspapers and crime literature. The word gnome, often applied by newspaper writers, was never used more appropriately.

Howe's first contact with Roosevelt seems to have been in Albany in 1910. Howe was a newspaperman assigned to the Capital. Roosevelt was a first-term senator from Dutchess County. Howe was then 39; Roosevelt, 28. Howe's first important service was in Roosevelt's campaign for reelection. Typhoid fever incapacitated the candidate, and Howe carried on the campaign alone.

In that campaign Roosevelt and Howe developed a principle of campaign strategy destined ultimately to capture both the governorship and the Presidency. Dutchess County was heavily Republican and rural. The two small cities, Poughkeepsie and Beacon, had Democratic leanings. Howe and Roosevelt decided to waste no time among Democrats. Their votes were taken for granted. Instead, they took to the back roads and the farms. Every Republican thus converted meant a solid and, it proved, a permanent gain. The young, ambitious and exceedingly personable heir to a baronial estate called himself a farmer. He and Howe—with some wry adaptation—learned the homey language of the open fields, the cow barns and the dairy. This succeeded beyond their dreams.

Years later, their strategy was rewarded with two successive elections to the governorship—with an immense gain the second time. New York City, Buffalo and other cities were left to the machines, which methodically turned out the vote. Roosevelt as candidate and governor labored for gains in Republican counties and succeeded. In the race for the Presidential nomination, all of Roosevelt's speeches, especially in the rural states, stressed the idea that farm recovery came first. Other segments of the economy, he added, would inevitably follow a rise in agricultural prices and prosperity. At the supreme moment in the convention, the delegates from the great industrial states sat unmoved in their seats while the South, the Middle West and the Northwest marched in triumph—*rus triumphans*. In the campaign that followed, Roosevelt's speeches were full of agricultural reform, government economy and Bryanesque excoriation of Wall Street—themes dear to the hearts of impoverished farmers. Labor was scarcely mentioned, except briefly at Boston near the end of the campaign. From the defections thus suffered in the Middle West, the Republican party did not recover for six years. Howe was largely responsible for this master strategy.

Reams have been written about the origins of the Smith-Roosevelt rupture, and as I have noted in my discussion of the former, the major difference was in fundamental character. Howe figured in the early irritations. In the mid-twenties Roosevelt, seeking a means of relieving himself of carrying Howe's modest salary, sought a place for his manager and friend on the payroll of the Council of State Parks. Robert Moses, friend and a major adviser of Smith, refused to use his position as park chairman to create a job for Howe. Moses' reason was that Howe intended to devote his major attention to the political fences of his protégé, rather than to the shrubbery and ravines of the parks. Moses thus earned the lasting enmity of both Howe and Roosevelt, which darkened the relations between Governor Smith and his successor.

Another job was provided for Howe, as executive for a voluntary National Crime Commission, of which Roosevelt was a major member. This provided Howe with an office in lower New York and with ample facilities and time to enable him to promote the interests of Roosevelt. Letter-writing was raised by Howe to mass production levels in the six years preceding 1932. At one stage at least three expert imitators of Roosevelt's signature were employed, signing letters dictated by someone other than the man whose name was printed on the stationery. No doubt, thousands of Americans are cherishing or handing on to their heirs Roosevelt missives dictated by another and signed by someone else.

It was while Louis was in the Crime Commission that I first met him. I had some expertness in the field, having conducted surveys in a number of states, including New York. I did a number of jobs for Howe, including a long report on payroll robberies and the wisdom of paying by check. For this I received no compensation except in valuable additions to my political education through contacts with a veteran. I saw a great deal of Howe in those years, and he occasionally talked to my Columbia classes on the practice of politics.

In 1928 he summoned me from Chicago to help Roosevelt, then running for governor, with the preparation of a speech on judicial reform. That was my first meeting with the man of destiny. Two years later, Roosevelt appointed me to a commission on judicial reform which brought me into occasional and later into continuous contact with the governor. My concern with judicial reform ultimately turned to Presidential politics.

This intimacy carried dangers in its wake, for Howe was a jealous watchdog. The utmost discretion was always essential in the conduct of anyone close to Roosevelt in those years, for Howe was determined never to lose his niche nearest the governor. As Basil O'Connor, Roosevelt's law partner put it, Louis was ready to "give the foot" to anyone who threatened his propinquity. I learned very soon that Howe entertained no cordial regard for Samuel I. Rosenman, who had risen with the help of Tammany Hall to the position of counsel to the governor.

Fortunately, I managed to maintain friendly relations with both Louis Howe and Sam Rosenman.[12] If either had suspected that I was more than politely friendly with the other, if either had been given the slightest reason to resent any association of mine with Roosevelt at that crucial time, he would not have hesitated for a moment to block me off completely. It was lamentable but true that anyone, regardless of the contribution that he might have been able to make to Franklin Roosevelt, would have found the going hard unless he had appeased both these men.

Louis was then in New York City, working at Roosevelt headquarters on Madison Avenue. The governor, who was deeply devoted to Louis, was characteristically careless about keeping in touch with Louis as often as Louis' insatiable interest, curiosity and affection would have dictated. He lived in an agony of appre-

[12] The text beginning here and extending to page 140 is substantially quoted from my book *After Seven Years.*

hension that "someone" (obviously meaning Rosenman) would smash all his well-laid plans. Louis was constantly torn between the *idées fixes* that his pre-convention work in New York was indispensable and that, in his absence from Albany, "someone" would "give Franklin bad advice or let his impulses run away with him."

I had a room across the street from Louis' and in the offices of the Commission on the Administration of Justice, and I went to see him frequently during February and March, as indeed I had been doing for years. I kept him informed of the developments that were taking place in my relations with Roosevelt—of the trips to Albany, the telephone calls, the correspondence—and I continued to do so thereafter. In some way this seemed to assuage Louis' fears, and it became clear from his conversation that he firmly believed that he had "planted" me in Albany to see that "someone" made no mistakes and to sound the sirens so that he could hurl himself into the breach if anything threatened his Franklin's availability. I confess that I did nothing to dislodge this idea from Louis' head. It comforted him. It minimized his potential opposition to the adoption of the kind of program I hoped to see Roosevelt champion.

Events moved fast during the spring and early summer. Finally, in late June the Democratic National Convention convened. The center of the convention, for me, was 1702 at the Congress Hotel—Louis Howe's suite.

I don't believe that Louis set foot outside his rooms during the entire period of the convention. There, in the inevitable confusion that washes over every outpost of a political convention, the doughty little man worked, worried, suffered, triumphed. Except that he threw his coat aside occasionally when he took a nap, I don't think that he had his clothes off during the entire week. It was a moment when his fondest ambitions, the fruits of a lifetime of labor, hung in the balance. And his nerves were raw with the strain, his body racked by illness.

The most vivid picture that I have of those days is that of Louis at the moment Roosevelt's name was put in nomination.

The convention was in an uproar. Over the radio came sounds of singing, marching delegates, blaring bands, and the futile poundings of Senator Thomas J. Walsh's gavel. Louis was lying on his bed, doubled up with suffering from his chronic asthma. For hours he had been sending directions to Arthur F. Mullen, the Roosevelt floor manager. Looking at that moment of victory like a man to whom happiness could never come and whose wasted body could hardly be expected to harbor the breath of life much longer, he groaned out between coughs, "Tell them to repeat *Happy Days Are Here Again*."

It is questionable whether Louis' intense activity was especially important at the convention. Jim Farley, after all, was the field marshal, attending sessions of the convention and negotiating with delegates there and in his own apartment. Probably Louis' chief contribution was made in keeping in touch with such party leaders as Senators Hull, Wheeler and Byrnes and in counseling with Farley and Ed Flynn. For the rest, the milling about that went on in his apartment seemed to have little enough to do with the actual political management of the convention.

During the agonizing six days of the convention my chief job was to get Louis to approve the acceptance speech. I had seen Louis constantly during May and June, kept him informed of what I was doing in Albany, and in general explained the shape our thoughts were taking. From those talks he had grown reasonably familiar with the ideas expressed in the acceptance speech and had no objection to them.

But though he admittedly did not demur at the philosophy of the speech I showed him, he rasped that the speech simply wouldn't do, simply wasn't appropriate to such an occasion. There followed, then, a fearful tirade which reached a crescendo with the shout, "Good God, do I have to do everything myself? I see Sam Rosenman in every paragraph of this mess."

So he spit it out—at last—the thing he really felt. It wasn't jealousy, solely, though clearly he resented not only Sam but the rest of us who were gathering around his "Franklin." It was the simple, primitive desire to play a major role in the crowning oratorical triumph of his idol's career.

In such a situation it was difficult, despite a long friendship with Louis, to do much with him. I explained that Rosenman had really had very little to do with the writing of the speech, but to that Louis bitterly replied that he knew better, that he had too much respect for my judgment to believe that I could have "perpetrated" this speech. "I don't expect Sam to understand, but you'd know it would go fine under the trees at Hyde Park and be a complete flop at a convention," he snapped. I argued that, convention or no convention, it was essential that a measured, comprehensive statement go to a country wallowing in the depths of a depression. But it was impossible to make Louis abandon the pretenses (1) that the speech was unsuitable and (2) that it was unsuitable because Sam had worked on it. Over and over again, he threatened to write "a whole new speech" himself, and the hours whirled by without his making a move to begin.

By the day of acceptance, however, Louis had prepared a speech. I tried desperately to get Louis to talk to me about it, but he flatly refused. He was too busy, he said.

When the governor's plane arrived at the airport Louis got into Roosevelt's car, sharing, as he had every right to, the triumph of that trip from the airport to the stadium.

But Louis had no chance to confer with Roosevelt in the car. Its path led through screaming, shouting, deafening crowds, and the governor was so happy and so busy waving at his admirers that Louis could not engage him in talk. Apparently, therefore, Louis decided on one of the most desperate courses imaginable. He undertook to get Roosevelt to accept his speech sight unseen at the very moment before Roosevelt was to address the convention.

After the Chairman had introduced Roosevelt, had announced to him the decision of the convention, and had completed a brief speech of his own, Louis handed Roosevelt his draft of an acceptance speech. Roosevelt, thoroughly aware of what the moment meant to Louis, took the document, extracted the other from his pocket, and laid the two beside each other. While the convention was cheering madly, he glanced over the first pages of the two speeches, removed the first page from his own draft, replaced it with Louis' and began to read.

In the following weeks, with a national campaign looming ever nearer my association with Roosevelt, of necessity, became quite close.

It was a difficult thing for Louis to accept. Functions which Louis had performed alone in the old days had grown to dimensions requiring the services of several people.

I remember, after Louis had indicated hurt feelings to Roosevelt, Roosevelt's saying to me, "Louis can be difficult. He can't bear to let anyone else have a direct line through to me."

Apparently my service in the campaign temporarily satisfied Louis that he had nothing to fear from my association with the President-elect. Our relations became more and more cordial and intimate. Howe, largely leaving matters of legislative and policy plans to me, was busy with Cabinet-making. A good deal of this had to do with the Secretaryship of State. There had been a great deal of talk about Owen D. Young, then chairman of General Electric, as a probability for the job. Louis told me that he believed that at any rate Young should have the "refusal" of the place. One day I met Louis on Madison Avenue as he was taking a cab. He told me that he was going to see Young. Shortly afterward, Young made a public statement to the effect that he could not be considered because of illness in the family. Louis apparently had had Cordell Hull in mind for a long time. In 1928 he had told me that Hull should be selected as a running mate for Al Smith. Ultimately, apparently, Howe prevailed, and Hull was selected.

The selection of Harold Ickes, made on impulse by Roosevelt, was a shock to Louie, but he ultimately grew to like the Chicago curmudgeon. When I first told Louis, in February, 1933, that I had, on the advice of Hiram Johnson and others, invited to New York for consultation a man named Ickes, Louie rasped, "There isn't any such name."

There were others whose appointment Louis steadfastly blocked. One of these was Joseph P. Kennedy, and it took a year suitably to reward this man who had contributed substantially to the pre-convention campaign.

In the months before the inauguration Howe also busied himself with meticulous planning of arrangements concerning the White House. His choice of a job was to be the President's secretary—"the" secretary in full charge. Under Hoover, there had been three secretaries, and it was assumed that this plan would prevail under the new regime. Much to the amazement of Marvin McIntyre and Steve Early when they received their commissions as Howe's colleagues, they were designated as Assistant Secretaries. Howe had seen to that. He also saw to it that I was appointed Assistant Secretary of State, safely removed from the White House.

In one respect, Howe's White House arrangements were abruptly upset. He planned that Marguerite LeHand, for years the confidential secretary of Roosevelt, should live and work in the White House proper—among the women. Missy had other ideas, and when she saw a small, cozy office between the President's and the Cabinet room, she gaily moved in—yards nearer the President than Howe. Her loyalty proved no less than Howe's, and her life, like so many others in those days of great events, faded out and ended before her allotted time.

I had occasion many times to observe Louis in his capacities at the White House. He certainly gave untiringly of himself, and his influence with Roosevelt was considerable. It seems to be generally believed that Roosevelt's drift down the stream of capricious experimentation can be explained by the death of Louis Howe. As a matter of fact, Howe was as much the lover of experiments as was Roosevelt. Fortunately, though, the two men rarely got the itch to carry out the same experiment at the same time. So the relationship actually was a rough corrective.

But there were times when Howe's self-assurance made him rush to conclusions and in turn bend the President's mind to decisions which were unwarranted, ill-considered, ill-advised and almost disastrous in their consequences. One of these was the calculated indifference of Roosevelt to the mounting bank crisis in February. Howe, who knew little of finance or economics, took a light and wholly political view of that development.

Another was in connection with the President's action in scuttling the London Economic Conference. When the President wrote his fatal message on that occasion, only Howe and Henry Morgenthau, Jr., were with him on the cruiser *Indianapolis*. As the story has been told on what seems to me good authority, Louis was skimming through the newspapers on the desk near his boss. He remarked that the stock market did not seem to be greatly disturbed by the trend in London. To draw a conclusion of such importance from that fact was inutterable folly, because a decision by the United States to refuse to cooperate in restoring gold as the world's currency standard would be desperately inflationary. However, after Howe's remark Roosevelt wrote the refusal that shook the world and, incidentally, Howe's friend Cordell Hull and myself.

When I returned from London and remonstrated with Louis, he gaily informed me that the declaration rejected by Roosevelt was a moral commitment to restore gold. Louis overlooked the critical fact that it left the time for such restoration completely open.

It was Howe who established the widely criticized custom of White House people's writing for pay in newspapers and magazines. Most of the press, he said, would be against the new regime. Therefore, it was necessary that the members of the Administration be articulate in print as well as on the stump. He said, further, that pay could be accepted because the members of a leftist regime would likely be impecunious. Hence, his own literary output for a year or so, Mrs. Roosevelt's, and ultimately that of many others.

The First Lady was always Howe's most dependable and friendly tie to the President. She regarded him as a political seer without parallel, and while his strength remained he counseled her in great detail.

Meanwhile, as illness inexorably sapped his energies, his concern over the course of Administration policy and his own part in it grew. Illness took him more and more from his desk near the President's office. But wherever he was, there was the telephone, and he continued to call Cabinet officers and others with orders and suggestions. Things became confused because, as his contact with Roosevelt lessened, Howe's orders and suggestions had a tendency to cross wires. Roosevelt, intensely busy with great events, had less time to placate Howe's ideas and fancies. At times, he was irritable and short when Howe sought him on the telephone. Finally, the doctors induced Howe to move to the Naval Hospital, where he remained some months before the end in April, 1936.

I was still, in a wholly unofficial capacity, in charge of the President's important speeches and messages. Semi-isolated toward the end and steadily growing weaker, Howe's earlier jealous concern over his prerogatives vanished and was replaced by a pathetic dependence upon me to see that no errors of judgment crept into the President's utterances. I scrupulously respected this concern and when every speech or message was in semifinal form, took it out to the hospital for his perusal.

He confided in me often in those days that he had always been desperately concerned over "Franklin's" impulses and solemnly charged me with minute watchfulness. There was something portentous in the fear in this frail remnant of a man, lest the man he had done so much to make President should destroy his career by such errors as Louis had always conceived that he and he alone could prevent.

In those last months Louie grew a beard, which added a shocking grotesquerie to his gnarled and emaciated figure. His breath came with such difficulty that he read or chatted with visitors while kneeling on the bed. And so the light faded for this Nibelung, while Siegfried, now grown to hero's size, moved on to a destiny reserved for only the few immortals of history.

The Ghost That Haunted The
White House

CHARLES MICHELSON was the most famous political ghost writer in history, and he is included in these chronicles as a convenient excuse for a discourse on that strange and, to some, very doubtful occupation. One would expect a ghost to operate in deep anonymity. But Charley was well known. He was widely written about and cartooned. He was anything but secretive about his ghost writing, and newspapermen who heard this senator or that Cabinet officer sound off knew that, while the breath came from the speaker, the words and music were Michelson's. He even designated his memoir as *The Ghost Talks*.

There are other paradoxes in any account of Michelson, aside from the fame of his anonymity and the substance of his ghostliness. His book frankly reveals a species of cynical truthfulness, perhaps unparalleled since Machiavelli wrote *The Prince*, but he spent the best-known period of his life making things seem other than they were. He told only the better part of the truth about the people he served and only the worse part of the truth about his political opponents. But he unsparingly told all the truth about himself. He passionately supported the Smith-Raskob-Shouse wing of the Democratic party, but on the day after the Roosevelt wing had won, he walked into Louis Howe's rooms in Chicago and set to work for Roosevelt. When the defeated group, Charley's former employers, later helped to organize the Liberty League, he produced reams of invective to hurl against them. He says frankly in his book: "Just why any personal opinion I might have had could have influenced me, I have never been able to figure. I never had a part in formulating Roosevelt policies. I was merely a propagandist and therefore naturally campaigned to the best of my ability for anything the President proposed." [13]

He says, too: "My concern in such matters was purely that of a political technician. If a course seemed to me to advance the prestige of the party and the administration, I was enthusiastic at its incubation. If it seemed to me a hindrance to political success, I was against it; but if such a policy was adopted, my business was to make it palatable to the country, with no reservations on the score of my personal views."

In his long years with Hearst and the New York *World,* in his labors for the Democratic committee in destroying the Hoover Administration, in the manifold duties, later, for this or that agency of the Roosevelt Administration or for the Democratic National Committee, he followed the line drawn by his superiors and turned in effective stuff. Withal, he was an observer of but not a moralist about those dissimulating men of political distinction whose right hand never inquired about what particular pocket the left hand happened to be exploring. That is why Charley's life and opinions can teach us so much about politics.

While he was often "loaned" to the Roosevelt Administration for this or that purpose, Michelson was for years officially an officer of the Democratic National Committee. During eight of those years, his boss was Farley. In the last two of the Farley years, the chairman and the President were drifting apart. Michelson operated on his conviction that Farley was never a New Dealer at heart nor was Garner—and probably he was right. He admired Farley's incredible skill in making friends for the party. He respected Farley's truthfulness, which he believed in Farley's case to be expedient. He quotes with favor Farley's words, "What is the use of lying to a fellow when he knows he is being told a lie?" In short, Michelson thought that, since Farley could not lie well, he had better be content with the truth. On one occasion Michelson's admiration found words: "Jim, you are the most honest man alive! You would not steal anything—except an election."

[13] *The Ghost Talks.* New York: G. P. Putnam's Sons, 1944; p. 176.

He was, in later years, amazed at the hurt manifested by various statesmen who believed the assurances of Roosevelt not wisely but too well. To Michelson such a matter was "merely another example of the President's sunny disposition to make people believe he is with them." To Michelson, a true politician should know that dissimulation is part of the game. To say one thing and mean another in politics, according to Charley, was no more to be resented than a third baseman who hides the ball and puts out a rookie runner.

Charley's cynical masterpiece was a bit of advice he gave Roosevelt when there had been no third-term announcement and Farley wanted the nomination. He said to the President: "But I think you will agree with me that no Democrat but yourself can be elected this year. Would it not be better—in the event of your not being the candidate—to let Jim Farley have the nomination? If he ran and was defeated, that defeat would be attributed to religious prejudice. If almost any other of the aspirants was nominated and lost, that defeat would be hailed as a repudiation of your administration and the New Deal."

This advice to save Roosevelt and the New Deal at the expense of Farley and the Catholic Church, it is needless to say, proved to be academic. Roosevelt, who probably at that time had decided to run himself, rejected it on the ground that it would be unfair to Farley.

Michelson lays on the table the soiled cards regarding the famous campaign book which was a device to raise money without violating the Hatch Act. It was a book of pictures of politicians and of pieces written by distinguished but friendly writers. With this editorial background there were sold pages of advertising at a rate of $2,500 a page. A circulation of 100,000 was guaranteed. There were editions for little $2.50 contributors and $100 de luxe copies for the fat cats. These latter copies were embellished by a genuine autograph of the President of the United States.

In this connection Charley says he had some discussion with the President on the subject of "righteousness." But with amusing cynicism, he attributed Roosevelt's hesitation to his hatred of "the drudgery of writing his signature so many times." Charley prevailed in this argument.

The Hatch Act may not have purified national politics, but Charley shows how magnificently it awakened his creative imagination. Another of his plans was to have the Federal government buy the Empire State Building and have the selling agent get ten men to contribute $5,000 each to the Democratic campaign fund. This fell through.

Another idea was to have the government buy a bit of virgin forest in the Adirondacks, for which Charley suggested a $20,000 contribution might be gained for the party. The bill had passed the Senate, and Charley asked the Speaker to recognize a sponsor in the House. The bill was passed, but the Budget Bureau alerted the President, who vetoed it.

This cured Charley, because he later found that "on this transaction nearly every lobbyist between Albany and Washington was in on the deal for a fat commission."

It is interesting to note that most of the plans to help the party that are told by Charley are those which fell through. It would, of course, have gravely injured the party to make his chapter on party finance a tale of the successes that must have been achieved. But the good ship did weather the sea—even in war years, when, according to Charley, the national committee secretary and treasurer "kept the establishment alive."

"These two," he says, "were the political heroes of 1941-1942. Their contribution had to come by a devious passage. It was on the same principle that our freight ships to the war fronts had to be routed around the Cape of Good Hope to avoid being torpedoed—which suggests that if the motive be virtuous and the desire intense, there can be no insurmountable obstacles."

Whether the virtue of the motive intensified the desire, Charley does not tell us.

Michelson's likes and dislikes among the people with whom he worked are a telling commentary on his political regularity. He disapproved of Heywood Broun, with whom he worked on the New York *World*, Harry Hopkins, Tommy Corcoran and

Stanley High. He liked Flynn, Farley, Marvin McIntyre and Steve Early.

But Michelson's fame will finally rest upon his stupendous product as a ghost writer, and, as I wrote at the beginning of this chapter, that art needs a bit of explaining.

The ethical question involved in the delivery by a public figure of a speech written by some unnamed and uncredited person can and should be argued at length. The net result of this practice so prevalent not only in politics but in business and labor management has been the growth of a cynical attitude on the part of the public. We often hear the comment among informed people, "That was a good speech. I wonder who wrote it." People are chary in evaluating a candidate on the basis of what he says.

This is really no essential loss, because in selecting a public servant the test should not be a contest of oratory. For most public positions, excellence in oratory is hardly more important a test than excellence in pie-baking or fiddling. Public administration involves judgment in decisions, skill in picking subordinates, the capacity to analyze problems and knowledge of economics, government and other fields of human activity. These qualities may reside in inarticulate people.

It is also true that the education of the public is one of the major responsibilities of a man in high office. I have stressed that in several other chapters in this book, notably in those about Tom L. Johnson and Alfred E. Smith. To accomplish that, words —spoken or written—are the chief instruments. Therefore, a public man can hardly be blamed if he enlists aid in preparing his speeches and public documents. The ethical question comes down to a matter of method or degree.

This ethical question never bothered Michelson. A part of the job of the National Committee during the time of his service was to attack Republicans, defend Democrats and win votes. This was largely done through speeches, whenever possible on radio time, or on notable ceremonial occasions or on the floors of Congress. The more notable the speaker, the more publicity.

Michelson's job was to construct speeches attacking Republicans in Hoover's time, defending Democrats in Roosevelt's time. In campaigns, his job was to do both.

He regarded writing a speech as a routine task. He knew that his products were not likely to be remembered long, nor would they be seriously answered. He racked his brain for catch phrases and rough frameworks of thought upon which to hang his sentences. Being a newspaper man, he delved in the papers for source material. He was especially fond of the business news. There one can find items to support any contention. In Hoover's regime, Charley picked out notices of business recessions and failures. In Roosevelt's day, business profits were fodder.

The technique of argument was varied. Sometimes the argument by example was used. The fallacy in this method is that the examples selected merely support the contention and may not be representative. In political badminton this isn't important, of course. Another device was to search for material to quote a man against himself. Another was ridicule by name-calling, phrase-making and irony.

Charley's speeches were often written without any idea of who the speaker might be. They were turned out, and then somebody had to be found who had an open date. Sometimes several prospects had to be approached.

Many of his speeches were written on order for senators, congressmen and others who came to him when they were invited for some ceremonial occasion.

As business grew, Michelson had to enlist an assistant or two. These were usually newspapermen who needed work. A great many speeches were farmed out, usually to working Washington reporters, anxious to earn an extra dollar or two.

The total output was tremendous and mediocre.

Michelson's background had allowed no great mastery of history, economics or other fields of knowledge. He said in his book that he never knew "beans" about economics. But with a depression going on, it was easy to find material to condemn the Administration in power. Later, with recovery on the way, it was easy to note gains.

Roosevelt scarcely if ever asked for or used Charley's speeches. He did not find that the Michelson style or subject matter fitted his personality or needs. Nor was Charley's knowledge not sufficient for the launching of new policies or for the explanation of complicated matters of statecraft. The history of Roosevelt's speeches needs a volume in itself and is hardly pertinent here.

Suffice it to say that in the formulation of Roosevelt's speeches and state papers in the four and a half years when I served in that ritual, the technique used could hardly be called ghost writing. Roosevelt had a sense of the general subject matter appropriate or necessary to the occasion, the timing suitable to the presentation of this or that project, and the public state of mind or emotion at the planned time of delivery. His temperament had a lot to do with it. He could work and think with some people. With others he was annoyed, impatient, bored.

It was my job to discuss all these elements of suitability, tone, occasion and time and to get his views of general subject matter, perhaps making note of his half-formulated ideas. Then it was necessary to draw from my own knowledge, from books, papers, records and from the knowledge of others to whom I had access.

In any event, after many drafts and a great deal of consultation with Roosevelt, the speech evolved. It became part of his personality; it matched his moods and met his feeling for words and style. It was no mere paper prepared to be read, as is the British Cabinet's speech of the King.

It should be added that such a speech cannot be prepared in council. From beginning to end, any conferring with others was my job. Only Roosevelt and I worked directly on the speech, and over that whole period Roosevelt strictly adhered to that rule.

The care, craftsmanship and research essential to the public statements, papers and speeches of a President or of a prospective President or candidate are too great either for his knowledge or time. The radio and other means of communication prohibit repetition. There must be help, and there is help.

The claim of Wendell Willkie that he "rolled his own" was neither a credit to his appreciation of what was required nor a tribute to the facts as I know them. He had a profusion and, may I add, a confusion of helpers. He was much more daring on occasions in "off-the-cuff" utterances, but those bursts never helped his progress.

The important thing is to provide the means through which a public figure can create the impression that he knows what he is saying and that he means it; to make sure that what is said is informative, enlightening and of some permanent significance. Mere ghost writing can never meet that requirement.

Holmes and the Sorcerer's Apprentices

FELIX FRANKFURTER

IN THE EARLY YEARS of the recent war, Richard Gardiner Casey, Australian Minister to Washington, resigned to accept an office in the British Cabinet under Churchill. This lightsome shift of allegiance from one sovereign state to another was an uncommon matter, even within the British Commonwealth. At least Casey's superior, the Prime Minister of Australia, thought so and protested. Casey said in his reply that, before making his decision, he had sought the advice of Felix Frankfurter and Harry Hopkins.

This extraordinary participation by a Justice of the Supreme Court of the United States in international job placement hardly created a ripple on the sea of news. Perhaps that was because over the years it had become so commonplace to know Felix Frankfurter as America's most eminent provider of suitable jobs for people and of suitable people for jobs.

No one except Frankfurter will ever know how many men have moved from one official or unofficial position to another or from no job at all to an important post because of his advice. But enough is known to justify my observations.

This activity has gone on under five Presidents, Democratic and Republican. It may be going on under a sixth, for a Frankfurter protégé is Secretary of State. Scores of others are top civilian brass in Washington, and Frankfurter is no man to permit the confines or traditions of the Supreme Court to limit his usefulness to the nation and to his friends. As a Justice he may, later on, speak with the wisdom of a Marshall or a Taney, but his enduring fame will rest upon his prodigious labors as a provider of jobs for men and men for jobs.

We are only incidentally concerned here with Frankfurter the jurist, the law teacher or the legal philosopher. If there are matters in the great marble hall opposite the Capitol that might add to the pansophy that is politics—and no doubt there are—they are barred to the inquisitive, even to the academic inquisitive. But in the years before his investiture, in 1939, despite the protection of academic mist and an acute talent for anonymity, enough was revealed to establish Frankfurter as a politician of superior, highly original parts. It is that period in his life that attracts the patient but amazed attention of this analyst.

Frankfurter, like Will Hays, is small, slight, sharp, talkative and immensely energetic. John Garner used to say that Frankfurter reminded him of the late Cardinal Gibbons. There the resemblances end. Frankfurter was an immigrant from Austria who knew no English until he was twelve years old. His habitat has been limited—Boston, Washington, New York. He once said that he considered New York City his intellectual fatherland.

His progress through City College in New York and at Harvard Law School was marked by exceptional academic work. He easily found employment in a New York law firm and almost immediately had the good fortune to attract the attention of very important people.

The first of these seems to have been Henry L. Stimson, who was destined to hold Cabinet office in three widely separated Administrations. Stimson had been selected by Theodore Roosevelt as district attorney for the major purpose of getting after the "trusts" whose base of operation was the lower end of Manhattan.

In those days of nascent "progressivism" and in that litigious environment Frankfurter attained the simple pattern of his statesmanship. He has not altered it in any important respect in the forty years that followed. The problems of economic life were matters to be settled in a law office, a court room or around a labor-management bargaining table. These problems were litigious, controversial, not broadly constructive and evolutionary. The government was the protagonist. Its agents were its lawyers and commissioners. The antagonists were big corporation lawyers.

In the background were misty principals whom Frankfurter never really knew at first hand and who were chiefly envisaged as concepts in legalistic fencing. Those background figures were owners of the corporations, managers, workers and consumers.

Despite his vast intellectual energy, his multitudinous contacts with men in academic life and in government, his copious reading, Frankfurter's economic and political ideas remained in this no man's land between the realities of business and the practical problems of government.

Perhaps he would reply to this that a reading of briefs and opinions on economic matters supplied the deficiency. That would be an issue of personal rating of values. I cannot believe that such secondary sources can supply the vital knowledge that can be gained by personal acquaintance with the managers and workers in great enterprises, by ocular observation of plants, engineering departments and production lines, and by first-hand knowledge of the vast network of sales and supply that characterizes modern industry.

There was good fortune in Frankfurter's relations with Stimson. That planetary figure—austere, sophisticated, ambitious—was a means of influence for Frankfurter for nearly forty years. No one but the two principals can know how much Stimson did to promote Frankfurter's protégés. It may even be—although this is wholly speculative—that the miracle of Stimson's elevation to the position of Secretary of War in the Administration of a man whom Stimson had roundly denounced was not achieved without a well-calculated nudging by Frankfurter at the White House. But this is a more recent event going a bit ahead of our present story.

Frankfurter, after five years with Stimson in the district attorney's office and in the War Department in the Taft Administration, was appointed to the faculty of the Harvard Law School. This was done in 1914, according to Fred Rodell of the Yale Law School, through the help of Lewis D. Brandeis, an influential Harvard alumnus.

In 1917, through a contact with Newton D. Baker, Secretary

of War, Frankfurter was called to Washington, where he soon became chairman of the War Policies Board. Another member of that board was Franklin D. Roosevelt, Assistant Secretary of the Navy. This established a friendly though not intimate relationship which continued until Roosevelt was President. He was not so fortunate in his relations with T. R. who violently denounced him during that period for some of his views, actions, and decisions on labor matters. As we look back at that controversy the indignation of T. R. seems to have been pretty farfetched. It was cut from a partisan pattern, since to portray Frankfurter as a sinister figure was a means of enlarging T. R.'s campaign against Wilson.

In 1919, Frankfurter returned to his teaching at the Harvard Law School. Frankfurter's position in the Harvard Law School was ideally suited to his temperament, ambitions and methods of operation. Contact with students—and this generally meant the most advanced students—gave him the opportunity to discover talent, which is always a much sought for commodity in certain government departments and in big law offices. The promotion of former students' careers provided a means for enlarging Frankfurter's contacts with leaders of importance in government and law. And it elicited lasting gratitude from those who were helped.

His privileged and protected position in the academic world enabled him to speak and write with little fear of the consequences. His views, not always clearly expressed, were generally regarded as somewhat unorthodox, although on examination they certainly were not unusual, even in the atmosphere of the 1920's. A favorite outlet was the *New Republic,* whose editor, Herbert Croly, was a close friend.

Frankfurter's contacts with organized labor were almost continuous. His service was sought as consultant and counsel in important labor litigation in the courts. Frankfurter took no fees for these services. He lived at a fairly simple standard and was never much interested in money.

His circle of friends was never wide, but it was select. It was limited chiefly to the legal profession, but there were professors of philosophy and a scattering of musicians, playwrights and editors. No little mutual admiration was the rule in the Frankfurter circle. An example of such praise is Archibald MacLeish's introduction to a collection of Frankfurter's writings published on his accession to the bench. [14]

Frankfurter's development of his relations with Justices Holmes and Brandeis, however, must stand as the most important of all his exercises in friendship. A man on the Supreme Court, especially an elderly man, has some need for means for articulation and promotion other than his own limited avenues of expression. In these cases Frankfurter became a sort of missionary for these truly remarkable men. In the case of Brandeis there never seemed to have been a very great need for interpretation. For Brandeis was not merely a somewhat weary and pessimistic dissenter, like Holmes, but a constructive statesman and a person of positive optimism. He was quite able to speak for himself within the confines of judicial comment.

With both of these jurists, as well as with several others in important courts, Frankfurter enjoyed close relations. For many lesser judges, as well as for Holmes and Brandeis, Frankfurter was able to provide able young assistants, which, of course, spread his influence in many directions.

Frankfurter wasted little time, either in law school or in social and official life, upon that great generality of people whom he might call dull or of mediocre intellectual attainments. Rodell says:

"The dull and mediocre students, the slow-witted, got short shrift. Moving too fast or too subtly for them, he left them behind—and as a result they had no more use for him than did he for them . . . But the bright boys, the end men of his minstrel shows, revered him." [15]

In all of Frankfurter's incessant activity in public affairs he has manifested a remarkable capacity for anonymity. The most re-

[14] *Law and Politics, Occasional Papers of Felix Frankfurter,* New York, Harcourt, Brace and Company, 1939.

[15] *Rodell,* "Felix Frankfurter" *Harpers,* October, 1941, p. 453.

markable feats of persuasion were accomplished through indirect channels. Law professors have remarked about how, when a specific faculty appointment was to be made, a shower of letters and telegrams would come from various sources—from judges, eminent lawyers and statesmen—commending a candidate. The comment would be made by those who were familiar with such manifestations, "Frankfurter is at work again."

It is remarkable, considering his tendency to avoid public notice, that in the Sacco-Vanzetti case Frankfurter came out openly and waged the hardest fight of his career. This was probably a completely unselfish act, for he had little to gain and much to lose. This case was destined to have vast repercussions.

In Roosevelt's first campaign for President and in the years after 1933, Frankfurter became an avowed supporter. Part of his activity consisted of the recruitment of people—mostly former students—for jobs in the Administration. To that aspect I shall presently return. But on measures in which Frankfurter was interested, he moved heaven and earth. In the years when I was in or close to the Administration there accumulated in my files scores of notes and telegrams from Frankfurter—suggestions regarding legislation, ideas for Presidential speeches and recommendations for jobs.

During that period and later, much of the Frankfurter volume of advice was cleared through Thomas Corcoran, who was a sort of Washington general manager for Frankfurter. At times, notably in the hot fight over the Holding Company bill, Frankfurter lived for a considerable period at the White House, almost completely unnoticed by the press.

It is important to note that, despite all this activity, Frankfurter actually had little or nothing to do with the major reforms of the New Deal. The notable exceptions to this were the Securities Act of 1933, the Securities Exchange Act of 1934 and the Holding Company Act. Also excepted were some railroad and labor matters.

Frankfurter thoroughly disapproved of the N.R.A., since his prescription for all economic ills was the antitrust act. Of agriculture he knew very little. Hence, he had no influence in the A.A.A. He had little or no contact with Henry Wallace. He disliked Rex Tugwell. Hugh Johnson disliked Frankfurter. Adolph Berle and Frankfurter entertained a mutual distaste which seemed to go back to the days when the former was a law-school student. For the whole philosophy of planning Frankfurter manifested intense opposition.

As early as 1934 or 1935 Roosevelt had told me of his intention to appoint Frankfurter to the Supreme Court. Frankfurter knew this. As time passed, Frankfurter was exceedingly careful to show no displeasure in the President's policies or actions. Extreme tact was required in all this, but it was probably enforced by a story that Frankfurter knew very well.

When Holmes, after his appointment to the Supreme Court, disagreed with T. R.'s views in the Northern Securities Case, the relations between the two men chilled. Holmes in a letter to Sir Frederick Pollock [16] told of this incident:

"We talked freely later, but it was never the same after that, and if he had not been restrained by his friends, I am told that he would have excluded me from the White House . . . I never cared a damn whether I went there or not."

Since this was a Roosevelt trait, Frankfurter was careful to maintain a deep silence when F.D.R. launched his plan to reform the Supreme Court. He probably did not approve of the plan. In fact, in an article written some years earlier, he had decried an enlargement of the court.

A close examination of Frankfurter's views on public questions reveals a rather narrow range of constructive ideas. In fact, they show little or no originality or deep comprehension of economic or social movements. Despite the voluble assertions of his friends, the record shows Frankfurter essentially to be only a man of action, a controversialist and a passionate defender of civil liberties. His views on business competition were as dated as those of John

[16] *Holmes-Pollock Letters: The Correspondence of Mr. Justice Holmes and Sir Frederick Pollock, 1874-1932,* Harvard University Press, Cambridge: 1941; Vol. II, pp. 63-64.

Sherman. Later there are some evidences of a limited belief in the Keynes ideas of spending on public works. In general, on most questions, including labor, he followed the formulas of Brandeis and of Herbert Croly.

This being true, it is not strange that Frankfurter's opinions on the Court since his appointment have earned him a reputation as a conservative. The fact is that he has always been a conservative. His reputation for radicalism arose largely from his participation in labor litigation, his defense of radicals on the grounds of civil rights and the radical behavior and views of some of his protégés.

One of his most effective political possessions was having the reputation among radicals as a sympathizer, while he could in truth align himself with conservatives. When, in the final days when the Holding Company bill was before Congress and Frankfurter was living in the White House, he counseled yielding on certain points, Roosevelt said to me, in Frankfurter's presence, "Felix sounds just like John W. Davis," a quip which was greatly enjoyed by all.

As remedies for what he conceived to be wrong with our economic society he fell back on large purple phrases such as "bold and laborious grappling with the basic forces in our economic situation" and "the reformation and transformation of our society." These seemed to be adequate to correct "maladjustments in industry" which he never specifically defined.

In the absence of specific governmental remedies he constantly fell back upon that axiom of uncertain reform—"experimentation."

The generality of his mind in economic and social matters may in large part be the reason why he was so passionately devoted to Holmes. For Holmes was so much of a skeptic and, unlike Brandeis, so loath to go to the trouble of analyzing the nature and effect of legislation in economic matters that he favored letting the states fool around with what he sensed was often half-baked legislation and learn by trial and error. This aspect of Holmes' philosophy was in perfect harmony with Frankfurter's generalities, just as Holmes' cynicism became a philosophical façade for the more direct and radical drives for power of other disciples of Holmes.

Frankfurter's writings are liberally peppered with quotations often inserted in lieu of a careful spelling out of an argument. Holmes ranks high in these citations. In some instances propositions that need no argument or proof at all are festooned with quotes from the great jurist.

In New Deal days if one protested that certain experiments were costing a lot of money, the Frankfurter protégés were likely to say (and I heard this many times), "Mr. Justice Holmes used to say, 'I like to pay taxes. That is how I buy civilization.'" That seemed to dispose of that.

Thus the Holmes' tradition became Frankfurter's most important and lasting intellectual contribution to his students. Ultimately he became the leading exponent of Holmes' views and his literary executor. A former student and Holmes secretary, Mark deWolf Howe, became the editor of the Holmes-Pollock letters and is writing an authorized life of Holmes. There is a significant note in Catherine D. Bowen's *Yankee from Olympus* that the author was denied access to the Holmes papers in preparing her book.

Archibald MacLeish has called Frankfurter the "ablest teacher of his generation." This need not be accepted as authoritative since such an estimate depends upon opinion and distinctions in values. It is not too much to say, however, that Frankfurter was the most influential, since he not only taught most of the ablest students but later actively promoted their careers. There can never be a complete accounting of the students and friends who were benefited by Frankfurter's personnel work. For a great many placements were carried out through secondary means. A Frankfurter protégé placed in a position of authority or influence would himself recruit schoolmates who had been taught and influenced by the master.

There has been much friendly and unfriendly comment about the influence of Frankfurter-selected legal secretaries to Holmes and Brandeis. It seems to be assumed that these selectees constituted Frankfurter's major contribution of men to government.

This is not true. This group includes several major figures, but it is only a small fraction of a much larger number of protégés. Frankfurter seems to have recommended nineteen secretaries for Holmes and twenty-one for Brandeis.

Four of the Holmes secretaries attained prominence in Washington—Thomas Corcoran, Alger and Donald Hiss and James H. Rowe, Jr. In the Brandeis group were Dean Acheson, James M. Landis and Calvert Magruder. Among the remainder of the forty recommended to the two Justices, twelve became professors in law schools and most of the rest went into private practice. In some cases these law teachers and practitioners have drifted in and out of government service, and some have been active in politics.

But this list, as I have noted, is only a minor part of the Frankfurter contribution. Solicitors for at least two of the great departments in the early New Deal were regarded as Frankfurter men, and in their powerful positions they were able to employ many lawyers. When Dean Acheson was Under Secretary of the Treasury a considerable number were brought into that department. Also, under Jerome Frank, who was general counsel of the A.A.A. in early New Deal days, there were several. It is interesting to note that Morgenthau and later Wallace as heads of these departments instituted purges which meant the shifting of these lawyers to more sympathetic departments. The S.E.C., the Justice Department and the N.L.R.B. were always well supplied.

In Corcoran's time there was a sort of *esprit de corps* within what was called the "well integrated group." Once, when Roosevelt seemed to be veering toward more conservative policies, one of the leaders remarked to me that the boys were considering a general resignation. This I took with a grain of salt. Needless to say, there was no mass departure. Instead, the number multiplied and moved into many agencies.

Certainly there was nothing contrary to the public interest in the recruitment of vital young men for government service, a fact which Frankfurter very ably defended in an article published in *Fortune* magazine in 1936. I note the fact here as an example of the projection of political power and the development of a political technique which is unusual—perhaps unique—in public life.

It offers, moreover, a paradox strange even in politics. For even those who dislike Frankfurter have been unable to point out any material or official gain that Frankfurter ever received from those whom he helped. Certainly this activity was not essential to the keeping of his job at Harvard. And Roosevelt would have appointed Frankfurter to the Supreme Court if he had never sent a lawyer into government service. One motive was undoubtedly a desire to help these young men. Another may have been the human love of exercising power and influence, as innocent of blame as a desire to win a golf or chess championship or to write a great novel.

This great ramification into public service of men inspired and helped by Frankfurter, together with Frankfurter's exaltation of Holmes as an ideal, presents a situation which Frankfurter no doubt never anticipated or planned. It is necessary to set it down, however, as an unpremeditated effect of Frankfurter's influence.

Perhaps it is best stated by MacLeish, who certainly was in the first rank of Frankfurter's friends. Speaking of the influence of Holmes on younger men he observes that the Holmes' "influence on his friends, which was one of the great forces of his time, was always the influence of a personality and a way of thinking." I think he means that it was Holmes the philosopher and man of the world that attracted disciples rather than Holmes the great lawyer.

MacLeish goes on, "It was not in all cases—however heretical it may be to say so—a fortunate influence. The skepticism and the philosophic detachment that sat so easily with the Justice Holmes himself, giving flavor and taste to his strong humanity as salt gives flavor to fresh meat, had a caustic and pickling effect on lesser vitalities, so that many of the justice's disciples were left only with the skepticism and the detachment and without the human and believing force." MacLeish is careful to add that Holmes did not have this effect on Frankfurter personally.

It is that point so ably stated by MacLeish that often occurred to me in days when I saw a great deal of some of the more active disciples of Holmes at work in Washington.

The adulation of Holmes is a very real thing. It has swept hard-headed lawyers into emotional—almost fanatical—expressions.

Jerome Frank, in a book published in 1930,[17] seeks to make the point, with much psychiatric language, that judges follow tradition because they have a "father complex." The final chapter is in praise of Holmes, "The Completely Adult Jurist." It would seem that the difference between Judge Frank and other judges is merely in the selection of a "father."

"Listen," said a young lawyer and noted devotee of Holmes to two pop-eyed newcomers in Washington shortly before the death of Holmes. "Come with me and I will let you see God." Meaning that he would take them to Holmes' house and give them a peek at the old man sitting in his study.

Holmes to Frankfurter was "the philosopher become king." MacLeish says that to Frankfurter Holmes was "a sovereign prescription."

It will clarify our thinking if we consider that Holmes was at least three personalities. There was Holmes the great gentleman and lover of the truth; Holmes the truly great judge who scrupulously applied the law of the land; and Holmes the off-hour cynic, wit and philosopher. It was the latter who inflamed the imagination of his devotees more than he knew or calculated.

It was one thing for Holmes who scrupulously followed a deeply ingrained, inherited code to entertain the sketchy philosophic notions that he often expressed. It was something else to drop these *obiter dicta* on life into the unproved and immature minds of some of his apprentices.

For some of Holmes comments are fairly strong spirits. Jerome Frank says, "Holmes has been telling us, in effect, that the Golden Rule is that there is no Golden Rule."

Ethics was defined by Holmes as "a body of imperfect social

---

[17] *Law and the Modern Mind,* New York: Coward-McCann, Inc., 1930.

generalities expressed in terms of emotion." *(Holmes-Pollock Letters.)*

Again he said, "I hate facts. I always say that the chief end of man is to form general propositions—adding that no general proposition is worth a damn. Of course a general proposition is simply a string of facts."

To Holmes the things that Jefferson called the inalienable rights of man were wishful thinking. He asserted: "I think that the sacredness of human life is a purely municipal ideal of no validity outside the jurisdiction."

Again, a man's work is "the total of human energy he embodies." The final test among men therefore is the force they can exercise.

And since the state has greater force than a man the state is the end—the right.

In a thoughtful article by Rev. John C. Ford, S.J.,[18] these philosophic conclusions are called totalitarian in the sense that they eliminate the significance of the individual or the individual's rights or dignity as an end of the state. Perhaps we should select a word with fewer immediate unpleasant associations than totalitarian. But these views of Holmes certainly are not democratic as that word has come to be accepted in American philosophy.

Father Ford presents a few quotations from Holmes the nub of which is much the same as those I have cited.

"Our personality is a cosmic ganglion . . . Functioning is all there is—only our keenest pleasure is in what we call the highest sort. I wonder if cosmically an idea is any more important than bowels." Again, "I see no reason for attributing to man a significance different in kind from that which belongs to a baboon or a grain of sand." In his old age, according to Ford, Holmes said, "O Cosmos—now lettest thou thy ganglion dissolve in peace." *(Holmes-Pollock Letters.)*

If we consider these philosophic quips in connection with the complete acceptance of Holmes as a source of wisdom, it is difficult

[18] "The Fundamentals of Holmes' Juristic Philosophy," *Fordham Law Review,* November, 1942.

to believe that they have not affected public policy and states-manship. It is probably true that these beliefs of Holmes have been shrugged off by most of those who admire and revere his memory. But it is a fact which I know to be true that they deeply affected the point of view and attitude toward politics and govern-ment of disciples who were also Frankfurter protégés.

Despite the high academic requirements for law-school admis-sion and the exacting routine of a first-class law school, these young men were in fact immature people among the tremendous facts of the economic and political world. In truth, they knew nothing of government except what they had read in books, mostly second-hand accounts of past events. They knew little of economic life except the *ex parte* lectures they had heard in class, the fragments that had appeared in economics or in law cases or the casual table talk at home. So the ideology of Holmes was strong spirits for such youngsters, and it is not strange that they took it raw and fast, like inexperienced boys at their first cocktail party.

The sorcerer in the story knew how to move the mechanism to action, but he also had the faculties and instruments of control. His apprentice knew only the initial impulse, and sought the exercise of power without clear conceptions of its uses, purposes or results.

That is why the comment of MacLeish has such pregnant meaning on the background of the political life of the past few years.

Soft Heart in a Hard Shell

HUGH JOHNSON

O F ALL THE FIGURES mentioned in this book, it is most difficult to write of Hugh Johnson. For to recall the days of my association with him, the causes in which we were joined, the disappointments we shared, the manner of the man and the atmosphere in which he moved through the last great ten years of his life is to feel again his vitality, his cosmic pretensions, his torrential emotion and his armored divisions of words. It means, too, a return of the feelng that came with his death—bitter regret that he burned his precious vitality so recklessly, that he could not have seen the frustration at the end of the war he opposed so earnestly, that he could not counsel us on the problems of its aftermath. Even more, there is regret that the country he loved could not have benefited for many more years from the ideas he created in such abundance, the color he gave to dull matters of state and the inspiration he generated by the written and spoken word.

With all the externals of a tough realist, a ruthless engine of discipline and judgment and a volcano of invective, he was in reality a man of tender and copious emotion, a sentimentalist and a dreamer of fine-spun fancies. No man ever secreted a softer heart in a harder shell.

Hugh Johnson graduated from West Point in 1903. Douglas MacArthur was a classmate. Johnson rose rapidly in the Army, but his restless mind moved to other fields, and a few years later he captured a law degree at the University of California. Fifteen years after graduation from West Point, he was a brigadier general. He planned the selective-service system of the First World War and helped in its administration. He moved into industry and learned at first hand the perils and problems of business in the 1920's. Meanwhile, he had written voluminously in many fields.

He had something of that universality of knowledge that was the mark of scholars and preachers of the Middle Ages, before knowledge was pigeonholed and skills were specialized. He was at home in fields of public finance, law, agriculture, industry, diplomacy, military affairs, literature and American folklore. I am chary about the use of the word "genius," but Hugh's capacity to absorb and retain knowledge calls for no other descriptive word.

Perhaps I can best portray what I knew of him if for the moment I abandon generalized characterization and recite some of the narrative of my personal association with him.

It began on the day after Roosevelt was nominated in Chicago in 1932. Early that fateful morning, when Roosevelt was flying from Albany, Bernard M. Baruch came to Louis Howe's apartment in the Congress Hotel. Baruch had not supported Roosevelt for the nomination. Instead, he favored Ritchie of Maryland and had accompanied a party of Al Smith's supporters to the convention. After the issue was resolved, however, he wanted to offer his support to the candidate through Howe, the candidate's agent. Specifically, Baruch wanted to see what Roosevelt intended to say in his speech of acceptance. I handed him my copy, which he read with hearty approval. Then he introduced a man who had accompanied him, for the moment unnoticed and lost in the luminous presence of Baruch. It was Johnson, who was employed at the time as Baruch's economist and adviser. In the confusion of the moment there seemed nothing unusual about Johnson, and during the rest of the morning, with articulate and vociferous figures all about, Hugh remained silent.

That first impression of self-effacement always stuck with me —perhaps because it was then essentially a true delineation of the man. Certainly, it was reinforced many times during the campaign when, despite his occasional emphatic contributions, he assumed toward all public contacts a veritable passion for anonymity.

Baruch, as one of his many contributions to that campaign, turned over the services of Johnson to me as the head of the group concerned in the formulation of policy and the writing of speeches. It was my province, therefore, to accept and make full use of this recruit. I did so with some eagerness, since the people whom I had enlisted up to that time were mostly academic, having altogether too little practical experience in politics and business. Johnson came from a broader field, with ample diversity of skills and knowledge. Moreover, I greatly needed at that moment to dilute the leftist tendencies of my earlier associates with some doctrinal base of a more conservative nature. And I assumed that no radical would be advising Baruch.

I was right on both counts, but later I came to realize that, in addition to these qualities, Johnson had brought to our group a most versatile, forceful and extraordinary personality.

By tradition a soldier, he respected prudence and order. He proved to be a faithful and fruitful associate and, with certain temperamental limitations, he carried out assignments faithfully.

Since the initiation of any new member in our group began with a trip to Albany and an evening with Roosevelt, I arranged that at once. That occasion is a vivid memory, with overtones of humor, and it aroused in me a feeling of growing admiration.

Hugh brought with him, as his initial contribution to the crusade a long memorandum which he had prepared in collaboration with Baruch. It was a review and indictment of the Hoover Administration. Johnson had read it to me beforehand. He never wanted people to read his contributions; he insisted on reading them aloud.

After dinner, Roosevelt and two or three associates assembled in the Governor's study and Hugh produced his philippic. Since I had heard it before, I slipped out and retired to my room to do a little work of my own. But that proved to be a futile effort. For the mighty roar of Hugh's declamation carried through the baroque walls of the Governor's "Mansion" like rain through a barren tree. So I rejoined the group.

At intervals Hugh would pause for breath or a sip of refreshment or for the receipt of expressions of audience appreciation. He was not disappointed, for in those intervals there rang through the house the high tenor of Roosevelt's laughter. The Governor had the time of his life. I well remember one climactic passage in Hugh's document. After a recital of the mistakes of the Hoover regime and the wreck that had ensued, Hugh had written: "If the skipper of the ship had only followed the honorable tradition of the sea and elected to die on the bridge, we might entertain respect and regret. But no! He seeks the vindication and reward of another term!"

Later, as we all moved to retire for the night, Roosevelt said to me aside, "It's great stuff. Water it down 70 percent and make it into a speech."

Later I learned how bitterly Hugh would fight any watering down of his contributions.

We had missed the train, and Hugh, Charley Michelson and I drew lots for the single room on the third floor. Charley won, and Hugh and I took the McKinley room with twin beds on the second floor.

There was gusty drama in everything Hugh did, even in preparation for bed. He ignored the pajamas that someone had laid out, stripped to his shorts, dashed cold water over head and torso and dropped on the unopened bed. Presently there came the measured uproar of sleep. In my own bed I was hopelessly wakeful. I wondered how I could gain the momentary silence necessary to lose consciousness. Finally, I devised a plan. I pulled a metal wastebasket near my bed and carefully calculating distance and direction threw the noisy missile into the bathroom. I simulated sleep during the ensuing clatter. Hugh was sufficiently awakened to fall silent. Then I prayed, "Dear God, take me before he sleeps again!"

Hugh was indefatigably industrious but no teamworker. Again and again I tried to get him to collaborate with others on speeches. But he had a way of vanishing at such times and of returning after an all-night and solitary session with a whole assignment in his own handwriting. When I tried to edit his stuff he would scream and swear at every blue pencil scratch, as if I were hacking his child apart before his eyes. But he never failed on an assignment, never faltered in an emergency and always opened up new vistas of thought and inspiration.

In the campaign that followed Hugh's literary output exploded like an elaborate fireworks display into a series of enchanting patterns. Those of us who worked with him had a preview of the color, spirit and versatility that were later to fix the eyes of the country upon him. We were captivated.

After the campaign I saw very little of him for some weeks. But I remember one occasion when I lunched with him in the dining-room of the Biltmore in New York. It is strange that almost every contact I ever had with Johnson is associated with a hotel. Hugh was always moving about, travelling, coming and going.

"The way to bring about recovery in this country," said Hugh, pounding the table, "is to mechanize the Army. That would boost the heavy industries." Hugh never ceased pounding away at that point, and as events proved, he was right. In the first place, such mechanization would have more rapidly stimulated the recovery of the heavy industries than did the snail-like development of PWA under Ickes. And furthermore, it would have helped to prepare us for what was to come. For in the very month that Hugh first gave me this advice, Hitler became Chancellor of Germany.

Ten weeks later, I met Johnson in Washington in the Carlton Hotel, where we had lunch together. He and Baruch had journeyed to Washington to offer their services, which, it must be noted, had been sadly neglected in the months since the election. Hugh outlined a plan for mobilizing industry for recovery, based somewhat on the principles of the War Industries Board, in which he had worked during the First World War. Other plans for some sort of industrial recovery had been coming in to the new

President and had been turned over to me for consideration and condensation. I asked Hugh to come to my office, talk over these ideas and develop them into a plan for industrial recovery. He rose from the table, accompanied me to my office in the State Department, pulled off his coat and tie and sat down at a desk. He stayed in Washington for two years, almost without interruption. First a bill was drafted and, despite argument within the inner circle, was accepted by the President and enacted into law. This was the National Industrial Recovery Act.

The act contemplated two simultaneous attacks. First, there was the great cooperative enterprise of tying together industries through the adoption of industrial codes of fair practice. Second, there was the $3,300 million appropriation for public works. The two were essentially joined, but Roosevelt made what it seems to me was a major error in separating the administration of the two. He gave the first task to Johnson and the second to Ickes. When this division was announced by Roosevelt in his office, Johnson bitterly expressed his disapproval and impulsively decided to quit. Frances Perkins tells the story of how she took Hugh away with her and finally persuaded him to stay.

The mistake in separating these functions was compounded by the fact that the development of industrial cooperation in the creation of codes should have been carried out slowly and with infinite diplomacy. Public works should have been rushed at top speed. Instead, Johnson rushed the codes and Ickes, suspicious in an inordinate degree, developed the public works so slowly that they had little immediate effect on the recovery of heavy industry. Because of the slow development of public works, it became necessary to throw Hopkins and his Civil Works Administration into the breach. This meant essentially a duplication of effort and delay in the necessary application of public money for public works.

In the job of NRA administrator, Hugh came face to face with monumental and complex obstacles. Emotionally he was not prepared to handle the extremely trying situations which arose. Hugh later said of his job, "When you feel that a thing ought to be done and feel it so hard that it makes your heart ache, and you want to do that thing so badly that you lie awake nights trying to think up ways that will let you do it, then the only question about doing it is whether there is a way to do it that you can depend upon."

Johnson stated simply that he "regarded NRA as a holy cause." After the fight for codes was lost, he could not understand how the whole nation had not felt likewise. He felt he had failed to get business and labor to exercise the virtues he had extolled throughout his life—fair play, faith, discipline and hard work.

Hugh later admitted that in the making of codes he should have proceeded with much more deliberation. He said, "For too little acumen, for too great complacency in not making issues and taking them to the White House I blame myself bitterly."

He also admitted that he lacked the tact and diplomacy necessary for the task. In his capacity as an administrator Hugh used intemperate language. He scolded and denounced; he quarreled bitterly with his counsel, Donald Richberg, and with Secretary of Labor Perkins. He applied to industrialists, perhaps with some justice, such characterizations as "men of the old Stone Age," "witch doctors" and "tom-tom beaters."

When the Blue Eagle cards were distributed, he said that a storekeeper who violated the code would have to "suffer the consequences." He said that it would be something like what happened to Kipling's Danny Deever—"And they've taken of his buttons off an' cut his stripes away."

"N.R.A. will have to remove from him his badge of public faith and public honor. And break the bright sword of his commercial honor in the eyes of his neighbors—and throw the fragments in scorn in the dust at his feet."

Hugh lifted his voice on many occasions. He had been given the power to impose the codes and, as he said, was never checked or advised to slow, stop or divert.

There were diversions. On one occasion Charley Michelson in his capacity as publicity director for the Democratic National Committee expressed some fear of Hugh's violent and indiscriminate attacks. In the course of his remonstrance, Michelson waxed personal: "It is true that he made faces at some of these (great corporations), and when the General makes a face, mothers put bandages over their children's eyes and everybody shudders. His scowl brings back a comment of the late Arthur Brisbane in describing an executive whose frown was terrible. He said, 'I have just discovered how you came to have that kind of a face. Your ancestors in the antediluvian period used to stick that face around the corner of the cave to scare mammoths away.'

"To this the General made response as follows: 'I know my face would stop a clock, but would the faces of Henry (Wallace), Henry (Morgenthau), and Harry (Hopkins) stop a Follies girl! And that beloved old sour puss of Charley's—he could rent it out as a gargoyle over a Chinese joss house to scare the devil away.' " [19]

But when Hugh had a job to do, he did it in his own way, by direct action and quick dispatch, unless a superior instructed him to change his tactics. And it may be added that his behavior as NRA administrator was regarded by Franklin Roosevelt as exactly what was needed to dramatize the New Deal.

Ultimately, the NRA bogged down and it was essential that it stop for reorganization and reconsideration. At that moment Hugh decided to resign and, except for a short time as WPA administrator in New York City in 1935, never returned to government.

For a time he wrote voluminously for magazines and lectured. Later, he became a regular columnist for the Scripps-Howard papers.

His disagreement with Roosevelt, after the Supreme Court had declared the NRA unconstitutional, was basic, although he made some speeches for Roosevelt in the 1936 campaign. Fundamentally, Johnson was a strict constitutionalist, a believer in private enterprise and he entertained a profound fear of Roosevelt's capricious administrative methods.

He also detested the new flock of advisers who rose to the

[19] Michelson, *The Ghost Talks*, p. 127.

surface in 1936. For the most part, they entertained a view of economic policy wholly antagonistic to Johnson's. He vented his invective upon them in such a characterization as "termites."

He was outspoken during the Court fight in 1937. His protest rose, when Senator Joe Robinson died in the midst of his defense of the Roosevelt plan, to a suggestion that the President had driven Robinson to his untimely end. At that moment Roosevelt invited Johnson to visit him in the White House and, according to Johnson's story castigated him about the column on Robinson. Roosevelt said solemnly as Johnson entered the study, "If Joe Robinson should walk into this room and read this column, he would say that the man who wrote it was a cad and a coward."

Johnson, fixing his livid gaze on Roosevelt, said in reply: "If Joe Robinson said that, I would smash him on the nose." And then, rolling his words with all the intensity of which he was capable, he added, "if he were President of the United States."

This acrimonious conversation went on for some time. There was a lighter touch, when Roosevelt accused Johnson of using the word "bagnio" in connection with the little group that constituted the palace guard in the White House. The dispute then came to be a matter of definition, Roosevelt declaring that when he was a student at Harvard that word was used to describe a house of ill fame. Johnson, out of the treasury of his encyclopedic knowledge, asserted that the word meant merely the group of advisers that gathered about an oriental monarch and the place where they assembled. This dispute, it may be added, was never resolved.

After the President had brought his indignation within the bounds of restraint, he appealed to Hugh on the basis of old friendship. This broke the dykes of Hugh's sentimentality, and the two men ended in expressions of love and friendship and much patting on the back.

This reconciliation, however, was wholly within the realm of temporary sentiment. It had no permanence, for Johnson continued his attacks on the Administration, with mounting intensity.

There were times in his life, after he had yielded to somewhat more indulgence in artificial stimulants than was wise, when he brought himself sharply to judgment. On such occasions he would often journey up the Hudson to an inn which looked out over the river and West Point. There he would contemplate the ivied walls and playing fields of his alma mater, fragrant with memories. He would recall what it had taught and given him, and he would resolve to remember more carefully the basic lessons of self-control that were there instilled into students. And when he returned to his work, there was always something of benign greatness in his demeanor.

Millions of Americans, big people and little people, were poorer on that day in April when, the burdens of war already upon them, the news came of Hugh Johnson's death. No man ever submitted to the stabs of little criticisms so magnificently, because he was always willing to admit personal shortcomings. He never spared criticism, but never wilfully struck a low blow and never failed to give his country the best he had of mind and heart. Only death could silence him—a conquest which neither threats nor flattery nor compromise nor fear was ever able to claim.

Uncle Mark's Daughter

RUTH HANNA McC. SIMMS

RUTH HANNA McCORMICK SIMMS would cock her quizzical eyes in perplexity if she knew that she was to be the focal figure in a piece about women and politics. But I am sure that she would agree with my conclusion—that there are or should be no women's politics as distinguished from men's politics. For she never asked that political life should provide a special preserve where women might play the game with a soft ball, frequent rest periods and short innings. And she was the one politician in a thousand who knew that women voters want no special appeal for them, no framing of political issues around the concerns of the kitchen and home and no labored interpretation of problems of government in the phraseology of the nursery or the powder room. To Ruth Simms a vote was a vote, and a citizen a citizen. Matters of state had no sex and therefore, so far as politics was concerned, there should be no women's faction.

She had little faith in, only tolerance for, separate women's bureaus in campaigns, for special literature for the "fair sex," or for "representative women."

All this seems simple, and almost every woman instinctively feels it. But such is the thraldom of tradition which binds politicians that very few ever realize its truth.

When women are addressed in politics as citizens, without smirks or womanly adaptations, they respond much as men respond. I have some justification for a judgment on this point, because for thirty years I have taught politics to college women. I learned very early that they wanted no women's course on this subject. They want to learn it as men do. They believe that just as mathematics or physics is offered, so should this course be offered in its essential subject matter.

I have taught politics on the assumption that there is no difference between a woman's approach to the subject and a man's. There are, of course, subtle differences in the minds and mental processes of the two sexes. There are differences in the degree of attention that boys and girls have received at home when politics or government is discussed. Fathers, bound by tradition, assume that such discussions with boys are more enlightening and fruitful. This develops a certain political timidity in women of college age or older. But this very reticence opens the golden opportunity to teach. College women are restrained, attentive and willing to read and learn. College men are generally voluble, discursive and sketchy in politics courses. Perhaps the little learning with dad at the breakfast table is a dangerous bar to knowledge.

At any rate, in my experience with parallel courses with men and women I have found the final grades of women to be about twenty percent better than those of the men.

In 1932, after some discussion Roosevelt was willing to accept this lesson and he made no special appeal to women. On the night before the election I was alone with him at Hyde Park. We listened to the Republican radio hour, nicely divided according to interests or supposed interests—a woman told women how to vote; a labor man appealed to labor, etc. Roosevelt wondered a bit about the wisdom of our own strategy, because Jim Farley had complained about his neglect of women in speeches. I must admit that I was somewhat apprehensive about my judgment. But the next day the proof came in. No candidate, I believe, has ever over the years so attracted women's votes, and Roosevelt never appealed to them as women.

Ruth Simms always took her responsible jobs in politics as a merited recognition of her experience and capacity, not as a gesture to a representative of womankind. She never took advantage of any prerogative which tradition accorded to women.

That is not to say that she was not a fighter for the political rights of women. Equal suffrage had no greater champion, and after that was gained she lent her energies to every effort to win the battle for complete equality. But equality was all she asked, not a special protected niche in the political scheme of things.

It was not easy to win from the routineers in the politics of the second and third decades of this century any recognition of the need for arousing the neglected political interest of women. Nor was it easy to get men in politics to accord to women the positions of responsibility that they deserved. Ruth Simms labored indefatigably to win places for women in the political home.

After suffrage had been won, she became Republican National Committeewoman for Illinois. At the same time, Mrs. George Bass occupied that position in the Democratic party of the state. The two women cooperated, despite party differences, to get political recognition for women. They often spoke from the same platform, urging women to join party groups and to be active in party affairs.

Miss Anne Forsyth, who knew Ruth Simms well in those days, wrote the following in response to my question on the subject:

"Ruth started the Republican Women's Clubs in the winter of 1923. She called a meeting in Chicago of the Congressional District leaders, women who had worked in the last Presidential campaign. These women made up the first State Board of the clubs and each one started the work of organizing clubs in the counties and towns of her district.

"It was up-hill work. Women were afraid of politics; they thought all politicians were crooked and they did not know the give and take so necessary to party success. However, the club idea spread, and the clubs became active and strong.

"Ruth had to tell the women over and over again that party organization in this country is set up by state law, that the party is just as good as its active membership and that the party must be reformed from within. Every summer she went on speaking tours through the state, with the thermometer at 102. She spoke every night in some church or hall and held leaders' meetings every day, urging the women to conduct their political reforms through party channels. Getting off a train at two in the morning in some southern town, she held a meeting at ten, talking to the men about the value of women in politics or to the women about the need of working with the men. Then came a big evening meeting, with a drive afterward to the next town, often in a model T Ford, to be ready for the next day.

"The women rallied to such leadership with enthusiasm. Her vital magnetism drew them to her, and the obvious sincerity of her statements gave them trust in her program. To overcome the prevailing political inertia was a real test of leadership. The fact that many of these clubs are still active measures the work done.

"From the first Ruth urged women to run for office and she gave vigorous support to the few who bobbed up, bent for the legislature. She supported a violent dry who talked against her in speeches, because Ruth was not so violent in her opinions. Her interest was in getting women into politics and she never deviated from that path.

"Slowly as she gained strength with the women, the men leaders of state politics opened the doors of inner sanctums to her and she took her place with the party planners. She was strong and popular with this leadership because she knew every turn of the game.

"Ruth's political methods, you see, were the orthodox procedure, kept well within the framework laid down by state law. She often dreamed of an awakened electorate, honest and intelligent enough to reform political practice. She talked about it in every county of the state, but she was willing to do it the slow, hard way and she worked at it with great success in Illinois."

Ruth Simms' early schooling was practical, infinitely rich and varied. Her father, Mark Hanna, for all his conservatism, must have believed, as she did, in identical treatment and responsibility of boys and girls. For early in her life he took Ruth under his wing as a companion, assistant and, later, as his secretary in political matters. His son, Dan, had great native ability, but his interests ran elsewhere.

History will name the Hanna era in American national politics as approximately the fifteen years preceding the great master's death in 1904. In the final eight years of his life, Hanna came as close to the power of a national boss as has any man in our history. It was the golden age of the Republican party, and Hanna's house was the citadel of power.

Ruth was about ten when Mark Hanna extended his power and interests from Ohio to the nation. It must have been at about that time that he conceived the idea that with proper management William McKinley, the attractive, experienced Congressman from Canton, Ohio, might go far. A Presidential nomination was out of the question in 1892, because Harrison was President and could command the nomination for himself. Hanna and McKinley worked loyally for the ticket, and although Harrison went down to defeat, McKinley's oratory won high praise and recognition. Hanna's protégé was governor of Ohio as a natural and logical step to the Presidency.

In those years of preparation Hanna's houses in Cleveland and Georgia were the Meccas of Republican politicians from all over the nation. Consider the basic education acquired by the little girl who sat and listened! When Ruth was sixteen Hanna was national chairman, mobilizing the tremendous forces that crushed Bryan. By this time Ruth was his constant companion and assistant. Mark took her with him to political meetings, large and small. She sat in when slates were made and campaigns were planned. She worked in headquarters.

She accompanied him on campaign trips and stood at his side as he harangued the crowds from the back platform of his private car. Occasionally, she would be presented and would make a few remarks herself. She learned Mark's speech so well that on one occasion, in North Dakota when he was ill, Ruth substituted for him with all her father's verve and gestures. There was time off in those years for private schools, but college would have been the gross waste of a concentrated education in the political life of Washington.

In the last year of his life Hanna's friends, quite without encouragement from him, began to call for his nomination for President in 1904. This was good news to the many conservative people who distrusted the unpredictable T. R. It was not pleasant news to Roosevelt, who was intent upon an election in his own right. Fate had its way with this potential rivalry, for a fatal illness came to Hanna early in that election year.

During that illness Hanna told Ruth that, far from aspiring to the Presidency, he had decided to retire from the Senate. His purpose was to devote the rest of his life to the relations of capital and labor. His efforts in that direction had been sympathetic and constructive. He never had shared the anti-union sentiments of the big employers of that time, and he counted Samuel Gompers as a valued friend.

Ruth well knew of this dominating concern of her father with labor problems. When she was very young, Mark had sent her to visit his mines, to know the workers and to get their point of view. She had an abiding concern for the employees in the many enterprises in which she had interests.

In 1903, Ruth married Medill McCormick, undoubtedly the most brilliant and temperamental member of the McCormick and Medill clans. This meant not only the joining of two families powerful in politics, but it added the life of newspaper publishing to Ruth's other interests. For McCormick, during a number of years prior to his election as United States Senator, was master of the Chicago *Tribune*. That brought Ruth into the virile politics of Chicago and Illinois, where she was destined to be an important figure for nearly twenty-five years. In that environment she indulged her passion for organization to the full. She got to know local politics and politicians all over the state. Her greatest interest was in the seamy life of down-town Chicago machine activities. "Miss Ruth" she came to be known in ward politics, where she was loved and respected.

In 1912 she and her husband temporarily left the Republican party and supported T. R. Medill served on the Bull Moose Executive Committee.

McCormick soon struck out for public office, first for the State Legislature and then for the United States Senate. In his campaigns Ruth was highly active and articulate.

Politicians soon came to value her judgment, respect her intelligence and enjoy her fine wit and humor. Her administrative ability manifested itself in every campaign. Always, she had a grasp of the situation. Detail as well as policy never escaped her. She did not forget the importance of personal contact with the lesser lights in the party. In political hinterlands she never talked down to party members. She had that gift of being at ease with the most diversified individuals and groups.

During one campaign she was almost childishly delighted when a co-worker reported a remark made by a housewife after a small-town meeting in downstate Illinois. "Mrs. McCormick!" the woman had declared, "Why she's wonderful. We were all a little afraid to meet her. We thought that with her position and her money she would act important. But she was just as common as the rest of us."

Ruth was a leader of the first order, and politicians knew it. During the early days of her public life one of her close associates went to a ward leader's office to talk over the local situation. The conversation turned to Ruth. The seasoned old ward leader took his cigar from his mouth and spoke: "Leadership! That's what that woman has. Nobody can teach it to you. It's like a big nose. Either you got it, or you ain't got it."

In 1916 Medill McCormick was elected to the Senate, and he and Ruth moved into the political atmosphere of Washington. In the years that followed she came to know the ways and wiles of the nation's capital.

As Senator, McCormick's chief distinction came in the League of Nations fight, in which he stoutly opposed Wilson. Ruth seems to have shared his views on that subject. In a backwash of party sentiment in 1922 McCormick was defeated for reelection. This was a disastrous blow to his proud and nervous nature, and he died in 1923.

Ruth carried on in Illinois politics. As I mentioned earlier, she was Republican National Committeewoman from Illinois. In 1928, she was elected Congressman-at-large from the state.

This inspired her to seek higher office. In 1930 she ran for the Senate and, in another backwash, was defeated.

By that time, she was weary of life in Washington and Chicago and through with aspiring to public office. Her three children were growing up and concerns other than politics crowded in.

In 1932 she married Albert Simms, whom she had known in Congress, and for some years she lived in Albuquerque, New Mexico, as quietly as her immense energy permitted. But she took an active interest in local and state politics. Shortly after her arrival she remarked to her husband, "I'm glad you brought me out here, Albert. Politics is the same here as in Chicago, only they do it in two languages."

She also occupied herself in founding and building up schools, an art gallery for Albuquerque, an orchestra, and directed the large concerns of her Colorado ranch and her newspapers in Illinois.

Tragedy came in 1938 when her son John was killed on a mountain climbing expedition. This was a mortal blow from which her spirits never recovered. During the next year, seeking to escape the memory of tragedy, she decided to go to New England to rest. She stopped in New York, and Joseph Medill Patterson of the *Daily News* and the Chicago *Tribune* introduced her to Thomas E. Dewey. Dewey was beginning his campaign for the Presidential nomination in 1940. She was impressed by Dewey and, no doubt remembering her father's early interest in a promising man named McKinley, felt that here was a President in the making.

Dewey was impressed by her vast knowledge of politicians and political conditions over the nation and impulsively asked her to become his co-manager, along with Russell Sprague of New York. Her spirit flared up once more, and, putting everything else aside, she plunged into the work.

Her methods of conducting a large part of Dewey's pre-convention campaign were those she had applied in Illinois—tremendous application to detail and, always, personal contact with party members, however small or remote. One observation is characteristic. Throughout the months preceding the 1940 Republican convention, New York managers of the Dewey organization shook their heads in despair at Ruth's long-distance telephone and telegraph bills. One day after telephoning to some unknown little man in a small-town South Dakota Republican organization, she turned to one of Dewey's doubting aides and said: "That's probably the first time he has ever had a long-distance call from New York, and the very fact that Dewey's manager thinks him important enough to call from New York will make him a strong Dewey worker. He will be so proud he will tell everybody in town that he had a call from the Dewey Headquarters this morning."

It was a commentary on the effectiveness of her job that the Western and Northwestern states where she labored so hard were the last to fall away in that momentous night in Philadelphia when Willkie won the nomination.

And the groundwork Ruth laid in 1939 and 1940 cannot be discounted as an important factor in Dewey's successful bids for the Republican nomination in 1944 and 1948.

After Willkie's victory in Philadelphia, Ruth, like a good political soldier, went to Colorado Springs and offered her services to Willkie. The candidate, completely surrounded by amateurs, apparently overlooked this opportunity to enlist a real veteran. In any event, she never heard from Willkie, but gave what she could to help a lost cause in New Mexico and Colorado.

Her political relations with Dewey were not resumed, for reasons that are shrouded in conflicting testimony.

In 1944, she was thrown from a horse on her Colorado ranch. The injury lingered, but from her room in an Illinois hospital she did what she could for Dewey's election. Her injury sapped her strength, however, and in December she died.

In many places in this book I have underlined the fact that competence in politics is no accomplishment to be picked up casually in a year or two, after half a life given to some other calling. Real political achievement asks for all you've got, including all the years of your life. Nowhere is that better illustrated than in the life of Ruth Simms. She had many advantages, including unquestioned natural talents. But she learned through hard work and intense application. She had forty years of politics before she finally decided to quit. And then she returned from private life whenever she felt the call.

Her concern for organization was intense. Her husband, Albert Simms, in a recent letter to me made special note of this. "She liked detail and was meticulous in supervising the activities of her various households. She wanted everything to run like a machine. I believe she would have mechanized everything in sight if it had been possible." Politics, among other things, is a capacity for infinite detail.

Ruth Simms was criticized in her lifetime, however, for over-stressing the need for expensive organization. This is a matter that permits of no generalization. It depends on immediate circumstances.

Her experience had taught her whom to trust and whom to watch in the world of politics. But because this or that politician was uncertain or unreliable was no reason in her mind to attack him. She assumed that whatever nucleus of value there might be in a person could be added to the sum total of party strength. As Will Hays put it once in explaining why he indulged in no political purges, "Politics is assimilation, not elimination."

I have already pointed out some of the infinite variety of Ruth Simms' interests. As long as these matters remained diversions, they added to the central core of her political wisdom. Woodrow Wilson once remarked that "Nothing that is human is foreign to the science of politics."

These diversions of hers, as in the case of T. R., were expendable bits of energy only because of the immensity of her reserves of drive and power. She never assumed that her background of wealth and of notable family would attain ends in themselves. They helped, but her personal vitality and desire to achieve ends were so great that they would have made Mary Jones a national figure.

She was incredibly generous with her time and energy. She

would frequently make promises that proved very difficult to fulfil. But she did not forget, and she did not fail to deliver.

There was an important strain of Quakerism in her heritage, and she hated war and national commitments that might lead to war. In this she followed in the tradition of her father, who, as the great historian, James Ford Rhodes tells us, bitterly opposed McKinley's surrender to jingoism when he called for war against Spain. (James Ford Rhodes, incidentally, was Ruth's uncle.) Her wholehearted opposition to Woodrow Wilson's course in 1919 was the result of inalterable conviction. It has become fashionable to call this "isolationism," but there are other, kinder and more accurate names. It was her way of expressing an intense love of country. Albert Simms points to this as "the basic and deepest foundation stone in her character. It amounted to almost an obsession."

No patriotic demand ever failed to elicit a response from her, just as every worthy concern in the community where she lived benefited from attention and material aid.

A year or so before her death, I prevailed upon Ruth Simms to speak to my class in politics in Barnard College. For two hours she veritably enchanted the hundred or so young women with stories of politics, of her father's interests and concerns with labor, and with homely advice about civic and political responsibility. Afterward, there were questions, and one student asked, "What is it that makes a good politician?" Without the slightest hesitation or a wasted word, Ruth answered, "Good manners."

Behind this simple prescription there was no mere stressing of the formal or the elegant. Ruth meant caring for people, respecting them, treating them as equals and sharing their fears, their earthly concerns and their ideals. She was literally revealing the moving purpose of her life.

Peter Pan in the Treasury

WILL WOODIN

IF THIS BOOK falls into the hands of any reader whose age is under 30, it is likely that among all of my *dramatis personae,* Will Woodin will be least known. However, in a financial crisis without parallel since Alexander Hamilton wrought his miracles eight score years ago, Woodin held the controls of the Treasury and brought us safely through. This labor cost him years of peaceful twilight, and since he had the means and talent for happy leisure, his sacrifice was very great. He was, among all the men I have known, the most kindly, sincere and unselfish. Retrospect brings memories poignant, moving and tragic.

Achievement in public office can be of two sorts. The first is rounded achievement—the details completed, the shadows retouched, the story told in persuasive and friendly prose. The friends of Will Woodin would covet for him that kind of public service.

But they must content themselves with the memory of another sort of public career—short, broken, the details incomplete—a fragment of artistry left by the maker.

One reason why the writers of the day-to-day history of Washington failed to portray the true proportions of this unusual Secretary of the Treasury was because he was so utterly and artlessly without pretense. When he did not know, he said he did not know. Time and again he sat down with newspapermen, and said that he was new at his job, that there were a lot of things he did not know, and that he wanted them to help him find out. The newspapermen liked it; even official Washington liked it. But the shock was very great.

The atmosphere that surrounds a successful candidate for high office is heavy with pretense. Ambition, selfishness and humbug press forward for attention. It was therefore something like a whiff of clear, thin air that I experienced when Will Woodin came to my room at the hotel in Warm Springs on a December night in 1932. Roosevelt was beginning to grapple with the vast economic problems of that critical moment and I was doing what I could to help. Woodin came down to Georgia by invitation, for he had been a loyal and financially helpful Roosevelt supporter since the difficult pre-convention days. He came in quietly and modestly and complimented me, a much younger man, by suggesting a first-name basis of contact. He said he would gladly supply what he knew of railroads and banking, "the only two things, outside of music, that I know a little something about."

He was a little, soft-spoken man with a face that suggested the innocent good will of an amiable child. It seemed incongruous to know that he was the master of a great corporation engaged in the manufacturing of heavy goods—the American Car and Foundry Company. He had been drawn into the life of an industrialist because he had to succeed his father. He told me that as a very young man his passionate interest was music. He traveled in Europe with the advantages of ample means. One day in Vienna he saw a zither in a store and bought it. The proprietor then had to supply him with a teacher, who traveled with him and instructed him. He played many instruments, but the zither seemed to be his favorite, for it lay beside his bed in the tremendous days of his service as Secretary of the Treasury. And this instrument had a part in his greatest decision in that office.

In the weeks that followed that meeting, it was his task to shepherd a group of railway presidents who were facing bankruptcy and disaster in that dark winter of 1932-33. Later on, in February, when Carter Glass finally refused the Secretaryship of the Treasury, Roosevelt faced a serious need. Basil O'Connor, Louie Howe and I one evening at Roosevelt's house on 65th Street urged the appointment of Woodin. Roosevelt agreed and summoned Woodin on the instant. Woodin accepted a job destined to shorten his life but to bring him official triumph.

From the moment of his acceptance I spent weeks with Woodin. We occupied adjoining rooms at the Carlton Hotel. One evening we were invited by Senator Burton Wheeler to dinner at the home of the patriarchal ex-Senator Jonathan Bourne, Jr. The two senatorial advocates of free silver discoursed for hours on their favorite monetary theme. Will was patient but non-committal. When we returned to our rooms, Woodin donned his bathrobe and began tinkering away at the piano.

"I am composing a lullaby," he said.

"Call it a 'Lullaby in Silver,' " I suggested.

It was so called, and it joined a succession of pieces that Woodin published, largely for his own amusement and partly to give employment to hard-pressed publishers.

In the weeks that followed it became a habit of newspapermen to make copy of the new Treasury Secretary's "faun-like" or "elfin" characteristics. One would think, to read the accounts of him, that he went dancing through directors' meetings wearing a conical hat, like one of Thomas Mackenzie's leprechauns, and playing on little pipes. The fact is that he was an extraordinarily hard-headed businessman and had the flexible mind which marks exceptional intelligence. That rare combination of flexibility and hard-headedness, plus his great imagination, was his essential qualification for his job in the Treasury.

Following Will's appointment came the long, draining days of the bank crisis. By March 2nd terror gripped the country. Twenty-one states had total or partial bank holidays. Although Roosevelt was confident of his ability to deal with the situation, Woodin and others were alarmed by the mounting gold withdrawals and bank suspensions.

The night of March 3rd was one of the tough nights in the fights for solvency. It was a long evening of tension, wondering whether Hoover would invoke emergency powers enabling him to control withdrawals of currency and gold, or whether it would be left to Roosevelt to do so.

At about one o'clock I ran into Will Woodin in the lobby of the Mayflower. I had thought he had gone to bed.

"Don't say it," Will said, "I really tried very hard. But I couldn't even get to the stage of undressing. This thing is bad. Will you come over to the Treasury with me? We'll see if we can give those fellows there a hand."

We found Secretary Mills; Arthur Ballantine, the Under Secretary; F. G. Awalt, the Acting Comptroller of the Currency; Eugene Meyer; and one or two others haggard and red-eyed in the Secretary's office. They had been calling the governors of all the states that had not already suspended or restricted banking operations and had induced them to agree to declare brief holidays. It remained to persuade Herbert Lehman of New York to overrule the bankers who were urging him to hold off.

Some time later I fell asleep and awakened with Will shaking me, "It's all right, Ray. Let's go now. Lehman's agreed."

I rubbed my eyes and looked at an unforgettable picture. Mills sat behind the desk of the Secretary of the Treasury, Woodin on the other side. For long days and nights after, Woodin was to sit behind the desk and Mills in front. Otherwise nothing was to change in that room. Mills, Woodin, Ballantine, Awalt and I had forgotten to be Republicans or Democrats.

We stood up then, and walked through the echoing halls past the soft-footed watchmen and the deathwatch of reporters and photographers who were to snap pictures of the same group of us, in the same clothes, bowed under the same weariness, for a week of nights.

Meetings and many men giving facts, advice, details consumed the hours of the next few days. The talk went around in circles. Finally, Will said to me, "I'll be damned if I go back into those meetings until I get my head cleared."

And that night, dozing, thinking and strumming his zither Will hit upon the solution. The emergency banking legislation was the child of his extraordinary mind. The way Will reached this decision was characteristic of him. Half businessman, half artist, he had succeeded in brushing away the confusing advice of the days previous and came cleanly to the simplest of all possible solutions.

Through it all his humor and good spirits prevailed. One evening just after the emergency bill was completed, Will emerged from a conference with Senator Glass.

Newspapermen were waiting outside to interview him.

"Mr. Secretary, is the bill finished?" one asked.

"Yes, it's finished," Will answered. He had gone many sleepless nights, but he managed a smile and added, "My name is Bill and I'm finished too."

The most dramatic incident during the opening of the banks after the bill was passed was the decision to open Giannini's Bank of America with its 410 branches in California.

Responsible officials in California were at first unwilling to permit the bank to open.

Woodin met the problem with such courage as I have rarely seen. He and Awalt checked the bank's figures and decided the bank was solvent. Then ensued a long telephone conversation with a high banking official in San Francisco—a conversation punctuated by some pretty strong language on Woodin's end. It wound up with Woodin's "Are you willing to take the responsibility for keeping this institution closed?" and the answer from California apparently was that the official refused to take that responsibility. "Well, then," said Will, "the bank will open." I shall never forget the look of joy on the faces of Hiram Johnson and William McAdoo when I stepped out of Woodin's office after that telephone call and told them the news.

There were half a dozen moments almost as tense. Nerves were frayed when the crisis had passed.

While I had been officially established as Assistant Secretary of State, there was no time in those crowded March days to get away from the Treasury or the White House. Arthur Ballantine held over as Under Secretary of the Treasury at Woodin's insistence. One day when Woodin and I were at the White House, the President asked when a new Under Secretary was going to be appointed. Woodin answered, "I want him," pointing to me. Roosevelt vetoed the suggestion on the ground that he wanted to keep me for general policy matters and the Treasury job would take full time. It was a wise decision on several counts. I had neither taste nor qualifications for the detailed Treasury tasks. And I am sure that with my own conservative instincts I could never have survived the experimentation of the next years. Later, Woodin selected Dean Acheson, who suffered the vicissitudes of the office only a few months. Even the obedient Morgenthau has written of his many troubles in his memoirs.

Woodin's health failed rapidly that spring and summer. A throat ailment that proved fatal a year later incapacitated him for days at a time. In late June, when I was at the London Conference, I called Woodin on the telephone at his home in New York in order to read to him for his approval a monetary declaration that we had succeeded in negotiating. While reading it there was a long pause. Later, I learned from Dean Acheson that Woodin had collapsed in his bed and that for a time the people present feared that the end had come.

In October, against Woodin's advice, Roosevelt adopted Professor Warren's fantastic and, as it proved, ineffective gold buying scheme. Shortly after Woodin retired on leave, Acheson resigned and Morgenthau was appointed Under and Acting Secretary.

Some time after that, I visited Woodin at his home in New York. He was in his library surrounded by his magnificent collection of Cruikshank drawings. With a most unusual touch of bitter sadness, he recalled his final departure from Washington. "Roosevelt couldn't have been more sweet in what he said about me. But he never asked me to stay." And then he paused a long time, "or to come back."

Roosevelt, however, could not sincerely have expected Woodin either to be able to stay or ever to return. Nor with a clear conscience could he have been the cause of such a sacrifice. It was kindness that left unuttered the words that Woodin had wanted to hear. For Woodin was mortally ill. His failing health, which might perhaps have been sustained for some time in a life of ease, had been spent in those eight epochal months in the Treasury. He died in the following spring.

Woodin's career, although its impression on history may be

dim, may resist the passing of time better than the finished product. The relentless erosion of facts may work havoc with the best planned memorial. The fragment is a fragment. It may pass into history with more assurance of permanence. That is true of Will Woodin's service to his country.

Durable Builder of Durable Works

ROBERT MOSES

ONCE GOVERNOR AL SMITH was asked why Robert Moses, his brilliant and indefatigable helper, had entered politics. Smith replied, "Why, Bob Moses has never been in politics." There was the very essence of politics in Smith's answer, because the most potent weapon in a politician's armory is a substantiated claim that his labors are without a political objective. And in Smith's case, the very foundations of the appeals that carried the great governor successfully through election after election were desirable legislation and public works conceived and carried out by Bob Moses.

Again, the most visible fruits of Fiorello La Guardia's service as mayor were the miracles wrought by Robert Moses, his park commissioner. And now a Democratic mayor supported by Tammany is secure and popular because he had the good sense to keep Moses in public service. These circumstances, if there were no others, justify the inclusion of Moses in any political hall of fame. Moses' works will certainly live as long and enjoy as much public praise as those of any man who held high office in the America of our time.

In projecting this estimate of the future, a singularly appropriate parallel suggests itself. Today, after a century, the tinsel Empire of Napoleon III is but a febrile tale of brazen pretense, stupid, corrupt diplomacy and ultimate national disaster. There lives the memory of the little Napoleon's Prefect of the Seine, Baron Georges Eugène Haussmann, in the indescribable architecture, planning, parks and public works of Paris. It is no mere vagary of temperament that the name Haussmann appears so often in the abundant writings of Moses. Nor was it merely to

include a biographical detail that Moses, in writing of Haussmann, said this:

"Baron Haussmann has been described as a . . . 'talker, an ogre
for work, despotic, insolvent, full of initiative and daring and
caring not a straw for legality.' Everything about him was on
a grand scale, both good qualities and faults. His dictatorial talents enabled him to accomplish a vast amount of work in an
incredibly short time, but they also made him many enemies,
for he was in the habit of riding rough-shod over all opposition."

That this estimate of Haussmann by Moses suggests an autobiographical hint is unquestionable. For Moses not only fits some
of those specifications but knows it and is not diffident about
letting others know it.

He fits all the Haussmann specifications, perhaps, except insol-
vency and contempt for legality! Moses knows and lives by the
law of the land. But law in the no man's land between private
possession and eminent domain is a blur of indefiniteness. Sometimes in overcoming the selfish resistance of a fee simple you are
dealing with a sort of legalized racket. Sometimes law has to be
changed by new legislation. More often, in the determination of
the paramount public interest the courts must be persuaded by
superior ingenuity and daring. For there is no little ground in
our jurisprudence for Aaron Burr's assertion that "Law is whatever is boldly asserted and plausibly maintained."

In pushing through the gigantic public improvements that have
been the concern of Bob Moses an infinite variety of private possessions must be absorbed. Compromise, personal appeals, threats,
loud talk and soft talk, compensation in kind and frontal assault
in the courts have been essential. Rebuilding a city suggests that
in making an omelet you must break eggs. And in the Moses
projects the number and nature of the eggs have been infinitely
varied. There have been noisome representatives of antiquity and
neglect. Some, as when he pushed great parkways through Long
Island estates, were well hatched and well preserved. In any
event, legal is distinguished from engineering talent in the Moses
administrative system. Moses tells his engineers to proceed with

their work and to let him face the legal and political music. "You guys keep to practical engineering," he says, "and if I ever catch you cracking a law book I'll kill you."

Since Moses' concept of planning is cosmic, integral and state-wide, and since in principle it flows in generalities out beyond the State of New York into many remote places through the nation and since the flood of his imagination covers all the relationships of community living, it seems like injecting a mere statistic to enumerate the official positions held by Moses at this writing. Here they are:

He is commissioner of parks of the City of New York—the one office from which he receives a salary. He is also chairman of the New York State Council of Parks, of the Long Island State Park Commission, and of the Triborough Bridge and Tunnel Authority. He is city construction coordinator. He is a member of the New York City Planning Commission, of the New York City Traffic Commission, and the official representative of the city on United Nations construction. His private consulting jobs throughout the country have been important and numerous. He is also his own best publicity expert, for his writings are distinguished and voluminous. He has offices in many places, among which he moves with remarkable efficiency and expedition. One of these is referred to as his "control tower," where, with a very small staff, he directs and supervises the activities of each of his commissions. His own office is mottled with maps of all parts of New York State, with marks and lines indicating finished or projected developments.

None of his chief engineers or managers is located in his central office. They have their own headquarters and exercise considerable discretion in their jobs.

Any competent administrator must delegate authority. But the proof of a great administrator is usually to be found in the quality of the men to whom he has delegated authority and how much authority he has been able to delegate without lowering his standards. Moses is a Houdini in freeing himself from the shackles of administrative detail.

Although he works without seeming effort, his activity is incessant. Moses is a big man, with a quick and infectious smile. His movements are fast and decisive. He works on trains, in automobiles, at home, anywhere and at any time. Some of his numerous staff have been with him since, 27 years ago, he began his great adventure in building with Al Smith. It is one of the marvels of those who know him well that, despite his demanding and critical disposition, he has been able to retain the services and loyalty of so many unusual people.

There are a good many reasons for this. An engineer assistant, who is himself highly trained in his profession, says that "compared with Moses, engineers are mere routine, short-sighted technicians with little imagination." His engineers credit him with unfailing judgment and astonishing vision. One of them says that Moses "acts toward us just as he speaks and writes to the public —brief, straightforward." Moses never holds back his opinions. While he is exacting in his demands upon his associates and friends, they respond cheerfully because they know he is equally unsparing of his own energy.

Moses, moreover, is a relentless teacher of his engineers. One of his original associates says, "He is always teaching, explaining. I am sure he has a definite curriculum in mind, and he is the best teacher I have ever seen. When a young man just out of engineering school gets a job with Moses—and there is warm competition for such places—Moses immediately starts teaching him the most elementary things. He has probably taught more engineers how to write English than all the engineering schools in the country. He will take a young fellow and put him to work drafting ordinary letters. If they are not written correctly, he will send them back to be rewritten. When his people face the problem of writing engineering reports, they are distinctly on their mettle, because Moses is a relentless and meticulous editor, and such reports have to be rewritten time after time."

Moses, like many other administrators, has found that the laborious work of the reformers of earlier years in setting up civil service requirements is one of the most onerous handicaps of a genuinely good administrator. He has probably spent more energy in finding ways to cut through the red tape of civil service than any other administrator of his time.

Moses had the good fortune to begin life with a comfortable amount of inherited means. When he left Yale he set his course toward the public service. After work at Oxford and Columbia, which yielded him graduate degrees, he joined the Bureau of Municipal Research in New York City. This institution originated with a group of people, early in the century, who conceived the idea that, instead of carrying on crusades against bad politicians and in favor of changes in the election laws, the best way to improve public service was to develop trained administrators and to work out standards of administrative service. Moses is probably the most brilliant and famous justification of the purposes of this bureau.

In the years from 1913 to 1917, John Purroy Mitchel, reform mayor of New York, literally invited the Bureau's personnel into the city administration. Moses, as well as other members of the staff, moved in and served in the City Hall. In 1916, however, Tammany replaced Mitchel with one of its most characteristic products, John F. Hylan, who had no use for reform and absolutely no use for the Bureau of Municipal Research. Out went the Bureau people including Moses!

For some time Moses was engaged in odd jobs in and out of the Bureau for Municipal Research. His interests turned from city to state government. I first knew him in that period, because it became my task as a candidate for a doctorate at Columbia to write a thesis, destined to be published by the Bureau, on efficiency and economy in state government. But while some of us wrote about better state government, Moses moved ahead and made better state government.

Al Smith appointed Moses, immediately after his accession to the governorship, chairman of a commission to report on the streamlining of the state government. The report recommended the consolidation of 175 scattered bureaus, agencies and commissions into 19 compact departments. It went on to propose a unified state budget with a state comptroller as a general and independent auditor. It recommended a short ballot and greatly increased the control of the governor over state administration. Smith was unable to get the necessary constitutional amendments through before his defeat in 1920, but on his return to office in 1923 he continued the drive and, in 1924, the Moses report, with few changes, became law.

Moses' labor on this task impressed Smith, always the friend of educated men in public administration. During the three Smith terms Moses was continuously engaged in the state service and became perhaps the Governor's closest friend and the dominant figure in the administration. Smith declared at the time: "Bob Moses is the most efficient administrator I have ever met in public life. He is the best bill drafter we ever had in Albany. He wrote all the reorganization bills. I know he went to Yale and Oxford, but he didn't get that keen mind of his from any college."

In 1922, before Smith's second election, Moses presented him with a plan calling for the creation, expansion and rehabilitation of state parks and the construction of highways for an expanding motorized population.

When this plan was presented to him, Smith snorted: "You want to give the state a fur overcoat when what it needs is a suit of red flannel underwear." But Moses persevered. He took Smith over the ground he proposed to turn into parks and the beaches he wanted to dedicate to the public. They traveled over Long Island, the Adirondacks, the Catskills. Finally, Smith was convinced, and the New York State Council of Parks came into being in 1924. Moses became president of the Council and chairman of the Long Island State Park Commission.

This marked the beginning of an adventure which resulted in the creation of vast arterial highways and parkways, beautiful parks and, as a crowning achievement, the great Jones Beach project. It took a long time to push these works to completion because, especially on Long Island, powerful and influential opposition developed. Owners of great Long Island estates, whose land was to be traversed by parkways and who feared the proximity of mobs swarming to centers of recreation, were especially concerned. The Moses proposals were fought in the state legislature and in the press. Ultimately, the job was done and it remains a monument to the imagination and persistence of Smith and Moses.

In the fourth Smith term, in 1927-28, Moses served as Secretary of State for New York. This job, whose regular duties are practically non-existent, gave Smith the opportunity of bringing Moses close to him for a variety of advisory and administrative tasks and at the same time to offer him a modest salary.

In the course of the Smith regime in Albany, the incident described earlier in this book occurred, which was to have lasting repercussions. Franklin Roosevelt, who was recovering from his illness, sought a convenient state job for his faithful helper, Louis Howe. It was suggested to Moses that Howe be put on the payroll of the Council of State Parks. Moses was willing to employ Howe but expected him to perform full service. This apparently was not the purpose of the suggestion, and Moses refused to grant the request.

When Roosevelt became governor, it would have been politically disastrous for him to have made the attempt to remove Moses from the state park job. Roosevelt, however, supplanted Moses with Edward J. Flynn as Secretary of State. Moses continued his state work without a salary.

In 1933 it became obvious that Tammany was destined to lose the mayoralty of New York City. Moses was the first choice of the leaders of the fusion movement as a candidate. However, Samuel Seabury, in one of his frequent bursts of intolerance objected because he saw in Moses the ghost of Al Smith's rule returning to New York. Moses then stepped aside in favor of Fiorello La Guardia, who was elected.

After his election, La Guardia gave Moses the pick of city jobs. Moses selected the park department and rapidly consolidated a rather roughly organized administrative set-up, which extended through five boroughs, into a single city-wide organization. He rapidly developed a gigantic plan for the development of city parks, and from the general outlines of this he has scarcely deviated in the years since.

He took time out in 1934 to run for governor as a Republican, but the tide of the New Deal and of the Democratic party was running high that year, and he was decisively defeated. This ended his interest in elective office.

Under the authority of state law there had been established a Triborough Bridge Authority whose function it should be to build and administer a great structure connecting Manhattan, the Bronx and Queens. In 1934 La Guardia appointed Moses chairman of this Authority.

Then began a controversy which adds no lustre to the memory of President Roosevelt. Apparently spurred on by Roosevelt, Harold Ickes, PWA Administrator, attempted to have Moses removed from the Authority before funds would be appropriated by that agency to assist in building the bridge. La Guardia, who was no man to fear threats or reprisals, promptly asserted that he intended not only to keep Moses until the end of his term, but to reappoint him. Thereupon, Ickes drafted a famous order, No. 129, which was aimed specifically at Moses. It stated that the PWA Administrator would honor no more requests for money where the supervising authority held both a state and local office. Moses, of course, held both, in addition to the chairmanship of the Triborough Bridge Authority, which was a separate corporation.

When Order No. 129 came to the city, Moses released a copy with a bitter statement. Virtually the entire press of the city backed him up, and it was not long before Ickes was immersed in what was probably the hottest water of his burning career. In the Ickes memoirs appears a full confession of his part in this particular business, with a complete exoneration of himself. He lays the entire responsibility on the President.

At the dedication of the bridge, in 1936, addresses by the President and by Public Works Administrator Ickes were the features of the day. Moses presided and in presenting Ickes indulged in a bit of literary allusion drawn from his own ample reading. He brought into his short remarks a reference to Dr. Samuel Johnson's tilt with Lord Chesterfield on the occasion of the completion of Johnson's great dictionary.

Early in the planning stage of the dictionary, Johnson had submitted his plan to Chesterfield and had waited expectantly but fruitlessly—on one occasion, at his very door—for some response from that notable patron of literature. Enraged, Johnson plodded through the work with little encouragement or help. Then, belatedly, Chesterfield condescended to write favorable notices. Johnson replied with one of the most devastating letters in all literature. Its import was that, since the author of the dictionary had been cast on his own at the initiation of the great project, it came with less than Chesterfieldian grace to join in the acclaim at the triumphant conclusion of the work.

Perhaps the allusion was lost on the President, although the intent was instinctively perceived. The more bookish Ickes might have dimly sensed the Moses purpose. But for the record and for posterity Moses had scored. Chesterfield had sought to move into the orbit of final acclaim. The President and Ickes, mere bookkeepers of the public's money in the bridge project, came at the outset of a political campaign to view and share the light of the achievement. It was Moses who had conceived the project and who, despite ill-concealed spite from Washington, had borne the labor pains. There was the bridge—which would never be disassociated from the name of Moses. It was a moment for triumph and, sparing a human impulse to remind the public of what had passed, to extend a generous hand. Never were these complex purposes so well put in words. Moses said in part:

"Enterprises such as this are too big for personal enmities. I have never been much, anyway, at harboring bad feelings for a long time—first, because it is not my natural disposition; second, because I am too busy; third, because objectives seem to be more important than personalities; and, finally, because it is a well established fact that venom and bitterness are bad for the chemistry of the soul."

Although there was a crying need of the Federal government for competent administrators, in all the years of the Roosevelt regime the indubitable talents of Moses were never summoned.

Despite an occasional spat with La Guardia—and Moses enjoyed these occasions no more frequently than did other La Guardia commissioners—he continued as park commissioner throughout the La Guardia years.

The Democratic party returned to power in 1946, after the election of William O'Dwyer. O'Dwyer, a reasonable and well-intentioned man, asked Moses to stay, and Moses, preferring the opportunity to continue his great works regardless of party affiliation, agreed. At this writing he seems assured of continuous tenure in all of his jobs, regardless of the comings and goings of mayors and governors.

In fact, O'Dwyer immediately began to use Moses in such a variety of municipal activities that La Guardia from his retirement taunted his former subordinate with the name "oberburgomeister."

In his capacity as chairman of the State Park Commission, Moses began with Smith, served under Roosevelt and continued under Lehman, whom he attempted to defeat for governor, and has enjoyed cooperative rather than cordial relations with Dewey. In these recent years since the coming of O'Dwyer, Moses has developed a genuine affection for his chief. He has urged that he be re-elected. This, it would seem, is a lesson in politics worth learning. Moses, who began long ago as a passionate reformer, has found that the opportunity to do a job transcends the lesser satisfaction of living under a regime which corresponds to his political predilections.

And what a job it has been! An attempt merely to enumerate the public works conceived and directed by Moses scarcely conveys the immensity of the achievement. It is almost sufficient to say that the traveler who saw New York twenty years ago and now returns will comprehend the works of Moses in what he sees from Montauk Point to Buffalo.

At the half-way point, Moses has built his own monument. He might, with vastly more justification than many other people who have appropriated Christopher Wren's epitaph, presume to say, *"Si monumentum requiris, circumspice."*

Flower and Victim of an Age

JAMES J. WALKER

IT IS THE THEME of Gene Fowler's absorbing book, *Beau James,* that Jimmy Walker was the product, the hero and the victim of an age. Unlike so many striking generalities of that sort, this observation is almost true. Walker would probably have never been selected by his political betters as a candidate in more sober times. His doings would not have assumed such carnival proportions and such fame. His downfall would have lacked the dark background of a world collapse. And fate would not have placed him in the pathway of an ambitious man on his way to the White House.

But the elements in the Walker tragedy are eternal. The circumstances out of which they grew belong to the classic pattern of politics. And the moral implications are old and tried and inexorable.

The Walker saga, however, like the adaptation of a dramatic theme by a master craftsman, blended into the background of those times. It was centered in New York City, which provided so many of the stereotypes by which the 1920's are remembered. He moved in an atmosphere of generous giving and rapacious taking, of rackets, bootlegging, champagne, fabulous night spots, gay theaters, Duesenbergs, private trains, Paris, Rome, Naples, Havana, Palm Springs, visiting royalty, receptions to heroes, ticker tape, graft, murder, suicide, waste, plenty and, to paraphrase a saying of Machiavelli, "low thinking and high living." Among the performers of his act were clowns, phonies, the idle rich, dissipated genius, bosses, governors and big business. Walker's concerns touched all the ramifications of politics—fran-

chise grabbing, gambling, subway manipulation, convention in-
trigue, patronage, political blackmail and legal dilly-dallying.

Because Walker disdained hypocrisy, he freely provided for the
speculation of the multitude and the mutterings and squealing
of gossip plenty of matter marked private but open to all. There
was in his *heldenleben* wit, song and romance; caprice, jealousy
and desertion; love, faith, hope and charity; disaster, frustration
and retribution; defeat, exile and disease; contrition, prayer and
ghostly absolution; humiliation, despondency and death.

Beau James was born in the arms of Honest John Kelley's
Tammany and died in the arms of the Church Eternal. His story
begins with the clank of horse hoofs on cobblestones and, like
that of Faust, ends amid the singing of angels. Before the rising
curtain are flickering gas-lights, and behind the falling drop are
funereal candles.

Little, bright, lovable Jimmy, born in a comfortable home, son
of a decent minor Tammany figure, didn't really care for politics.
He liked music and happy companions. He wanted to write
songs. His product was second rate, corny; but his hopes were
rooted in a public taste which was good corn ground. He learned
music by ear, played by ear; as a statesman, he learned by ear
and acted on instinct. His father and his father's friends planned
his career. He didn't elect a career in statecraft. Jimmy never
elected. Always he was elected. He drifted into law and public
life, but his heart tarried on Broadway.

The austere Charles Francis Murphy, whose life was a sym-
phony of horsehair sofas and roll-top desks, was amused and interested by this little man of charm and color. He promoted him
from the Assembly to the State Senate and, no doubt, played
covertly with the idea of higher honors. For Walker attracted the
attention of what the great boss called those "interesting" people
on Broadway. He knew Walker needed balance and guidance,
but he felt that he could supply them. The sixteen Walker years
in Albany were marked by no particular achievements. Only once
or twice in a generation, in fact, do any real issues of statesmanship arise in a state legislature; and when they do, the strings are

held by strong governors and bosses. But Walker brightened the dullness of those legislative sessions and provided bits of copy for bored newsmen in the exile of the Capital.

It was Al Smith, Tammany and, later, Edward J. Flynn, the new boss of the Bronx, who decided that the bumbling Mayor Hylan had to be ousted and that Walker fitted the need for sharp contrast and attractive vote-bait. And so Jimmy became Mayor of New York with all the perquisites and power of that great office. Fowler says Walker worked hard at the job for exactly six weeks. Then his interest turned to the fripperies of the office rather than to its duties and opportunities. Walker's mental capacity was first-rate. He was sharp, analytical and, at moments when he chose to apply himself, very effective. But he was the victim of his brilliance. He conceived the idea that in the City Hall, as in Albany, he could get by with a few moments of quick application and reserve the rest of his time for the ceremonial aspects of his job and for personal pleasure. He took long, numerous and gaudy vacations. He permitted himself unofficially to be surrounded by what he would have called "moochers," some of whom were compensated only by the public attention they received; some of whom, of a more acquisitive strain, found profit in this propinquity. A succession of well-to-do friends contributed large sums to the fulfilment of Jimmy's extravagant tastes. Walker lived as he liked and gloried in his genuine lack of hypocrisy. All this was attractive to the public, suspicious as it was of the dull but respectable pretensions of most statesmen.

Walker as mayor created bright illusions that made waste trivial, graft tolerable and neglected duty a happy bit of humor. Vice and peculation lost much of their bad name by shedding their vulgarity and stealth.

New Yorkers who, despite the reputation of their city, are in the main quiet burghers, lived vicariously in this bright figure the festal dreams hitherto permitted only in moments of bibulous ease and escape. They knew or should have known that theirs would be the bill for this pageant. But in those years anything could be afforded. They loved meanwhile to believe that generosity, wit, charm and beauty could so easily sit with the great business of state. They loved the dream and the figure that dominated it. And now, twenty years later, they still love it and his memory. In 1945 a newspaper poll showed Walker an overwhelming choice for mayor.

Walker's second election was at the end of what Fowler calls "the age of festival before a great hush came over the world." When Walker on election night in November, 1929, turned to Grover Whalen and said, "Well, Grover, this election proves that a man can wear his own clothes," the economic foundations of the world were sinking into a vast quicksand.

When the early blast of the collapse was over, these actors were still there, but they stood incongruous, like the tired and hapless members of a disbanded musical show, still in costume in the bus station of a remote town, waiting for a cheap ride home.

In the first year of Walker's second term scandals broke loose in endless succession. Magistrates, judges and police were revealed as common blackguards.

On this day of retribution and judgment, there arose out of the past a massive figure—humorless, virtuous, churchly, puissant and legal—Samuel Seabury. Fifteen years had passed since Judge Seabury, as Democratic candidate for governor, had been honored by a Tammany stab in the back, which had been augmented by a bit of double-dealing by Theodore Roosevelt. Here at long last was the chance to square accounts with perfidious Tammany and to strew land mines in the way of T. R.'s cousin, then governor of New York. Beau Jimmy stood a frail and unprotected figure as the potential piacular offering for those sins.

Among the many crimes of which the man of episcopal ancestry stood innocent was that of low aim. The three Seabury investigations, as I shall show later in this book, began with lowly magistrates, procurers, stool-pigeons and bed houses. The Seabury plan, however, from the first was to strike down Walker, maim Tammany, if necessary embarrass Governor Roosevelt's Presidential ambitions and perhaps present himself to the nation, as did

Samuel Tilden years before, as a suitable occupant for the White House.

From the autumn of 1930 to the early summer of 1932, Seabury labored with tireless energy and superb legal skill toward that end. It is passing strange that Walker seemed unaware of this ominous movement. He played and dallied while Rhadamanthus toiled in the night. For an entire year a Republican-controlled legislative committee opened the gates of the city for Seabury's investigators. Everything that later contributed to Walker's downfall had been blazoned forth in the papers. Walker spent days and weeks trying to fathom the mercurial impulses of Betty Compton, whom he ultimately married. He took long vacations from New York. He toured Europe and consorted with the King of Iraq and the Prime Minister of England, and he delayed as long as possible the inevitable interrogation before Seabury.

His conduct as a witness was unbelievably inadequate. He was undocumented and unrehearsed. He could not defend his administration, because he apparently knew little of the vast government over which he had presided for six and a half years. He was quite innocent of any knowledge of his own personal finances, his own bank account or the safe-deposit box of which he had been a joint owner for years. Faced by the flood of evidence accumulated by his enemy, he stood helpless. A sea of deadly facts rolled over him—neglected duty, misplaced trust and colossal indiscretions. Walker had no defense but evasion, amnesia, cheap theatrics and shallow, unbelievable rationalizations.

Roosevelt, meanwhile, was working desperately to snare the Presidential nomination. He wanted the New York delegation, but he could get along without it if he could build up sufficient strength in the Middle West, the South and the Far West. Smith was on the prowl for delegates, too, and stood pretty well assured of a majority of the delegates from the machine-controlled states. Hence, Roosevelt, in contemplating the inevitable day when Seabury would demand Walker's removal, was facing a dilemma. If he removed Walker, he would anger the bosses in the big urban centers. If he evaded the issue or upheld Walker, he would convey to those who hated Tammany in the states west and south of New York the impression of an amiable but weak executive who was not averse to a bit of dealing with iniquity.

Very important people who were near Roosevelt and who also had their roots in Tammany urged him to limit his action to a reprimand. Others, who knew the country better, realized how important it was publicly to oppose Tammany. Whacking Tammany is a traditional way by which New York politicians have won national support. In my conversations with Roosevelt in those spring days in 1932 I repeatedly mentioned this practical consideration as well as the ethical problem involved in Walker's gross neglect of duty.

On one occasion while talking over the subject Roosevelt said, half to me and half to himself, "How would it be if I let the little mayor off with a hell of a reprimand?" Then suddenly, as if answering himself, Roosevelt said sharply, "No. That would be weak."

It seemed to me that from that moment Walker's removal was inevitable.

Shortly after Walker's examination, the Governor rather sharply reminded Seabury that if there were any evidence against a public official, it should be submitted to him and he would act promptly. Seabury, thus challenged, submitted a series of charges which Roosevelt promptly asked Walker to answer. Walker took his time and replied after Roosevelt had been nominated for President.

Meanwhile, I had recommended Martin Conboy to Roosevelt as a suitable and able choice for counsel in the hearings before the Governor. I knew Conboy well and realized that, although a Democrat and in earlier days a friend of Tammany, he was deeply concerned about the decline in public morality.

Moreover, Conboy was a distinguished Catholic layman, and his selection for this task would make it certain that Roosevelt could not be attacked on the ground of hostility toward the church in which Walker had been a somewhat casual communicant.

In my own opinion, there would have been some difficulty in

convicting Walker of positive and deliberate violation of the law in the various derelictions charged by Seabury. Together, however, they proved gross neglect of duty. It seemed to me, and I so suggested to Roosevelt, that the basis of removal could well be considerations which might cause a probate judge or surrogate to remove a careless but not necessarily faithless guardian. This opinion of Walker's neglect I still retain, although it must be admitted that in certain respects a guilty man would have acted precisely as Walker did in some of the transactions involved.

Conboy took his job very seriously. He lived in the Executive Mansion with Roosevelt during a long examination of the evidence gathered by Seabury and during the actual hearings in the Executive Chamber. He coached Roosevelt magnificently, and the amazing showing of Roosevelt in his examination of Walker is largely due to this fact.

It was perfectly apparent, at least to me and even to Seabury, whom I happened to meet in Albany during those hearings, that Roosevelt was pursuing Walker with an intensity that would lead to only one conclusion. He was sharp, aggressive and accusatory.

Toward the end of August there came a respite of two or three days, during which Walker returned to New York City. Meanwhile, his brother George died and Walker attended the funeral on September 1st. Rumors were traveling over New York that something ominous was impending in Albany.

On that evening a group of politicians and personal friends of Roosevelt called on him and spent the evening with him at the Governor's Mansion. It was reported that this group included James A. Farley; Frank Walker; Arthur Mullen, national committeeman from Nebraska; Basil O'Connor; and Samuel I. Rosenman, who had been the Governor's official counsel.

I am unacquainted with the individual motives of these men in seeking their interview with Roosevelt. However, from Roosevelt himself and from witnesses who were present I learned that the preponderance of the advice given to Roosevelt that evening was that he should not remove Walker, but that he should close the case with a severe reprimand.

I am not sure that this story has ever appeared in print, but in fairness to the memory of Roosevelt, it deserves telling. There was considerable argument and some table pounding. Toward the end of the conference one of these gentlemen arose, and, after lighting a cigarette, hurled the match at the Governor with the sneering remark, "So you'd rather be right than President!" Roosevelt calmly accepted this affront with a comment somewhat to this effect: "Well, there may be something in what you say."

At this dramatic moment the telephone rang and the news of Walker's resignation was delivered to the Governor. The case was ended, and Roosevelt emerged from the whole affair before the people of the country in an entirely new light. He had shown not only strength and skill but political courage of a very high order.

I have made it clear, I believe, why I feel that Roosevelt would have removed Walker. I might add that this belief is supported by the testimony of Al Smith, Mrs. Roosevelt and Walker himself.

Walker's statement, issued at the time of his resignation, was a bitter attack on Roosevelt. He freely used such words as "unfair," "un-American," "unlawful" and "indefensible." He ended his statement with the threat and promise that he would run for mayor again and submit his case to the people of the City of New York. Whatever may be said of the thirteen remaining years of Walker's life, it cannot be denied that he paid bitterly for his failure. This period has been told with sympathetic understanding by Gene Fowler in his remarkable *Beau James*.

Walker's boast that he would carry his case to the electorate of the City of New York proved to be an empty gesture. Shortly after his resignation he sailed for Europe and there he made the decision not to run again. On his return the following month, he so informed his political friends, and in November returned to Europe where he remained in exile with his wife, Betty Compton, for nearly three years.

In the first year of that period, in July, 1933, I met him in London during the World Economic Conference. I invited him and Betty for lunch in the American Embassy where I was staying at the time. Jimmy looked less resplendent than in his New York days, but was asking for no sympathy. His comments on Roosevelt and others who had participated in his downfall were friendly and without rancor.

He had been employed by a newspaper syndicate to write some articles on the Economic Conference and he asked me to explain why, considering the fact that the British had not pressed the collection of reparations from Germany, the United States insisted on the payment of the British debt to us. I lumbered into action and explained at some length that the reparations had been arbitrarily fixed, but that the debt owed to the United States by Great Britain and other nations stood for money and goods actually given to them.

Walker displayed the sharp intelligence that had always served him so well. "Ah," he said, "the reparations are a fine, but the debt is a debt." This is the best summary of that difficult economic problem that I have ever heard.

After Walker's return to the United States, he lived quietly with his wife for some years. He made a living by odds and ends of law practice. In 1939 it became the duty of Mayor La Guardia to appoint an arbitrator for the garment trade, and Walker's friend, Edward J. Flynn, quietly went to work to bring about Walker's appointment to this job, which paid a liberal salary. The appointment of Walker by a political opponent of former years required some managing, and Flynn succeeded in having President Roosevelt suggest the appointment to La Guardia. La Guardia made the appointment.

Walker's final days were shrouded in domestic and physical problems. Betty Compton capriciously divorced him, and subsequently Walker declined to remarry her. Later, Betty and a new husband, together with Walker, two adopted children and one child born of the new marriage lived in fairly happy and comfortable circumstances for some time. Betty died in 1944, and Walker, two years later.

Walker never should have been mayor. In private life he would have made and spent great amounts of money, enjoyed gay pleasures and happy friends, indulged his romantic fancies and enjoyed occasionally the comforts of domestic life. He would have been a popular public figure, capturing always the applause of his listeners.

It was not so ordained. Fate and ambitious politicians, knowing his weaknesses, miscast him in high office. Much of the blame for what followed must attach to Al Smith and others who promoted his candidacy in 1925 because it seemed that only Walker could beat Hylan. For this tragic misjudgment Walker paid bitterly and paid alone. Perhaps that is where the story should end.

But the moral implications of politics cannot rest there. The historian must hold his guard high when he deals with a life so compact with seductive charm and personal tragedy. This is true even though in Walker's story, as in the moral code of the movies, sin was expiated by punishment, retribution and suffering.

If a civil state is to be created fit for free men and dedicated to the pursuit of happiness by the many as well as by the Walkers and their friends, there must be in the seats of power faithful and industrious public servants with a high regard for law and order. To that end Walker contributed nothing.

That he was guilty of a crime as crimes are known in the law and before the courts I gravely doubt. For a crime is a compound of act and intent, and Walker spared no time for that intent which is essential to guilt.

His moral failure was in neglect, indiscretion and in the violation of the conventions of public service.

I have already sufficiently stressed Walker's gross neglect of the onerous but essential details of government. There remain his positive violation of the conventions of public service and his open and palpable indiscretions.

"If civil society be the offspring of convention," says Edmund Burke, "that convention must be its law." The written laws governing the morality of public officers are efforts to specify the sound prudence and maxims that ensure good and honest public service. But such laws are, in the nature of things, imperfect and belated. Conventional conduct demands more than mere compliance with the law. And such conventions grow with custom and adapt themselves to changing times and conditions.

In Governor Roosevelt's opinion in removing Sheriff Farley some months before the Walker hearings, it was written that when any public official lives at a standard beyond his revealed earnings or is in possession of sums of money beyond his probable legitimate income, it is his duty to disclose and make public the sources of such means. I had the honor of drafting that opinion for Governor Roosevelt and I know that he intended to establish a new and original standard of official morality. After that declaration it is hard to see how Roosevelt could have failed to remove Walker or could have rationalized such a failure.

For Walker held in his private possession and spent prodigally sums beyond the dreams of most public officials. True, when Seabury disclosed that large sums had been paid to Walker, he disclosed their sources. In the main they came from this or that friend. But in his defense Walker claimed that such matters were none of the public's business, unless it were proved that they were bribes. He lightly dismissed the possible ramifications of personal interest or private gain in some of these donations. In short, he denied the validity of the Roosevelt dictum in the Farley case. The burden was on Walker to prove the unselfish character of these gifts. Such lavish giving and careless taking cannot safely exist in public business. Convention must supplant law in such matters, and Walker was contemptuous of convention.

Roosevelt once drew upon Dante for a distinction between the sins of the cold-hearted and those of the warm-hearted. Our maximum sentences are always reserved for the cold-hearted grafters and the cynical public cousins of private theft. Walker was no kin of such crude blackguards. He took and he gave in the pattern of an age of fine manners and happy escape. But in the vast and complex background of the office Walker occupied, manners, however gracious, are not enough. And indiscretion, however artless, is a risk that high office cannot afford.

There, Almost—with the Grace of God

SAMUEL SEABURY

THE WAY of fate with Samuel Seabury had many ironical turns. In youth and early manhood a rebellious critic of legal and economic orthodoxy, Seabury ultimately became a pillar of legal respectability and sound economic institutions. A brilliant political success until his defeat for the governorship in 1916, he was never after granted the high office which his capacity and services deserved.

After incredible labor he placed a dilemma before Governor Franklin D. Roosevelt which seemed fatal to a presidential nomination. Roosevelt turned this challenge into a potent means of winning his election. Then, since Roosevelt interpreted this Seabury challenge as a deliberate effort to embarrass him, Seabury was denied high office in the new Administration. Finally, after doing more than anyone else to elect Fiorello La Guardia mayor, Seabury saw the "Little Flower" become a faithful Roosevelt disciple.

However, it may well be that Seabury in life's twilight can draw massive gratification from the classics in philosophy, which he has read so copiously, and from the deep religious traditions which are his inheritance. He has seen the city which denied him the honors which he so earnestly sought enjoy, through his efforts, fifteen years of the best government in its history. Although 8 million people are rapidly forgetting him, those same people are immeasurably better off because of his work.

And in addition to these elevated philosophic compensations, he can as a human being enjoy the subtle intoxication that a man can feel after paying off his enemies with compound interest. For Seabury, like Edmond Dantes, came back from long absence from public life and struck down one by one the forces that had connived at his downfall years before.

Tammany will never recover from the prodigious blows inflicted by Seabury in the years after 1930. One after another of its overlords have fallen, either directly from the Seabury attack or from the weakness and incompetence that followed its defeats at the polls. Even now, with a Democrat back in the mayor's office, Tammany is feeble, divided and essentially leaderless. Bosses have succeeded one another in such rapid succession that few New Yorkers can name the man who sits on the crumbling throne from which the redoubtable and famous Charles Francis Murphy once ruled the city and state. Seabury in the quietude of a comfortable seventy-six has outlived them all—Murphy, Curry, Walker, Untermyer, Roosevelt, and even his handpicked Mayor La Guardia. All, that is, except the Methuselah of San Simeon.

Seabury had almost every advantage that might have won high place—even the presidency. His antecedents were luminous, impeccable. He was the direct descendant of Samuel Seabury, first Bishop of the Episcopal Church in America. In the Seabury succession were notable churchmen and judges. Samuel's father was an exceedingly distinguished clergyman.

To see Seabury in his home among the solemn portraits of his ancestors was to know how conscious he is of the benign approval of lordly shades.

His personal dignity suggests the austerity of a Stuart portrait. One of the historians of the Seabury investigations, Milton Mac-Kaye, wrote: "His dignity was Jove-like . . . there was a conviction, among his associates that anyone who called him Sam, chucked him in the ribs or offered him a cigar would be promptly dealt with by a heaven-sent bolt of lighting." [20]

Seabury rose to immense standing at the bar early in life. A prodigy in law school, a city judge at twenty-eight, a Supreme Court judge at thirty-three, and a member of the great Court of Appeals at forty-one, he moved majestically toward higher and higher things.

[20] *The Tin Box Parade.* New York: Robert M. McBride & Co., 1934, p. 298.

Despite these antecedents and early successes, he was no stuffed shirt. As the judge in the famous trial of Lieutenant Becker for the murder of Herman Rosenthal, his performance was legally magnificent. After his defeat for the governorship, his achievement in private practice was not only highly profitable but a mark of distinguished ability and hard labor. He was a lawyer's lawyer. A high priest of the bar. His skill and judgment in hearings and at court in the long investigations of the early 30's were extraordinary.

In his earlier years he indulged in that flair for radicalism that is often marked in young people of unassailable social status. Like Tom L. Johnson, he was a believer in Henry George's single tax and in municipal ownership. He was elected to the Supreme Court as a candidate of Hearst's Independence League. Neighbors on Long Island, he and Charles F. Murphy—a man also in the massive mold of dignity—played golf together. Seabury was a T.R. Progressive in 1912 but, as with others, he was double-crossed by that variable statesman in 1916 and defeated for the governorship.

With that rebuff compounded by T.R.'s shift, Tammany's treachery and the perverse way of New York voters with whatever savors of sanctity, Seabury conceived a holy crusade. MacKaye says with much truth that Seabury, "an egoistic man felt, away down deep, that he was divinely ordained to destroy Tammany Hall and all its works for the glory of God and the deliverance of the town."

The gate of opportunity to fulfill this ordination opened in 1930. A series of noisome disclosures of judicial misbehavior in the lower courts and of questionable conduct higher up broke out in that year. Governor Roosevelt called upon the Appellate Division of the First Department of the Supreme Court to exercise its power to investigate the magistrates' courts. As a result, Seabury was appointed as a Referee to investigate and to present facts and, if warranted, charges to the Appellate Division, which had the power of removal. Seabury moved in with relentless force. Appalling squalor, political influence and evil practices were almost immediately revealed. Some magistrates resigned under fire, and others were removed.

I came to know Seabury in the early days of the magistrates' investigation. I had written a book, *Our Criminal Courts,* which was published that year. It was in part a summary of my findings and conclusions after ten years of specialized study and investigation in law administration in various states. The book was given to Seabury, I believe, by my friend Basil O'Connor, Roosevelt's law partner. Seabury apparently felt that I could be helpful and summoned me from California where I was on a vacation. I was a member of his staff for a year or more, formulating plans for reforming the courts and working on his final report to the Appellate Division.

The trail of incompetence and sordid politics led to the New York County District Attorney's Office. Before Seabury had finished with the magistrates, Roosevelt gave him another job, that of commissioner to investigate charges against District Attorney Crain, an aging, soft-spoken ex-judge and Tammany Sachem. Nothing personally reprehensible about the old man was discovered. He was simply slow, incompetent and gullible. Seabury gave me the not-too-difficult task of assembling the statistical and graphic evidence and of presenting it in public hearings. I did this with considerable zest and, I believe, proved a case of gross inefficiency, despite the artful cross-examination of Samuel Untermyer who was retained as Crain's lawyer.

But it was characteristic of Seabury's incredible legalism that despite this statistical proof he felt that only on the basis of proved incompetence in specific cases could a charge of gross inefficiency be proved. In his report to the Governor, Seabury seemed for a number of pages to be recommending Crain's removal. Then his tone changed and he satisfied himself by a severe castigation of the district attorney. I ultimately had the satisfaction of seeing the successors of Crain, including Thomas E. Dewey, justify their administrations in successive reports by substantially the same statistical methods which I had used against Crain.

Seabury was after bigger game than an aged D.A. In 1931

he undertook his crowning work of investigating the entire city government of New York City. In this he served as counsel for a committee created by a Republican legislature which was intent upon blasting Tammany and, incidentally, upon blighting the presidential aspirations of Governor Roosevelt. Since I was by this time an appointee of Roosevelt on a State Commission on the Administration of Justice, I had no part in this final Seabury effort.

The story of the final acts in this play of exposure, inquisition, ambition and ultimate triumph I have described in my discussion of James J. Walker.

After the downfall of Walker and after the conclusion of the legislative inquiry, Seabury brought his immense prestige to the task of defeating Tammany in 1933. He was the very center and heart of the Fusion movement that selected and elected Fiorello La Guardia and kept him in power for twelve years.

Occasionally in those years Seabury reappeared on the municipal scene, usually to denounce Walker's final efforts to benefit himself.

While Walker was in Paris during his three years' exile from New York, James A. Farley called on him and wished him well. Seabury disapproved in these extravagant terms:

"It is not an edifying sight to see the Postmaster General of the United States make a pilgrimage to see Mr. Walker, and to hear that he eulogized him in Paris . . . I think it was a disgusting spectacle."

Farley countered effectively by replying:

"Walker and I have been personal friends, as everybody knows, for twenty years. Perhaps Judge Seabury can't understand what it really means to love a friend."

In 1937 Walker was appointed to a minor and apparently temporary job as counsel by the State Transit Commission. Seabury again made himself heard. He wrote a letter to the Commission attacking the appointment and characterizing Walker as the "Captain of the Tin-Box Brigade."

Finally, in 1940, Seabury denounced his old friend La Guardia for designating Walker as impartial chairman of the women's garment industry. Seabury said that La Guardia had "stepped down from his position of political leadership among those who are striving for decent municipal government in the United States." He said also that La Guardia made the appointment to get votes for Roosevelt and had thus "adopted the tactics of his ally, Boss Flynn."

These blasts at a beaten enemy were hardly in the tone of a man who was content to live with his philosophic laurels. They were, I regret to say, some evidence that the reformer had outlived the statesman.

They underline the fact that Seabury's greatest achievement was—however useful—essentially negative. Unlike Tilden, Cleveland, T.R., Hughes, F.D.R. and Dewey, those New Yorkers who marched to glory over the recumbent but resilient body of Tammany, Seabury was not satisfied with half measures. More than any of these, he was determined upon extermination, not mere defeat. And he probably did more to that end than any of the others.

They, however, moved on to more eminent and constructive matters than the buffeting of bossism.

Despite the usefulness of Seabury's contribution to municipal government, there was something sad in the picture of this man of immense talent at the summit of his life standing before a legislative committee exposing the peccadillos of a lot of cheap rogues and snides. It was like Voltaire at four-score bandying billingsgate with the President de Brosses.

But Seabury lived a massive consistency, perhaps no sure qualification for great political success.

Divide, Provide et Impera

HUEY P. LONG

WHEN THE NEWS of Huey Pierce Long's tragic death reached an incredulous world, the requiem took the form of various paraphrases of *Sic Semper Tyrannis:* "The Kingfish is dead. There will never be another—thank God!"

My feeling was a sense of tragedy—a tragedy of wasted talent in a nation that bitterly needs the first-rate.

The notion that Long was merely another wild prophet of the backwoods, a cunning despot, a clangorous demagogue, fell far short of the whole truth. Long was all those but vastly more. He was a Dr. Jekyll and Mr. Hyde—with a difference, because in Long the Dr. Jekyll lived in easy camaraderie with the Mr. Hyde. Few men—certainly none who have gone so far in public life—have exhibited more pure native intelligence alternating in swift incalculable turns with more vulgarity and empty-headed noise. At one moment Long was a buffoon, a loud-mouthed, loose-tongued blatherskite and ranter. Yet in five minutes he could turn this side of his nature off and become the cool, earnestly persuasive and logical man who delivered that masterpiece of argument at the Chicago Convention of 1932.

He had, combined with a remarkable capacity for hard, intellectual labor, an extraordinarily powerful, resourceful, clear and retentive mind, an instrument such as is given to very few men. No one can tell what services he could have rendered his state and nation had he chosen to use that mind well.

He did not choose to use it well. He misused it, squandered it, battered it, as a child might treat a toy the value and purpose of which he did not understand. He used his mind so erratically as to seem, a great deal of the time, not only childish but insane.

He used it for his own reckless, grandiose, and shoddy personal ends. He used it for petty revenge on petty enemies. He used it to destroy the only foundations on which some of his reforms —and they were genuine reforms—could securely rest. He destroyed many things with his mind. Among them was himself.

The basis of Huey Long's power was threefold: his very real achievements in his own state; his uncanny ability to arouse the masses; and his development of an efficient and ruthless personal political machine.

It cannot be denied that in Louisiana Long was a builder. His enemies have paid too little attention to his achievements, because his methods were bad. His supporters were blinded to the evil of his methods because his achievements were necessary and real. Huey Long helped his state to break through the crust of smug conservatism and backwardness that oppresses much of the deep South. He abolished the poll tax. He reduced public utility rates, improved the schools, brought the care of the crippled and insane up to date. He built roads (which usually did not extend into those parishes which failed to support him at the polls); he built a thirty-four story state capitol (every American's local pride is flattered by a high building, no matter how superfluous); and he made Louisiana State University outstanding among the institutions of the South.

Like Al Smith and other first-rate but self-taught men, Long had a genuine sense of the value of education. He was immensely proud of "his" medical school, which grew in a few short years to high rank as a Class A institution. I well remember a personal incident that occurred in connection with the university.

It was a part of my job in the early days of the New Deal to act as a friendly contact with a number of people who were troublesome to Roosevelt and with whom he never seemed to be at ease. Huey Long was in this category.

On a hot day during my last month in the State Department, in 1933, Huey came to see me about his law school. He wanted a dean—"a good one and no politics in this." He wanted that dean to come to Louisiana, take plenty of public money and build a school equal in distinction to his medical school.

"How much can I get a good dean for?" he asked.

I told him that the Harvard dean probably received $15,000.

"That's easy. I can pay more if I have to. Name your man."

I was not as familiar with law school talent as I had been a few years before, but I told Huey that I had directed the graduate work of a young man at Columbia who was Dean of Law at the University of Oregon. He might do, I thought.

"Call him up," said Long.

I did so, and Huey forthwith offered him the job at twice his salary.

"Think it over," concluded Huey.

That night I received a long telegram from my former student, asking a number of questions. "Could Long thus hire people for the Louisiana State University?" "What about the president and trustees?"

My answer was that if Huey offered the job it was his for the taking.

My friend went to his president, got a substantial raise and remained in Oregon.

I may add that the man was Wayne Morse, now United States Senator from Oregon.

That was Long's way. He moved ahead with almost hysterical speed, over-riding custom, protocol and all those impersonal procedures that republicanism has built to curb government by fiat and impulse. If the law stood in the way, Huey changed the law or, by shrewd artifice, moved it aside. He charged upon his objectives with the savageness of a mad bull. It was as if he sensed that there was little time for him and that he must complete in a few years the achievements for which others took many.

I spent many hours in the three years before his death talking with him about the affairs and problems of the nation, politics, philosophy and people. In those hours he tossed off the demagogue as an actor wipes off grease paint.

Long's idea of a solution for the farm problem anticipated by two or three years and greatly simplified those of Wallace and Roosevelt. It was his "Drop-a-Crop" plan unfolded in his state two or three years earlier.

"It's all in the Bible," he said, slapping the Gideon in his hotel room. "Let 'em raise all they want. Let the government build storehouses for the surplus. Lend 'em money only if they need it. And when a year's crop is stored, declare a holiday on planting a specific crop. Base the moratorium on the necessity of getting rid of pests."

Anticipating the coming decision of invalidation of the A.A.A., he said his plan might have trouble with the Supreme Court.

One day I suggested jokingly that under the Constitution the Supreme Court could be enlarged by the addition of 531 new members, one for each member of Congress, for purposes of constitutional interpretation. The normal nine members could be reserved for run-of-the-mill law cases, as in the case of the law lords in the British House of Lords.

"How do you know all that?" asked Huey.

"It's my business as a teacher of government to know that," I answered. "But it's my duty as an American with some common sense to warn you never to try it."

Huey, however, had tried to tinker with the Louisiana courts nine years before Roosevelt's court scheme appeared. As governor he had proposed increasing the number of appeals judges of the state from nine to fifteen—the same numbers as were in Roosevelt's plan.

Huey's career in Louisiana, from his rise to the governorship in 1928 to the end seven years later, can be divided into three phases.

The first of these Huey spent in subduing the old order, punishing his enemies, gathering trusty henchmen, spreading the net of state power over recalcitrant New Orleans and initiating the vast system of public improvements and benefits that he had promised in his campaign for governor. This period was briefly interrupted by a revolt which aimed at his removal from office. But impeachment failed in a disorderly, brutal legislative rout.

Following this, there was a period when it actually seemed that Huey, dividing his time between Louisiana and Washington and scheming for national power, was slipping in his home state.

Finally, profiting from the mistakes of the early period, he turned with cold, ruthless efficiency to the building of a dictatorship. In two years he reached the summit of his power. He was never so seemingly secure as at the moment of his death.

It became fairly clear to me in 1933 and 1934, as I had occasion to talk with him and observed his activities during that period, that sometime, perhaps after the election in 1932, he had roughly planned a cosmic course of political conquest and personal rule. The psychopathological questions involved I cannot pretend to define in scientific terms. But it is apparent to anyone versed in the history of power-seeking that when consummate ability is linked with grandiose visions of achievement, success is not unattainable. Even Huey's erratic behavior, so often attributed to mental abnormality, was probably an "antic disposition" thoroughly under control. His course of action contemplated three lines of endeavor: first, the complete consolidation of his power in Louisiana, which would free him for wider conquest; second, the use of his senatorial forum in Washington to hold national attention; and, most important, the direction of a campaign of "education" and agitation through the states for the purpose of seizing the reins of government at some future time, perhaps in 1940.

No one has summed up not only Huey's ruthless methods but the extent and ramifications of his local power better than a native Louisianian, Harnett T. Kane. "At the summit of Long's career," wrote Kane, "no other man in America has had the powers he held in his hands.

"He possessed the state government, the Governor, the university, all commissions and departments; the Legislature, the public schools, the treasury, the buildings, and the Louisianians inside them. The courts were his, except in isolated instances, and he had the highest judges. He had a secret police which did anything he asked: kidnapped men, held them incommunicado, inquired without check into private matters of opponents. He ran the elections. He counted the votes. He disqualified any man or woman whom he wanted disqualified. He could order the addition to the rolls of any number of voters that his judgment dictated. He was becoming local government in Louisiana. The officials of no town or city were secure. Let a brother or an uncle offend, and Huey would have a mayor or an alderman out of a job and his own man appointed in his place. He was reaching into local police affairs; he was controlling municipal finances by new boards. He could ruin a community by cutting off its taxes, preventing it from adopting substitutes, and then forcing new obligations to break its back. He was moving in upon the parish district attorneys, using his attorney-general as a club.

"His power was becoming that of life and death over private business. His banking examiners, his homestead agents, his Dock Board, his Public Service Commission and State Tax Commission were instruments of financial salvation, or of ruin. He served as attorney for the state without hindrance, dug back far into the past records of companies on the wrong side, shook heavy payments from them and took a full third as a fee, by law. There was secrecy about most of the state's records. The law forbade officials to give out financial information; they could be put in jail for doing so. Others did not need a law to guide them in closing their records. . . .

"A Louisiana man could lose private position because the dictatorship decided that one of his friends or relatives had aggrieved it. He could be arrested on a faked charge and held as long as the machine wanted, without the knowledge of his friends. He could be tried before a machine judge, receive a sentence, appeal —and in the end find himself turned down by Huey's highest court. If he were on the other side, he could steal, gouge, maim, perhaps kill, and know that he was not in jeopardy; and he could grow rich without capital, without ability, with nothing to his credit except the 'right connection.' "[21]

All this power was dependent upon Long's hold upon the affec-

[21] *Louisiana Hayride.* New York: William Morrow & Co., 1941; pp. 128-130.

tion and support of the voters of the state. There was never any question about that. Huey had purchased that support by what he, the beneficiaries and also detached observers must call good works. As a true Machiavellian he could not rest secure on the lasting gratitude of those who profited by his largesse. And so he made certain that opposition should be suppressed by whatever methods were at hand—blackmail, obscene slander, intimidation and threats. And, above all, power was protected by a tight grip on election machinery, the law and the courts. For if perchance his people should forget his benefits, he held the means to manufacture a paper majority at the polls.

Meanwhile, single-handedly and in an intensely hostile environment, he gave Washington such a show as it had not seen in generations. His prescription for gaining attention was simple. He ascertained what was expected of a new senator and then did the exact opposite, with dramatic trimmings. A new senator solicits the friendship and fatherly interest of his elders. Huey selected such respected conscript fathers as Carter Glass and Joe Robinson as objects of ribald insult. He rejected routine work by resigning all committee assignments. He spoke incessantly and without preparation on whatever suited his fancy, treating our most revered deliberative body as if it were a shoeless rabble at a lynching. With cold calculation he broke with the Administration he helped to elect and hurled reckless insults at the President, the chairman of his party and the President's Cabinet. He contemptuously rejected patronage with the remark: "I've got all the jobs I need at home." Senators detested him, feared him, avoided him.

A day or two before Roosevelt's inauguration, Huey came to my room at the Mayflower, kicking the door as he entered. Two or three people were there, including Norman Davis, embodiment of diplomatic correctitude and a well-known friend of the Morgan Company. Huey seized an apple, took a sizable bite, walked up to Davis and tapping a clean, correct shirt front with the bitten apple, shouted, "I don't like you and your goddamned

banker friends!" Words failed. After Huey left, I found a senator hiding in the bathroom. "All clear," I announced.

Huey's assault on Washington was absorbed, not to say frustrated, by the sheer power of numbers, of tradition and of specific
gravity. Under the shrewd direction of Vice President Garner,
Long was nagged and worried like a wild boar among dogs.
Younger senators taunted him, interrupted him, outshouted him
and brought his last attempted filibuster to a humiliating fizzle.

But Huey was accomplishing his calculated end in Washington. He was not interested in respect or influence there. He was
merely using a high place to reach his real audience in the highways and byways of the nation.

His break with Roosevelt was part of his plan. He had little
respect for Roosevelt's mentality or his program. "He ain't
smart," Huey once remarked to me. He admitted at the same
time, however, that Roosevelt had a tremendously effective way
of disarming a critic.

"I go to that office intending to give that fellow a lecture
which he needs. Then after a while I find myself leaving without
speaking my piece. He's hard to talk to."

Farley he regarded as an amiable nobody whom he attacked
merely because he was part of the Administration. He loved to
provoke Roosevelt's friends into attacking him. Hugh Johnson,
with all his skill at word mongering, hurled a radio philippic at
the Kingfish. This merely gave Huey a free national hookup for
a reply. He used this time not to bandy words with Johnson but
earnestly and seductively to preach his national share-the-wealth
program. He was hunting for bigger game than Hugh Johnson
or Farley.

Huey calculated that a complete break with Roosevelt's New
Deal was essential to his plans for a national share-the-wealth
movement. His objective was a one-party nation, with himself
as National Kingfish. Since most of the votes he needed were in
the Roosevelt party, it became necessary to dispose of Roosevelt
first. This would be done by bringing about a Republican victory
in 1936. Then, he reckoned, the Republicans could be counted

on to play into his hands. And by 1940 Huey's movement could take over the remains of the Democratic party and sweep the country.

I was and am unable to estimate Huey's national strength when his threat took definite form in the spring of 1935. But I do know that Democratic leaders at that time had a genuine case of jitters. Polls taken by Farley's lieutenants indicated that in a three-way race Long might get as much as ten percent of the vote. Those polls were crude affairs and perhaps not reliable, but it is true that Long's threat to go into the neighboring states of Mississippi and Arkansas and defeat Senators Harrison and Robinson was real and formidable.

Roosevelt's feelings were mixed. No doubt, he detested the crudities of the Kingfish and resented his personal attacks. Moreover, while he was not overly meticulous in devising short cuts to his own objectives, he was repelled by Long's open grabs for power. At one time he toyed with the idea of using Federal troops to restore "republican" government in Louisiana. I was present when he discussed it with an eminent lawyer whom he later appointed to high judicial office. He was strongly advised to forget the idea, and he took the advice.

The Long threat profoundly affected the course of Roosevelt's policies in 1935. In June, after his N.R.A. had been invalidated by the Supreme Court and he had delivered his "horse and buggy" interview, Roosevelt dug up and presented to Congress a drastic, half-baked tax plan. This was in part due to the Long threat. It is also true that down the years after 1935 the New Deal turned to policies that were indubitably in line with those earlier perfected in Louisiana.

It cannot entirely be coincidence that the whole direction and philosophy of the New Deal changed at about the time when Long went to his gaudy grave. Roosevelt, Wallace, Hopkins and others had become Kingfish disciples to a degree that they probably never realized. As I have indicated in discussing Roosevelt in previous pages of this book, the Second New Deal, which arose in 1935, differed in principle from the first. In the first the objective was to bring to economic life the means of cooperative action without essentially disturbing the competitive spirit which energizes it and makes it productive. The second sought political power by a simple process of redistributing existing wealth under the guise of social justice and uplift by law. That drift swept through state and local governments. It elevated the methods of an old-fashioned district leader to the height and size of a national purpose. For the intelligensia it provided the sophisticated distinction of a philosophy of national evolution. And for the sentimental it offered the sweet seductive aura of charity. It opened the gates of power to those whose only qualification was a promise. And it spared lazy statesmanship the labor of analyzing the complex and changing civilization in which it craved eminence.

It swept on and has reached great altitude—we cannot venture to believe the summit—in the election of Truman to the succession of Washington and Lincoln through the simple device of expansive promise. It has bent men, like Robert A. Taft, against their instincts to pay for their place by rival promises of largesse from the treasury.

It is taking from some and giving to others. It is not new. Caius Julius Cæsar used it when he won his contest for popularity in Rome. The Medici used it in medieval Florence. Hague used it in Jersey City. It differs from the technique of the old ward boss only in that it is more direct. Bath House John Coughlin levied a private tax on those who had, and with part of the proceeds bought the allegiance of those who had not. The new redistribution uses the power of government to make the exchange. It yields greater returns; it has a better name; it exalts government as an intermediary; and it can plausibly be called "progressive" or, if you will, "liberal."

For all this Huey Long must bear a heavy responsibility.

I am not disposed to moralize as I draw this portrait of Long. That has been done in millions of words—in the press, in fiction and near-fiction, in the pulpit and in the history books. He did set up a dictatorship over and within the forms of democracy.

His methods, however adroit, followed familiar patterns of chicane, blackmail and graft. His lieutenants—mostly crude fellows —fell easy victims to the criminal law, and ultimately the machine he left was defeated.

All these twice-told matters are true and important, but I want to confine my reflections to a footnote about another familiar bit of moralizing that rises from Huey's career. He was born into a state with much poverty, illiteracy, sickness and debility. He found fertile ground for prejudice and divisive class conflict. He was able to make ammunition for himself out of the very weaknesses he found, for the ignorance he found and professed to cure enabled his nostrums to find eager acceptance. And he could preach "justice" to those to whom justice meant overthrowing those who were different. Divide, provide and rule. To maim a maxim, *"Divide, provide et impera."*

This immense influence on his time gives Long a singular place in our national history. In his nervous haste, in his complete disdain of cant or hypocrisy he drew a pattern of action that may influence the future course of politicians more than we now realize.

Certainly, his imprint upon his state is indelible. His machine, a tawdry mixture of clumsy workmen, fell apart. Its main characters went to jail. Reform had its day. But the grave of Huey Long before the State House is too shallow to confine his lusty spirit long. His brother sits in the governor's office and his son occupies his seat in the Senate of the United States.

Far from Europe

A FEW YEARS AGO in a Hollywood restaurant the late Wallace Beery told me the following story:

In the course of a rambling vacation Beery found himself in one of the ghost towns that abound in the old mining areas of California and Nevada. An old desk in an abandoned office attracted Beery and he arranged to take it home. In the bottom of the desk, under the drawers, he found an old photograph. On the back was the signature of Hiram Johnson.

Feeling that this might be a memento of value to Johnson, Beery decided to send it to him. In all innocence he addressed it to "Hiram Johnson, Governor of California, Sacramento."

After some time Beery received from the United States Senate an acknowledgment from Johnson: "I have not been governor for nearly thirty years. But my grandchildren can tell me the name of Wallace Beery's last picture."

Beery's error, however, was a true reflection of the attitude of California toward its great native son. It is always Johnson the governor that they remember. Ask the oldtimers out there about Hi Johnson and they will tell you the tumultuous story of the mighty young lawyer who claimed their votes when, early in this century, their state was racked with growing pains, when brawling and corrupt politics was the order of the day and the Southern Pacific ruled the roost. They will tell you how Johnson prosecuted public men who figured in graft scandals and how, in 1910, he was chosen as a candidate for governor by the Lincoln-Roosevelt League, a bold group of recalcitrant Republicans who found their party dominated by unwholesome and rapacious influences.

They will tell you of the Johnson campaign of that year—a

campaign the like of which was never known before and has never been seen since. Johnson in an automobile barnstormed the state from Yreka on the north to San Diego on the south. Johnson had an unparalleled gift of slashing, bitter invective. He was utterly indifferent to the potentialities of libel law. His enlargement of his opponents' sins was prodigious. No holds were barred. And with shrewd political sense he dramatized one antagonist and endlessly repeated one theme: "Kick the Southern Pacific machine out of California politics." His followers were an army of burning resentment and reform.

He won the election, and the Republican organization, thus shattered, never revived. In fact, the blows inflicted by Hiram Johnson upon party regularity in California were so severe that never since then has there been real party government in the state.

Since Johnson's victory in 1910 carried with it complete control of the legislature, the new governor brought about revolutionary changes in government and law. The Lincoln-Roosevelt League platform was enacted. For the most part this was a collection of the measures characteristic of the great wave of reform of those days: initiative, referendum and recall; direct primaries and non-partisan ballots for the judiciary; labor measures such as employers' liability, minimum wage and an eight-hour day for women; child labor prohibition; reformed criminal procedure; pensions for the aged; free public school textbooks. There were stiff regulatory measures for the railroads, utilities and investment houses to restrict the power of corporations in state politics.

These monumental reforms by one administration in so short a period were greeted by the early progressives over the nation. Theodore Roosevelt regarded Johnson's achievement as "the beginning of a new era in popular government . . . the greatest advance ever made by any state for the betterment of its people."

Johnson rode the crest of the popular acclaim induced by these reforms. The people of California never let him down. He could with wide acceptance and belief cry out, as he did in later days, "I saved California, single-handed and alone."

The pattern of the Johnson philosophy has been held ever since in California. Nearly four decades of legislation have only broadened and deepened it. Earl Warren, with his proposals for socialized medicine and his battles with the oil companies and his belief in non-partisan government, is hewing to the Johnson tradition.

Much needs to be said of the wisdom and results of the Johnson program and philosophy on the background of California's experience, but I shall come to that later.

At the historic Republican convention in Chicago in 1912, Governor Johnson led the California delegation. There he eloquently attacked the steam-roller tactics of the conservatives. After he had finished his address, the roll-call commenced. Each time California was called, Johnson, his eyes glittering, rose from amid the Californians and shouted defiantly, "California will not answer to its name on a fraudulent roll-call!"

Outraged at Taft's nomination, Johnson split with the party and joined Theodore Roosevelt as his Vice Presidential running mate on the Bull Moose ticket. Taft fell before Wilson, and Johnson returned to California to serve on as governor.

By 1916, Johnson had thoroughly learned the intricacies of politics and had perfected a political organization of his own, the power of which no former machine in the state had approached. At that time he decided to run for the United States Senate.

In that critical year California's affection for Johnson proved to be the decisive factor in the defeat of Hughes and the reelection of Wilson. The incident that probably threw California's vote to Wilson was a totally over-publicized trifle. It hardly needs repetition here, except for its momentous result, its indication of Johnson's hold on his state and the political incompetence of Johnson's enemies. Hughes wholly inadvertently failed to pay his respects to Johnson when, in the course of campaigning, they happened to be in the same hotel. Regrets and apologies failed to allay the ire of Johnson's friends.

While Hughes went down to defeat Johnson won the Senate seat with ease and took up his duties in Washington with the same feeling of high purpose and unbending conviction that he had displayed as Governor of California. As senator, Hiram Johnson was not a creative legislator. Rather, his stature in history comes from his great opposition stands.

This was particularly true of his struggles against proposals designed to bring the United States into international affairs. In 1919 came the spectacular League of Nations fight. Johnson took up his verbal cudgels and joined with Senators Reed, Lodge, McCormick, Brandegee and Borah to form what was called "the battalion of death." Together, these men waylaid Wilson's every attempt to get the United States to join the League.

Once before, Johnson had had occasion to come to grips with Woodrow Wilson. It had been in California. President Wilson had seen fit to send his Secretary of State, William Jennings Bryan, into California to oppose a bill before the state legislature which denied Japanese the right to own agricultural land. Wilson made two mistakes. As Chief Executive of the Federal government he stepped out of line by entering state affairs. Second, if he had known anything of Californians he would never have sent in an "outsider." California is, politically, posted land.

Johnson took Bryan into the governor's mansion as his guest, debated publicly with him, matched him speech for speech, and after two weeks sent him back to Wilson defeated.

When in 1919 Wilson took his appeal to the country, it was Hiram Johnson who dogged his trail and spoke against participation in the League.

After many days of speeches throughout the West, Wilson's health broke down and he returned to Washington. Johnson, too, returned to Washington, but to smash any hope of the United States' joining the League.

In 1920, secure in his grasp on his home state and immensely popular with those followers of T.R. who were ardent supporters of the 1912 Progressive party, Johnson sought the Republican nomination for President. In a sense he was the heir of the T.R. leadership. But reaction from Progressivism was in the saddle, and Harding was nominated.

From then on to the end, Johnson was, even more than his

great contemporary, Borah, an independent in the Senate. Nominally a Republican, he voted as his personal inclinations dictated. This independence was intensified when his fellow Californian, Herbert Hoover, was President.

In 1932 Johnson and other insurgents made a direct break with their party's candidate. Some of the circumstances surrounding Roosevelt's successful bid for Johnson's support are still very clear in my mind.

Roosevelt's political managers, largely superstitious folk, were extremely dubious about the advisability of including California in the candidate's itinerary. "Remember Hughes," they said. Nevertheless, Roosevelt decided to go.

I well remember the suspense that prevailed on the train when we passed over the California line and moved toward Sacramento, where Roosevelt was to make his first set speech. After some discussion in the morning, Roosevelt, with characteristic boldness, decided to make this speech a direct bid for Johnson's support, and I was delegated to put the words together. Under a blistering sun before the state capitol Roosevelt said, among other things:

"I am particularly glad to be here in Sacramento today and speak to the townspeople of a man who has done so much to further progressive thought and courageous public action. I refer to your own Senator Hiram Johnson, long a warrior in the ranks of true American progress.

"I rejoice that he said yesterday that a government that thinks only of a favored few and that forgets farmers whose homes are being taken away from them, and toilers whose wages have been decreased to the danger line 'is unworthy of the name and unfit to govern.'

"I believe in this doctrine myself 100 percent."

Johnson in a day or two responded with a generous declaration of support.

That this support was deeply appreciated by Roosevelt was evident. In the course of Cabinet-making, Roosevelt tried hard to secure Johnson as his Secretary of the Interior. Johnson had no interest in this onerous job. Then Roosevelt turned to Senator

Bronson Cutting, who also declined. Finally, with time running out, Roosevelt turned to Johnson again.

In the afternoon of February 22, 1933, Roosevelt told me that he had finally found a Secretary of the Interior. He said that he had called Johnson that day and had again offered him the job and that Johnson had again declined. Then the name of Harold Ickes came up, whether at Johnson's or Roosevelt's initiative I do not know. Johnson heartily approved of Ickes.

Ickes had been brought to New York that day on another matter and Roosevelt had seen him in the morning. Ickes was then called, and he accepted.

I recount this in detail because my story differs in a slight degree from that of Ickes. Ickes says that Roosevelt talked with him about the job in the morning.

There is no doubt about the final offer to Johnson and Johnson's endorsement of Ickes.

The warm Roosevelt-Johnson relationship continued for two or three years. In the spring of 1933 Roosevelt wanted very much to include Johnson in the delegation to the World Economic Conference at London. I was delegated to persuade Johnson to accept. I went to Johnson's home near the Capitol to talk it over with Johnson and Mrs. Johnson, that stalwart companion of all his years whom he affectionately called "The Boss." She agreed that it might be useful both to the firm nationalist Johnson and to the European representatives thus to bring them together. But Johnson, ever-apprehensive of Europe and of international conferences, overruled us. Senator James Couzens of Michigan was then appointed.

Another incident never before made public should be added. In 1935, Roosevelt told me of his ideas about appointments to the Supreme Court, if, as seemed probable, three of the elderly justices, Sutherland, McReynolds and Brandeis, should retire. This meant that in following geographical preferences there should be a western, a southern and an eastern appointment. Roosevelt said he had in mind Hiram Johnson, Joseph Robinson and Felix Frankfurter. The ultimate fate of these preferences is now written in history.

In those early Roosevelt years Johnson supported virtually all Roosevelt's domestic proposals, but fought him on our adherence to the world court. By the beginning of the second term however, there is no doubt that Johnson began to question the authenticity of Roosevelt's earlier isolationism and that several incidents made him feel that the President was more concerned with the acquisition of personal power than with the tenets of 1912 Progressivism. To Johnson these deviations were matters of fundamental principle.

And so, when, in 1937, the Supreme Court enlargement plan was proposed, Johnson joined the opposition with all the fire and vehemence that was in him.

When on that epochal day in July the Senate voted to send the Court bill back to committee, it fell to Johnson to pronounce the final benediction. He arose in his place to inquire if this meant the final end of the proposal. He was assured that this vote of the Senate meant just that.

"Praise be to God!" said Johnson with all the warm emotion of his being.

From then on, Johnson was a lone fighter once more. His participation in debate grew increasingly rare. His heart was heavy with domestic sorrow and with the agony of seeing his country drawn into the orbit of war. He was attentive upon routine matters such as roll-calls and the needs of his California constituents. But for the most part he remained in his office under the dome in the Capitol, an establishment which he preferred to the newer Senate Office Building. There he sat, consulting from time to time with younger men of the old Progressive tradition and with devoted friends of earlier days. Reelection in 1940 was easy. He was selected by both Democratic and Republican primaries and elected without opposition. He made one impassioned speech for Willkie.

During the war I called to see him. It was clear that the fire of many years was burning low, but that what was lost in volume and range was still concentrated in intensity. In a lesser man with a different history, some of the affirmations of which Johnson was fond would be set down as copy-book resolutions. Behind his desk was a picture of Lincoln, and near it were Lincoln's words: "I am not bound to win, but I am bound to be true; I am not bound to succeed, but I am bound to live up to what light I have."

Such words, which have often been used to hide the motives of slavish conformity, were in fact literally accepted by Hiram Johnson. His life was their embodiment.

At this last meeting he told me he could not go on much longer. The infirmity of age was heavy upon him. I protested, saying that, despite the fact that events had plunged the United States deeply into world affairs and despite the fact of Roosevelt's leadership in such dangerous waters, there was need for such voices as that of Johnson, sounding warnings, establishing the hard core of opposition and constantly reminding the country of its responsibilities at home. There was work for him to do, I urged, and knowing how sensitive he was to appropriate expressions from the poets, I repeated Robert Frost's lines:

> "For I have promises to keep,
> And miles to go before I sleep."

"Write that down," he said.

I did so on a piece of Senate stationery.

"I can use that," he said with a spark of the old determination.

The miles before him were few. In August, 1945, he died, and Governor Earl Warren appointed in his place William Knowland, a man who, like Warren himself, had determined upon a life of public service in the years when Hiram Johnson was the inspiration and guiding star of his state.

In all the years since the defeat of Woodrow Wilson on the League of Nations issue, Hiram Johnson has been portrayed in the Eastern press as the veritable embodiment of insensate isolationism. He has been indiscriminately denounced as a man blind to world realities who would so weaken his country's power of resistance as to endanger its very existence. A whole generation has grown up indoctrinated with this concept of the man and the statesman. Amazement that the State of California should, despite these considerations which to an Atlantic seaboard mind seem self-evident truth, elect and elect this man gradually sub-sided into a resigned comment, "That's just like California—try-ing to be different."

But fact is much deeper than that. Hiram Johnson was not purely isolationist. From his home vantage point in San Francisco, the map of the world takes on an aspect unlike that envisioned in Boston or New York. Through the Golden Gate the Califor-nian Johnson could see the vast oceans and land masses of a world that challenges the ultimate destiny of his country. Beyond that, far to the west, around the curve of the earth, is Europe —an attenuated series of fingers on a hand withered by internal hatreds, duplicity, false expectations and war. It was not the world that Johnson feared. It was Europe. To him, our pre-occupation with Europe was a diversion—a dangerous and en-feebling concern with an interminable series of insoluble problems. And to him the only possible course of action was to turn our back to Europe and, while making sure of our own national health, turn our faces to the West.

In the field of domestic policy Johnson lived to see much of the drastic reformation of the law in economic affairs which he enacted as governor become the accepted order everywhere. In large measure the early New Deal was merely the acceptance of that order in the Federal field. To the end that such measures, subjecting ruthless private competition to the restrictions of public law, have equalized opportunity and enriched the lives of the hitherto underprivileged, Johnson's contribution is a lasting assur-ance of his place in history.

In smashing the Republican machine in California through the initiative, referendum, recall, direct primary and the like, Johnson wrought better and worse than he knew. The result has been the incapacity of the state in all the years since to operate the affairs of government through two responsible parties. Since purely independent voting in the Johnsonian sense is not given to the generality of people, loyalties other than party affiliation have held the balance of power. For this the Johnson reforms must bear a heavy responsibility. For while law may strike down public evil, it cannot generate public wisdom.

He'll Never Walk Alone

SAM RAYBURN

"THE WAY to get along is to go along," Sam Rayburn said after a moment of pause.

We were sitting at breakfast in his small suite of rooms in the Anchorage Apartments in Washington in the spring of 1949. I had asked him to tell me how a man got ahead in the House of Representatives. Rayburn's answer was characteristic of the man—short, salty and simple. There is none of the Webster about him—nor of the Claghorn.

I was about to pursue the point and ask how a man decided with whom to go along. Knowledge born of old friendship stopped the question. I thought I knew, and I valued his respect for what I knew. I shall presently answer the question myself.

I turned the conversation to the room—the simple apartment I had not seen since Rayburn was elected Speaker nine years before, although I had been a very frequent visitor in the seven years before that. I remarked that nothing had changed much. "No, I had this room enlarged a little and I took another room. My sister comes up and stays with me sometimes in the winter."

Sam Rayburn, like Garner, hasn't swelled with his official rise. He has seen enough of greatness and the great through his keen, reflective eyes to know the transitory nature of high place. He has shrewdly refrained from letting his standard of life rise with his position in the State Department's Emily Post list of precedence.

My mind went back to another breakfast with Rayburn in December, 1932. We were on the train leaving Atlanta. I had met Rayburn at Warm Springs. We talked for a while about the new Administration coming to power in March and casually about legislation. Rayburn, a cautious man, peered behind him and across the aisle. Then he leaned toward me and said in a low voice:

"I hope we don't have any god-damned Rasputin in this Administration."

I started with the guilty feeling that he might be referring to me. It appeared later that he was referring to someone else close to Roosevelt who had already started to ruffle Congressional tempers by meddling orders. It was Rayburn the Congressman talking; Rayburn, the very incarnation of the spirit of the House of Representatives—suspicious of Executive interference, jealous of its own prerogatives, power without swank, immobile, holding fast to its rules and customs and proud of its traditions. Individually, the House member may reach for every crumb that falls from a bureaucrat's desk, but collectively the House can and does defy the President or the Senate almost every legislative day.

I was to learn a great deal from Sam Rayburn about Congress and Congressional politics, for we became warm friends when the eventful Hundred Days began. I learned what some other, luckless members of the Administration never seemed to understand—that the chairman of a powerful House committee is accustomed to ask for help and not to receive suggestions or orders.

Shortly after Roosevelt's inauguration, Rayburn, then chairman of the Interstate Commerce Committee, asked me to get someone to draft a bill regulating the issuance of securities. I asked Felix Frankfurter's advice, and he sent down Ben Cohen and James M. Landis. The measure was drafted, and Rayburn, with consummate skill and speed, put it through the House. He did not even stop for committee hearings. In substance, that measure is the present act on the subject. Next year, there came the Securities Exchange Act, prepared and passed, it must be said, with a bit more consideration for the parties and interests affected and with more committee consideration. The following year the Holding Company Act was passed after a bitter fight. I had no part in that. These Rayburn achievements which, in each case, were joined in active collaboration by the appropriate Senate committees, greatly added to Rayburn's stature in the House.

In 1934 Rayburn aspired to the position of majority leader of the House. I went to Roosevelt to ask him to give Rayburn a lift. He declined, with a sententious lecture about the two coordinate and independent branches of the government. This was wasted on me and, as it proved, it was wasted on the man who delivered it. For when Barkley aspired, in 1937, to the same post in the Senate, Roosevelt pulled all the necessary strings. Rayburn bided his time and ultimately won the leadership. Then two deaths ensued in the Speakership—those of Joseph Byrns and William Bankhead—and Sam's life ambition was realized.

I always wonder about stories of decisions born in early life, but Rayburn says that when he was a boy in Texas he heard the towering Senator Joe Bailey deliver one of his opulent, all-embracing orations. He went home and resolved that some day he would be Speaker of the House. This may be a bit of dreamy retrospection. Or it might ironically be suggested that, after an early taste of Bailey's senatorial oratory, Rayburn decided upon the wind-protected House, and that so far as his own speaking is concerned, that he would be the antithesis of the great Texas spieler.

Rayburn began in the Texas legislature, where he was Speaker of the House at the age of 29. Then, 36 years ago, he went to Congress where, because he is a Democrat, has a safe district and neglects none of the attentions a district ought to receive, he has had a continuous and unbroken career. His safe grip on his seat in the House, the seniority system and the friendship of John Garner made certain Rayburn's progress. But there is something more, and that is roughly phrased in Rayburn's aphorism that "the way to get along is to go along."

In the long years of Republican rule, Rayburn pretty much "went along" with Garner, his elder by several years and his senior in service by a decade. Garner was the moving spirit of the able and influential Texas delegation and, as ranking minority member of Ways and Means, the dominant Democrat in the House. In the critical hours of the 1932 convention, when Gar-

ner made Roosevelt's nomination possible, the quiet, efficient
Rayburn served as an intermediary between the Roosevelt people
and the Texas candidate.

When Garner moved over to the Senate, his influence in the
House remained very great and it is hardly subject to dispute
that he had a great deal to do with Rayburn's rise to the majority
leadership. In Roosevelt's second term, however, as Garner's
convictions on spending and labor opened a fissure between him
and the President, the old Rayburn-Garner ties perceptibly weakened. Rayburn's position of House leader under the personal
Presidential government of those years made it difficult for him
to do much but go along with the President. Garner had no
such compulsion.

There is much more of contrast than of similarity between the
two Texans. Garner, as I have tried to show in foregoing pages,
is a man of aggressive convictions. He is more showy than Rayburn. He has more intellectual certitude and is more disposed to
blurt out disagreement. Moreover, although the parents of both
Garner and Rayburn migrated from Tennessee, where Rayburn
was born, to Northeast Texas, their outlooks on life came to be
quite different. Rayburn remained in Northeast Texas and absorbed the mores and shared the interests of that country. Garner's West Texas is a different civilization.

Rayburn grew up in a country in which the people, according
to an informed writer, William S. White, "take no great stock
in money for itself, or property for itself, except for the proper
maintenance of one's family and 'connections' and a proper station in life, and therefore they do not really fear economic reform,
not even sweeping economic reform." Rayburn's philosophy fits
these specifications. He cares little for money or for the power
lent by money. Once in a moment of deep reflective nostalgia he
said to me that if he were assured of an extra $100 a month he
would go back to Bonham and live on his farm. Rayburn's farm
is a farm. Garner's numerous holdings are ranches.

Garner is a businessman of very considerable parts. He lives
where startling fortunes have been made. He respects business

success and has no prejudices against financial power—except public utilities. Garner has limited sympathy for what is called the underprivileged. He is not unkind, but he believes that people ought to care for themselves, to be self-reliant. Rayburn is more likely to suffer for those who fail.

Finally, there has always been an issue of political policy between the two men. Garner, of the cattle country and closer to Mexico, believes in tariffs. Rayburn, close to cotton, is no protectionist. Hence, Rayburn was always a darling of Cordell Hull. Garner and Hull had no mutual admiration. Garner moved to the very periphery of the Democratic party when he lost his admiration for Roosevelt. Rayburn was loyal to Roosevelt and remained an active party man, supporting its candidates, and working for the principles of the platform. So far as differences with Roosevelt and Truman are concerned, Rayburn probably never disagreed flatly or argued principle. He has told them frankly when he felt the House would not support them.

Had Garner been Speaker in Roosevelt's terms, he would have fully realized and exercised the immense potentialities of the office. It would have been what every civics text tells you that it is—the second most powerful office in the land. He would have been a Speaker in the tradition of Clay, Reed and Cannon. Even Roosevelt would have felt his curb.

Rayburn as Speaker is in another tradition. He has assumed a dual role. He is the House's ambassador to the White House and the bearer of the President's wishes to the House. Very infrequently has he aggressively pressed in the House any measure unacceptable to the President. Often, he has gone along with a Presidential measure with lingering doubts.

But he also "goes along" with the House when its will is unmistakably shown and when it has a case for party regularity as good as has the President.

He has the affection of the House membership, probably beyond any Speaker of our time. And this affection is heavily reinforced by respect for his judgment. An able member of the House recently analyzed Rayburn's advice to new members, including himself. He said that Rayburn tells new members—as he actually schools them in off-hours—to work hard, master the issues, learn the rules of the House and follow party leadership unless there are strong reasons for doing otherwise.

Rayburn keeps close contacts with the members. A bachelor, he has plenty of time for breakfasts and dinners for them at his apartment. He is no driving party leader. When a member has strong reasons for deviating from the party line, he brings his conscience to Rayburn. The Speaker may on a whip check take a recalcitrant member aside and say, "We need your vote. We would love to have you with us, if you can see your way clear to be with us. But be sure you take care of yourself first."

If a member decides not to go along, Rayburn never browbeats him. He never threatens. And to his lasting credit, he has never punished a member for breaking the party line by unfavorable committee assignments, withholding of recognition or the exercise of any of the other great powers of his office.

Once off the reservation, members do lose something of the intimacy which Rayburn offers to so many. On one occasion when I visited his office while he was majority leader, I asked about a Congressman with whom we both had been very friendly in earlier years. In the second Roosevelt term he had been strongly anti-Administration, and as a member of the powerful Rules Committee had made no little trouble.

Rayburn said, "I'll call him up and have him over for a visit." I noted that Rayburn, somewhat sadly, I thought, had to tell him how to reach the office of the majority leader. Friendship remained, but probably through no fault of Rayburn's they had not been seeing much of each other.

Rayburn had hopes—vague in 1940 and spirited in 1944— that he would have the nomination for Vice President. In 1940, Roosevelt blasted those hopes by asking as a personal favor that Rayburn make a nominating speech for Wallace. Rayburn complied. In 1944, the fantastic process described elsewhere in this book eliminated Rayburn because he was a "Southerner." This is always regarded by Rayburn as an inaccuracy and an injustice. "Bonham is more western than southern," he will explain. And the map bears him out.

Rayburn hates publicity. No member has ever so austerely renounced even the suspicion of demagogery, of baiting opponents or of underlining class distinctions. Prejudice is foreign to his gentle and open-minded nature.

He speaks only on rare occasions and then shortly, succinctly and with no flourishes. During the 80th Congress he made one of his infrequent speeches, on the passage of the Taft-Hartley bill. Two paragraphs sufficed. The first said members had been afforded too little time to study the draft. The second was:

"I do not know all that is in this bill. Few do, or can. But from what I know of it, I know that what you are doing here is not fair. The bill is not fair. I'm not going to vote for it."

That was all.

In the first session of the 81st Congress, after his election once more as Speaker, Rayburn received the greatest tribute of his life. It was not in the form of an elegant Congressional encomium. It was a simple change in the rules of the House.

It was decided by vote that powers held by the Rules Committee should be curbed and that the Speaker might under certain conditions bring bills to the floor. Rayburn did not object to this grant of power, but he restrained his colleagues from granting still more.

This was a substantial reversal of the historic action of the House in 1910, when in the midst of a bitter battle a handful of recalcitrant "progressive" Republicans joined the Democrats in curbing the power of Speaker Cannon. This was the first battle in the war that divided the Republican party and elected Woodrow Wilson. Thirty-nine years had passed until Rayburn was honored by a return of a substantial part of the authority wielded by great Speakers of the past.

Somehow, as you watch the disorder of the House, with its members engaged in endless meanderings over the floor, as you see but cannot hear some Congressman reading something that no one seems to heed, there is reassurance as you turn to the Speaker's chair. There sits Rayburn, generally with eyes closed or with his hand over his face—calm, confident, silent, but nevertheless a symbol of great authority and order. You view with less alarm.

Despite These Honors

JAMES F. BYRNES

J UST ABOUT 40 years ago, a frail looking court reporter in South Carolina closed his notebook and took to the tempest-ridden political trails. Over the red clay and through the pines he travelled and finally, in 1930, he knocked into political oblivion the great ranter of those days, Senator Cole Blease. *Who was Who* describes Blease as "The only South Carolinian who has been mayor of his city, senator from his county, speaker of the House, president of the State Senate, governor of the State and U. S. senator." Blease was also a blatant demagogue. Jimmy Byrnes, the man who beat Blease, redeemed the state of Calhoun and Hayne by topping the Blease record without resorting to the Blease methods.

Few men in America have enjoyed as diversified and satisfying a career in public life as has James F. Byrnes. He attained almost every governmental distinction except the Presidency, and he narrowly missed that. Leadership in the House and the Senate for 24 years; membership on the Supreme Court; the direction of the most important civilian war agency and, finally, Secretary of State—these appointments came not because he wielded political power in the usual sense or because he was a sycophant before the throne. They came because the people with whom he worked relied on his judgment and respected him. The Senate is a vital testing ground, and Byrnes had its support for 16 years.

In Congress Jimmy was superb. It was there that his unique skills reached their full development. It was from that body that he progressed into the Judicial and Executive branches of the Federal government. On leaving Congress he carried with him and applied the techniques he had practiced as a legislator.

My friendship and association with Byrnes began approximately two years after he had entered the Senate. Already, he was one of its most important members. Usually, a new man in the Senate faces several years of living in the shadow of his elders. His responsibilities include learning the ropes and serving apprenticeship in committees of that august body.

But Jimmy knew the ropes. There were few, if any, political knots he couldn't unravel. He had practiced his infinite skill in complex legislative work before entering the Senate, and when, in 1931, he took over Blease's seat, he commanded the respect and confidence of many senators, including those two great chieftains, Joe Robinson and Pat Harrison.

Jimmy's background had fashioned him perfectly for his undertakings in the Senate. As a sharp, energetic and good-tempered youth he had cultivated and worked with people with whom he was able to get things done. Important figures in Charleston helped him and advised him. He jaunted impressively through a host of jobs and offices—court stenographer, editor, lawyer, district attorney and, finally, congressman. Skill in politics came easily for young Jimmy. During crowded years of activity he had perfected and refined his natural talents. Few men can match Byrnes' acute perception, power of observation and shrewd judgment. Also, and perhaps most important, he has the manners of his Carolinian background—graceful and warm—indispensable to a finished politician.

He could get action, whether by persuasion, compromise or both. It was not surprising that Robinson and Harrison snatched up Jimmy Byrnes the moment he entered the Senate and put him to work on important and responsible jobs.

What Byrnes didn't know about the Senate when he entered it, he knew a few months later. For him, politics was never a nine-to-five job. It always involved homework—thinking during hours when the Senate was not in session and associating with his colleagues in lobbies, hotel rooms and lounges. He quickly soaked up knowledge of the political habits and behavior of every last member of the Senate. This knowledge went beyond the chamber in which they gathered to the areas which they represented. Filed away in Jimmy's retentive brain were the ever-shifting local political situations throughout the United States. He knew what local interests influenced every senator. He knew to which clique or cliques members belonged. He knew the eccentricities of his many colleagues. He knew human nature.

He knew how and when to move. Like a natural and well-versed quarterback who calls the right plays at the right time and generally puts the ball over the line, Jimmy recognized or sensed proper methods and timing for the many situations that arise in the Senate. At times his accomplishments in this respect were uncanny.

In the 1932 Democratic convention and in the campaign which followed, Byrnes was extremely helpful to the Roosevelt camp. In Chicago he lined up the South Carolina delegation for Franklin Roosevelt.

When the campaign of 1932 got under way, the so-called Brains Trust was altogether too heavily weighted with academic men. I realized this and more. It was also clear that Roosevelt, as governor of New York, had been too remote from Washington and the issues before Congress to be certain that in his speeches there would be no explicit repudiation of his party's record. The people I had collected to help him could only partially fill the gap. I talked with the candidate and told him that we needed a couple of real, live Democratic senators thoroughly familiar with what had happened in Congress during the long Republican captivity.

We talked over the range of eligibles and decided upon Senators Key Pittman of Nevada and Jimmy Byrnes. Together, they provided quick comprehension of issues, native political sense and long experience in Congress. Byrnes had served eighteen years in the House before his election as senator. He had been on the train with us some time before, and we were all greatly impressed with the range of his knowledge and with what is indispensable in a campaign—lightning-quick thinking.

Neither Byrnes nor Pittman was a candidate himself that year, and neither had to worry about his home fences. They were as good as elected for life.

After Roosevelt persuaded them to join us, we occupied adjoining rooms on the train and in hotels for the many weeks until election. Needless to say, I enjoyed the advantage of a postgraduate course in politics from that association.

During the famous hundred days following Franklin Roosevelt's inauguration, Byrnes rendered yeoman service to the new Administration. I seriously doubt that any other man on Capitol Hill could have achieved the parliamentary victories realized by Byrnes.

An instance which stands out in my mind bears witness to his political art. It had to do with the Thompson bill, which dealt with securities legislation and which had been introduced in both Houses.

The Administration found itself in a difficult position. It appeared that the bill would go through Congress in short order. The Senate committee had already reported it out.

I called Joe Robinson. Was there anything that he, as Senate leader, could do to get the Administration out from under the Thompson bill?

Robinson was doubtful. He could promise, at most, to hold off a Senate vote on it until the House had acted. For the rest, he could simply say he'd try.

But with the help of Byrnes, Robinson came through. With infinite skill they set to work. No one unfamiliar with practical politics and parliamentary procedure can quite appreciate the contrivings involved in this operation. Robinson and Byrnes decided not to get the bill referred back to the Banking and Currency Committee, but to pass the Thompson bill in the Senate and substitute the House bill, which was acceptable, in conference. The ultimate success of this maneuver was a triumph of bold and intelligent strategy.

This is only one example of Jimmy's ingenuity. In the years that followed, no one did more than he to bridge the gap between the White House and the Congress.

And Jimmy knew how to get action. As he explained: "When you're trying to get something done, there are certain men you can talk to and certain men you can't. You've got to know which are which, and who's best to send to the ones you can't go to yourself. . . . Never promise anything you can't deliver. Above all, never promise the President; let him do that. . . . When you get a man on your side, ask him to do something right away. If he gets to working for you, he will stick. . . . During a debate mingle every minute with the men on the floor. That way you know what's happening and when to put the pressure on. . . . If you haven't got the votes, talk along. If you have, keep quiet. Many a bill that might have passed in thirty minutes has been lost because somebody started to explain it."

Byrnes' appointment to the Supreme Court in 1941 was not only a measurable expression of Roosevelt's gratitude for Byrnes' service to his Administration, but a mark of Roosevelt's desire to improve his relations with the Senate. The Supreme Court fight and the attempted purge had left deep scars. Stalwarts in the Senate felt that Roosevelt had not played fair with Joe Robinson, whom, they believed, Roosevelt should have appointed to the Court. Byrnes was a senators' senator, and no appointment could have so improved Roosevelt's standing with Congress.

Byrnes as a member of the Court no doubt felt judicial life trying after the excitement of so many years of legislative and political service. Nor were the personal associations in the Court congenial for Byrnes, despite his great capacity for getting on with people. Black, Murphy and Frankfurter were not men with whom he could lighten weary moments. Eternal quibbling over legal concepts was not to the Byrnes taste.

And so, despite the honor and security of the job, Byrnes left it in 1942 to assume the temporary and indeterminate labor of Director of Economic Stabilization and, later, of Director of War Mobilization. This work was another of Roosevelt's interminable concepts of seeming to delegate authority without actually divesting himself of power. Byrnes carried on, however, not only because of a sense of loyalty to Roosevelt, but because he wanted to help the war effort.

The story of how it came about that Byrnes, despite all the prestige and offices that came to him in his long career, his undeviating loyalty to his party, and his very considerable ability, was not finally nominated for Vice President will no doubt some time be told in detail. It is to be hoped that Byrnes himself will undertake that task. For it is a tale of political wirepulling—or shall we say rugpulling?—and of political prejudices that has few equals in history.

Suffice it to offer here a bare outline of the circumstances, taken from the stories of Flynn and Farley and from such personal knowledge as I can offer without violating any essential confidences.

It was clear in 1939 and 1940, when Garner had decided not to run again and it became apparent that Roosevelt could be "drafted," that a popular party choice would be Byrnes. Unquestionably, he warmly entertained the idea himself. His name, like King Charles' head, kept popping up in all speculation.

Roosevelt, who was probably veering toward Wallace but who realized that he had to dispose of all rivals first, offered an objection which is thus given by Farley in his *Jim Farley's Story:*

"I had a talk with Jimmy Byrnes," Farley quotes Roosevelt as saying. "Of course, the Catholic issue would hurt there. You know he had been a Catholic until he reached the age of 21 and had graduated from college and law school. And then when he started going around with the girl who became his wife he began attending a Protestant church. Finally he became a member of it. Jimmy realizes that this would hurt his candidacy."

"I could not suppress a smile," Farley comments. "Jimmy has seen no more of the inside of a college than I had. Roosevelt found it hard to believe that those about him had risen without his educational advantages."

Later, when the nomination of Roosevelt was in the wind, Roosevelt asked Byrnes to work for Wallace at the convention and to speak for him on the floor. Byrnes, burying his own ambition, complied.

As we have seen, Byrnes, a year later, was appointed to the Supreme Court.

It is quite clear that by 1944 Byrnes felt that his substantial services and loyalty to Roosevelt and his party had earned him the right to the succession, which, of course, was nomination for the Vice Presidency. Realistic Democrats in that momentous spring season made no bones about the value of that nomination. As one of the other potential candidates remarked, "Only one heart-beat stands between that job and the Big Chance." And it was recognized in high political circles that the prospects of the heart in question were none too favorable.

Earlier in this book I have described the decisive activities of Edward J. Flynn in winning the Vice Presidential nomination for Truman. At the expense of some repetition, I shall tell here the aspects of that story that concerned Byrnes and how, once more, the South Carolinian tasted the bitter fruit of frustration—more bitter this time than in 1940, because he had so much reason to expect the nomination.

In Flynn's account of his pre-convention conferences at the White House, he thus records his argument to Roosevelt against choosing Byrnes:

"In a subsequent meeting with the President I told him of my conclusion that Wallace would be a serious handicap to him on the ticket. The problem then was to find a man who would hurt him the least. A review was made of the other candidates. Byrnes, who was the strongest candidate, wouldn't do because he had been raised a Catholic and had left the Church when he married, and the Catholics wouldn't stand for that; organized labor, too, would not be for him; and, since he came from South Carolina, the question of the Negro vote would be raised. For these reasons he would, as I said, hurt the President."

It is not clear from the Flynn account that this argument was decisive with the President, although, as Flynn says, he was told to talk with National Chairman Hannegan and others about

Truman. Flynn, after that conference, spoke alone with Roosevelt before he left Washington.

Byrnes, of course, for two years had been enjoying almost daily contact with the President because of his offices as stabilizer and mobilizer. His office was in the White House. Some time before the events described by Flynn, he had talked with Roosevelt about his ambitions for the Vice Presidential nomination. He derived the clear impression—and Byrnes was no man to indulge in vain imaginings—that Roosevelt had said that Wallace was to be jettisoned, that he had made no commitments and that the nomination of Byrnes would be agreeable to him. Byrnes further had the impression that Roosevelt preferred him. With that assurance, Byrnes moved to get the nomination.

After the final talk with Flynn, Roosevelt prepared to leave for Hyde Park for a weekend before a long trip to the Pacific. Before he left Washington and, I believe, after he saw Flynn, Byrnes saw him again. The President asked Byrnes to go to Chicago to help Hannegan at the Convention. The assurances made earlier were still firm. Later, on the Friday before the opening of the convention Byrnes talked with Roosevelt, who was at Hyde Park, over the telephone. Things still seemed all right to Byrnes.

Kelly and Hannegan later visited the Presidential train when it stopped in Chicago on Saturday and discussed the Byrnes nomination. They immediately telephoned Byrnes, asking him to come to Chicago. The fact that they believed that the President was agreeable to the nomination of Byrnes seems to be proved by Flynn's description of the violent argument that he was compelled to make to convince them that Truman, not Byrnes, was the man.

It seems, although I have no first-hand evidence of this point, that it was at the end of the train conference that Roosevelt told Kelly and Hannegan to clear the matter with Sidney Hillman.

Thus, when Flynn arrived—and he is the authority for this— he found that Byrnes was as good as nominated.

After hearing of the Kelly-Hannegan conference with the President, Byrnes went to Chicago. He saw Hannegan and Kelly at once. They told him that his candidacy was approved by the President.

On Monday, Flynn entered the scene, with the results told in my chapter dealing with him. In clinching his argument with the President against Byrnes, when he succeeded in reaching him by telephone at some point in the West, he said with great emphasis that Roosevelt could not carry New York State with Byrnes on the ticket. In any event, Roosevelt agreed. He so informed Kelly and Hannegan, and later the letter demanded by Kelly was made public.

This letter, which stated that the President was agreeable to the nomination of Truman or Justice Douglas, seems to have been written before Roosevelt left Washington. That seems to be verified by the account of Grace Tully, the President's personal secretary. She says that the President wrote the letter before he left Washington. Later, after Hannegan talked with Roosevelt on the train in Chicago, she was told to retype the letter and put the name of Truman ahead of Douglas. Thus, apparently, Hannegan had three strings to his bow: Truman, Douglas and Byrnes whom he seems to have preferred.

However, Flynn and the unpredictable ways of Roosevelt sealed the fate of the Byrnes candidacy.

And thus, despite the claims of Byrnes' long service, undeniable loyalty to party and President, he was denied the final honor that would have made him the thirty-second President of the United States.

After the death of Roosevelt, there were enough senators who knew how close Byrnes had come to the Presidency to provide the assurance that if Byrnes wanted to be Secretary of State, any other appointment would not be confirmed. President Truman gladly made the appointment and gave Byrnes full freedom of action.

An evaluation of Byrnes' career as Secretary of State would be outside the purpose of this book. His record of that tremendous eighteen months of international politics, well told in his book *Frankly Speaking*, is enough to make Americans thankful that in that period of reconstructing our foreign policy there was a man at the helm who was flexible in mind and adept in political negotiation. A heavy hand or an uncompromising disposition might not only have invited war but have destroyed the chance to cement the Western nations in a common cause.

At the outset it seemed that the agreements achieved at Potsdam would with no great delay create the foundations of stability in Europe. But shortly after it became clear that stability, if it ever came, would be bought at a heavy cost. For many anguishing months Byrnes stuck to a policy of patience and firmness, with the emphasis on patience. Later it became evident that the emphasis must be on firmness. Byrnes, however, was sufficiently sophisticated in his appraisal of the Soviet negotiators with whom he had to deal to lead them to a point where all Western nations could see unmasked the purposes of the Kremlin. As a result Western Europe is not divided as it would have been if any doubt had been permitted as to America's will for peace and Russia's recalcitrance. Byrnes permitted the Soviet to provide the pressure that has made possible Western unity. This must stand as one of the most substantial of American diplomatic victories.

The Almighty's Proxy

HATTON SUMNERS

IN 1940 MR. ROOSEVELT airily remarked that he saw
no reason why the Seventy-sixth Congress shouldn't go home.
It was the first of three Presidential attempts to profer the national
legislature its battered hat. All failed. Each time, Congress
hitched itself back in its seat and stayed. And each time it did,
the country gave it a rousing cheer. Clearly, the people back
home found the presence of its hired hands on Capitol Hill com-
forting.

Despite Congress's traditional role as a source of innocent merriment, the country loves the old scamp. The explanation isn't in
the Constitution, the textbooks, the newspapers or the stories of
Congressional leaders. The answer lies in the mystery of what
we loosely call character. And if it must be defined beyond that,
you can do it only by unraveling the stuff out of which a Congressman is made. Take Hatton W. Sumners, if you will. The
mystery of Congress is the mystery of Sumners—and the humor,
the power and the glory as well.

It happens that Sumners is a great many things. He represented Dallas, Texas, but he also represents the salty common
sense that we like to think is peculiarly American, and our abiding
faith in certain fundamentals that are at once infinitely simple and
enormously sophisticated. He represents himself. He is representative government. Called by Washington correspondents "the
ablest and most potent advocate in Congress," "wisest as well as
smartest," he was the most beloved man in the House. Affection
for him transcended political allegiance or philosophic compati-
bility. In Congress he had the affections of John Nance Garner
and Fiorello La Guardia, north and south poles in the ideological

realm; Joe Martin and Sam Rayburn, north and south poles in politics.

This would be easily enough explained if Sumners were one of those agreeable people with a faculty for mutual easements and accommodations. But Sumners was sometimes uncompromising, often ornery and always ready, when need be, with disagreeable truths. The butts of such treatment took it and liked it chiefly because no part of his pungency was achieved by throwing salt in the wounds of his victims.

There was, for instance, the way he saw fit to offer condolences to a mournful conclave of Republican friends after Willkie's defeat: "You Republicans thought you were entering a horse in a horse race," he drawled, "but the horse decided he was entering a rodeo."

Pious mummeries quiver and die when impaled on a Sumnerian phrase. But unlike most whose wit is barbed, Sumners would just as soon serve at the receiving end of his jokes. A vast comic legend has sprung up around his passion for thrift—personal and governmental. But Sumners laid its foundation stone by telling on himself the story of an old colored panhandler of his acquaintance who stopped him one day and said, "Good mawnin', Mr. Hatton. Sure is glad to see yo'. Yo' ain't got a quarter for the old nigger, has yo'?" Sumners ran his hands through his pockets and, after completing his search, replied, "I declare I did have a quarter, but I don't seem to be able to find it right now." At which point, he insists, the darky rejoined, "Mr. Hatton, please, suh, look again. 'Cause if yo' had it, yo's still got it."

Having thus established his aversion to ostentatious spending, he feels perfectly free to keep an eye on others, and there's nothing at all they can do about it.

It was attention to incidental matters that made it possible for Sumners to break all records in the House by returning unexpended committee funds year after year. This was not without its salutary effect on the business of the House. It made it possible for Sumners to rise on the floor from time to time and denounce certain expenditures as "barbaric."

And as long as Sumners could make his Judiciary Committee accomplish what it did with as little money as it expended, there were limits beyond which other committee chairmen could not go.

Unlike those political hucksters whose youthful vicissitudes are perpetually on display, Hatton Sumners scarcely ever refers to his. But their assembled history goes far toward explaining his poignant awareness of a dollar's value. The Sumners family, which moved from Tennessee to Texas, had all the economic provocation of the Joads without their moral corrosion. Its hegira was less a retreat than a quest. And its leader was a boy of eighteen.

There were no educational technicians to provide projects to teach young Hatton how to think. Nature and a rickety economic system did the needful thing.

As a young man Hatton decided to become a lawyer, and under unusual hardships and with the help of one Mr. Wozencraft, a Dallas city attorney, he went through the University of Texas Law School and passed the bar.

Three years later, in 1900, he was elected prosecuting attorney.

He soon found plenty of outlets for his energy in that job. Dallas was a city of 42,000 in 1900, but it still bore the marks of its frontier beginnings. The town was infested by gambling houses, and their proprietors had established a flourishing *entente cordiale* with the local political potentates. To a young man of Sumner's mettle, the situation was insupportable. Nature had given him no warnings when it chose to strike, and even then Sumners believed that human government must follow the laws of Nature and God.

There was something Elijah-like in Sumners' attack. Armed with a six-shooter and assisted by a few dependable officials, he burst unannounced into the roaring dives.

After two years of posting bond, the mobilized underworld of politics defeated him at the polls—fraudulently, he believed and claimed.

In 1904, under a legislative primary law, he managed to get back in as prosecuting attorney. He resumed the raids, but the cases lingered on the court calendars. So Sumners decided there was nothing left to do but drive the houses out of business by the sheer repetition of raids and court appearances. A court promptly cited him for contempt. Now nearly at his wit's end, Sumners marched into a "businessmen's prayer meeting" attended by many of the "best" people of Dallas. He listened for a while to a choice selection of pious irrelevancies and then rose, an angry prophet, to scourge his respectable audience.

"Here you are," he shouted, "chasing God around! Yet you won't lift a finger to help me, or Dallas, or yourselves!" Sumners came out of the meeting with an embattled array of influential people behind him, beat the contempt charge and finished the job of cleaning up the town.

Thus are statesmen made in America. A youthful, ambitious prosecutor; a mass of unenforced laws; cynical politics; slumbering burghers. Mix, and you have a hell-raising row. But the by-product is the thing. A public quick to applaud a fighter and inordinately interested in anything relating to crime will cry lusty approval and vote and vote and vote the enforcer into office. Congress is full of these promoted reformers. Some graduate there from the short-pants-Sir-Galahad class; some never do.

Elected to Congress in 1912, Sumners came to Washington hoping to get on the Committee on Agriculture. Once in Congress, he found himself fascinated by the work of the Judiciary Committee, one of the most powerful in the House. It has always had the reputation of drawing the best legal talent available. On it have served Edward Livingston, Daniel Webster, Stephen A. Douglas, not to mention three Presidents and a dazzling array of governors, supreme court justices, senators, cabinet members and state chief justices.

It is a measure of Sumners' capacities that, given the kind of legal training he had when he entered the House, he was able to add distinction to the committee's record. He was its first and only member to have appeared in the Supreme Court in its behalf as "friend of the Court," and he did this not once but three times.

The House proudly called Sumners "the only man who ever

overruled the Supreme Court." He got that title in the 20's. Chief Justice Taft had sent the Judiciary Committee a request for a bill making some change or other in court procedure. Sumners told the committee that no legislation was needed; the change could be made without it. When the word reached Taft, he asked Sumners to call. Would Sumners explain, Taft asked severely, on what he based conclusions that differed from those of the court? Sumners did. Taft's boundless good nature, as always, transcended pride.

"Well," he roared, "I can't deny it! You're right. We don't need the bill." And then, shaking with laughter, "I guess that makes you the only man who ever overruled this court."

That was the beginning of a warm friendship between Sumners, Taft and most of the other members of the court. Taft had a habit of dropping in on Sumners in the House Office Building with Sutherland, Van Devanter or one of the other justices in tow—a disregard of social precedent monumental in a city of precedents.

But Sumners' authority did not come from his associates, his achievements, or his eminent position among the leaders of the House. His personal weight derived from something deep within himself—a reserve force that didn't need the conduits of office or title. He was no leader in the formal sense; no field marshal of party groups; no dispenser of rewards or executor of punishments. Yet there were moments on the floor when, singlehanded, he persuaded the House to defy its appointed leaders; moments when he stood armed, it seemed, with the force of Nature itself; moments when the lawgiver stood transfigured as a prophet.

The essential thing about a prophet is, as Carlyle once remarked, his conformity with Nature—with the Nature which "burst up in fire flames . . . proclaiming with terrible veracity that forged notes are forged." Counterfeit reform produced a comparable reaction from Sumners. For Sumners, too, goes back to first sources for his judgments.

Whenever he wants to think hard he goes off "to commune with the ways of Nature."

Observations about the birds, trees and clouds are the fruits of Sumner's communings—items that sharpen his analysis when he speaks of statecraft. "No people who failed to use their capacity for self-government," he will say, "were ever able to retain it. No people who lost their capacity to govern themselves were ever able to remain free. Why? Because Nature will not permit strength to remain where it is not used. The fish in the Mammoth Cave have become blind. The athlete who ceases to use his muscles becomes incapable of using them. In such situations Nature has no delicacy in the choice of its instrumentalities. People learn to govern by governing; retain the ability to govern by using it; lose the ability to govern by not using it. That is the plan of Almighty God, and no man under the dome of this Capitol can overrule that plan."

Sumners could have told the House that the men who wrote the fundamental law were successful because they relied upon verities proved by Nature and experience. They were "not creators but discoverers; not founding fathers but finding fathers." Madison, Hamilton, Jefferson and Marshall merely gave eternal truths a local habitation and a name.

Whenever Sumners thought that his colleagues were being pushed around too much in the name of "The Chief," he rehearsed these beliefs.

Standing before the House with God as his "Big Boss," Nature his handbook, and the nation's great dead his intimates, Sumners could laugh at the Administration's demands for a puny conformity. Sumners wouldn't obey Administration orders blindly. And the Administration finally limited its complaints to deprecating mutterings. It had been burned so deeply in its attempts to put pressure on Sumners that it risked no purges and tried, for the most part, to avoid a direct issue with him.

Very early in the New Deal, Sumners began to teach the Administration that the Constitution vests the power to legislate in Congress. In December, 1932, when President-elect Roosevelt attempted to get the lame-duck session of Congress to rush through farm legislation Sumners, among others, balked. The legislation did not go through in that session.

I had an intimate view of the Sumners belief in legislative independence in the summer of 1934. I dropped in to see Sumners in his office on Capitol Hill. I found him in a dark and angry mood.

"Sit down," he growled, "and let me tell you a story—a story that, I am sorry to say, is true."

It seemed that President Roosevelt, on the eve of his departure on a long vacation trip, had called Sumners on the telephone. Rather sharply he reminded the Judiciary chairman that no action had been taken on a batch of bills enlarging Federal power in racketeering and kidnapping cases. The bills had been prepared by the Department of Justice and introduced by some obedient Administration congressman. There had been no hearings and no serious consideration of the bills because Sumners, who was no admirer of the Attorney General, felt that they were badly drawn and unwisely enlarged Federal power over local government.

I knew something of the bills and of the reason why Roosevelt had so abruptly called Sumners. Louis Howe, as I have indicated elsewhere in this book, was a sort of armchair criminologist. He knew little of law and cared still less about Federal-state constitutional relations. In his concern to dabble in all matters of state which involved his personal whims and predilections, he busied himself in the criminal enforcement side of the Department of Justice. He had apparently seized the moment of Roosevelt's leave-taking to urge the President to call Sumners and demand action on the bills. Roosevelt had done so with little deliberation and with nervous urgency.

Sumners in no uncertain terms, but politely, told the President he would take his own time in bringing the bills before the committee and added the general observation that the legislative side of the government was constitutionally independent of Executive directions. To that the President had no reply and probably forgot all about the matter.

I, too, had a special interest in the subject, because a year be-

fore, when I resigned, the President had designated me to study
the subject and to report my findings to him. I had not completed
the report.

Sumners then suggested that we read the bills together and
select the ones that deserved consideration and passage. We did
so, and after considerable amendment some of the more reasonable ones were enacted. It may be added that some of the bills
were so badly drawn that a labor union or a ladies sewing society
might have been prosecuted as a racket. Roosevelt, of course, had
never read them.

"Once bitten, twice shy" not being one of its mottoes, the
Administration three years later blundered into precisely the same
situation, but this time at a frightful cost to itself. Administration
strategists made the inexcusable error of interpreting Sumners'
normal going along with much of his party's program as a disposition to obey commands. Probably the mistake was made because,
at the moment of its making, the Administration was so flushed
with victory, so confident of its ability to rush the Court bill
through Congress that it never occurred to it that a Hatton Sumners might knock its plans into a cocked hat.

When the President announced his court proposal to the Vice
President, the Speaker, the majority leaders, the members of the
Cabinet and Hatton Sumners and Henry Ashurst, chairmen of
the two judiciary committees to which the bill would be referred,
he did it by handing them the bill, reading a few snatches from
his message and leaving, without discussion.

Sumners sat through that ordeal with a growing sense of devas-
tation. Silently he filed out with the other leaders, joining a
group of them in a taxi. A very few minutes passed. Then his
decision, his choice between party allegiance and the convictions
of forty years, was made.

"Boys," he said, "here's where I cash in my chips."

Beyond any member of the Senate or House, Hatton Sumners
had reason to object to the bill. For he had long since recognized
the need for new blood in the court, and was well on the way
toward doing something about it—a bill permitting Supreme

Court justices to retire with pay, which was about to get through the House. As he put it to the House, "If you went to a mechanic with the gas line of your car stopped up, he wouldn't put dynamite under the car and blow it up. He'd open up that line and see if he couldn't get the engine working. He might do something more radical later, if that did not work. But that's what he'd do first."

Sumners, facing a Presidential command which not only violated some of his deepest principles but threatened to tear down the results of years of quiet, shrewd labor, squared himself for the fight. He determined to do his utmost to keep the Court bill suspended in the limbo of his committee, knowing as well as he knew the laces in his shoes that it would be almost impossible to get it before the House without his committee's O.K.

In the course of the long months while Sumners held the court bill in his committee with no hearings, I saw him occasionally in his office. In his quaint way he described his attitude toward this effort to subordinate the Supreme Court to the Executive:

"When God Almighty made a fish he did not put lungs into it. When he made an animal, he did. He always knew that when he made a creature it was necessary to decide what kind of creature it should be and where it was going to live. If we want a free republic, we need the organs that will keep it free. If we want something else, we will need different sorts of organs. Following the dictates of nature, the founding fathers created three coordinate organs of government. The result is a republic. If we decide upon two or one, we shall have something other than a republic. That is the issue now before Congress and the country."

After the Administration strategists recognized the hopelessness of attempting to get the bill through the House, they shifted camp to the Senate, but things went badly there from the first. The fight in the Senate grew bitter.

In desperation, the Administration began to look for an opening in the House again. Perhaps it was still not too late to get the bill away from Sumners' committee and through the House.

Sumners met the attack head-on. On July 13th he rose in his

place to speak. Mountains of oratory had piled up during the long debate; history had been ransacked; precedents endlessly invoked. It was no part of Sumners' strategy to heap Ossa on Pelion. He spoke seemingly without preparation, in homely phrases. "There is not enough left in the Supreme Court controversy to justify the hurt resulting from its continuance," he said. The retirement plan had been passed by Congress and was working. The fight was won. And as to saving face for the Administration, "if these advisers who are counseling the President to force that bill into this House under pressure which they may be able to command, when we are trying to preserve strength and unity required to do the nation's work, if they force that bill into this House for the sake of saving their faces or their hides, they ought not to have hide enough left to be worth bothering about."

When he had finished, the House rose, cheering and applauding as it had not done for years. There was not the slightest doubt that Sumners had carried the day. That was the end of the battle in the House. Coupled with the death of faithful Senate Leader Joe Robinson that very night, it was the effective end of the battle altogether.

Judged by the lofty standard of "conformity to Nature's laws," the long record of Sumners' votes presents some anomalies. Pretty plainly Mother Nature most often appeared to Sumners wearing the ears and tail of the Democratic donkey. Sometimes Sumners criticized Administration measures and subsequently voted for them.

Yet political expediency was not the sole or even the chief reason for Sumners' going along. The fact is that Sumners wasn't a Borah or an elder La Follette, perpetually defying anyone who asked him, for the sake of harmony, to yield a little here or there. He believes heart and soul in the wisdom of collective judgments. He respects representative government because it is cooperative government. When he was in Congress he did his level best to go along with his party because he thinks that is the way to make representative government work.

But the bent of his mind has always been against executive

dictation to Congress. He resisted it because, he says, "the aggregate wisdom of the people is the only safe guide of a republic." "It is no disrespect to the President that we shall do the business for which the people have selected us," he once told the House. "You are part of the Government, the policy-fixing agency of the Government. . . . Whoever is President, in the nature of things, needs the counsel of you as an independent, vital organ. Your counsel, mind you. And who are you? You are the American people. The American people as nearly as the American people can assemble on this continent."

After his seventeenth term, Hatton Sumners retired from Congress. A bachelor with modest personal requirements, he lives in his ripe years with the comfortable assurance of investments shrewdly made in a Dallas that has grown to metropolitan proportions in his lifetime. He expressed the hope, when he retired, that his remaining years may be used in carrying to the people of the nation his convictions of what is good for republican government.

Unlike Texas' other retired statesman-philosopher, John N. Garner, Sumners travels a good deal. When the opportunity calls, he makes speeches expounding his principles of government. Like Garner, he probably votes the Democratic ticket with deep reservations. For he is unreconstructed, unsocialized, unrelenting in his fear of bureaucracy and centralized government. He broods with his ever-present Almighty on the strange ways of those statesmen who have forgotten their traditions.

Index

Index